Safeguarding Young People

from the same series

Safeguarding Adults Under the Care Act 2014
Understanding Good Practice
Edited by Adi Cooper and Emily White
Foreword by Lyn Romeo
ISBN 978 1 78592 094 3
eISBN 978 1 78450 358 1

Working with Domestic Violence and Abuse Across the Lifecourse
Understanding Good Practice
Edited by Ravi K. Thiara and Lorraine Radford
ISBN 978 1 78592 404 0
eISBN 978 1 78450 758 9

Adult Safeguarding and Homelessness
Edited by Adi Cooper and Michael Preston-Shoot
ISBN 978 1 78775 786 8
eISBN 978 1 78775 787 5

Safeguarding Young People

Risk, Rights, Relationships and Resilience

Edited by **Dez Holmes**

Jessica Kingsley Publishers
London and Philadelphia

First published in Great Britain in 2022 by Jessica Kingsley Publishers
An imprint of Hodder & Stoughton Ltd
An Hachette Company

1

A CIP catalogue record for this title is available from the
British Library and the Library of Congress

ISBN 978 1 78775 359 4
eISBN 978 1 78775 360 0

Printed and bound by CPI Group (UK) Ltd, Croydon, CR0 4YY

Jessica Kingsley Publishers' policy is to use papers that are natural,
renewable and recyclable products and made from wood grown in sustainable forests. The logging and manufacturing processes are expected to
conform to the environmental regulations of the country of origin.

Jessica Kingsley Publishers
Carmelite House
50 Victoria Embankment
London EC4Y 0DZ

www.jkp.com

Acknowledgements

I am hugely grateful to all chapter authors who have given their time and expertise so generously to produce this book, during an extraordinarily busy and challenging time.

I am particularly grateful to Whitney and Marley for offering their personal reflections on the key messages from research, and for challenging us all to think more deeply about how young people experience the support of professionals.

A heartfelt thanks is also due to everyone who reviewed, commented on, critiqued and corrected this book – and a special thank you to my wonderful colleagues at Research in Practice.

This book is inspired by the hard work, tenacity and creativity of those working with and caring for young people. Thank you for all that you do – it is, and should be, a labour of love.

Lastly, to JL, thank you. I promise to find a less nerdy hobby in future.

Dez Holmes
Editor

Contents

Chapter 1

Introduction

Dez Holmes

Introduction to this book and its aims

I would there were no age between sixteen and three-and-twenty, or that youth would sleep out the rest; for there is nothing in the between but getting wenches with child, wronging the ancientry, stealing, fighting.

William Shakespeare – *The Winter's Tale*, Act 3, Scene 3, 59

As a society, we seem to have been concerned by the behaviour of young people for as long as records go back. With each new generation comes fresh dismay – from the 'tyranny' of 'chattering children' discussed in ancient times (and usually misattributed to Socrates), to the moral panic surrounding Mods and Rockers in the 1960s (Cohen, 1972), to the present-day media and political focus on youth crime.

None of this is to suggest there aren't real problems facing young people today; there are. Rather, it is to acknowledge that any efforts to safeguard and support adolescents operate against a backdrop of ongoing societal anxiety, and to argue that any policy solutions need to take account of this emotional context rather than simply apply layer upon layer of new guidance. Work with young people facing harm, done well, is relational not only transactional; emotional not only procedural; and is as concerned with 'what matters' as much as 'what works'. Policy, sector leadership and direct practice must all contend with these wider complexities, and must engage with thinking and feeling as much as *doing*, if we are to continuously improve our offer to young people.

Working with young people, particularly those facing harm, can be a challenging area of practice and leadership. Our understanding of the types of harm that can affect young people has developed a great deal in recent years, with 'extra-familial' harm – that is, harm outside the family or family home – now recognized in national safeguarding policy and statutory guidance (HM Government, 2020). Most, if not all, local areas in England have sought to adapt and improve safeguarding approaches in order to better respond to teenagers (Association of Directors of Children's Services, 2021), and the evidence base is ever-evolving as we learn new things about, and from, young people.

Policy and practice are often developed in response to crisis or concern, arguably leading to reactive and defensive approaches; social work in particular has been noted as becoming preoccupied with managerialism as a response to risk (Webb, 2006). The attention of the media and policy makers should not however be seen as a wholly unhelpful catalyst for change. In the case of young people facing extra-familial harm, the sharp focus instigated by identification of failures has been a powerful lever for change. The contemporary understanding of and professional response to child sexual exploitation – until relatively recently described erroneously as 'child prostitution' – was catalysed by a series of local and national inquiries that laid bare the inadequacy of our response to this abuse. The even more recent articulation of child criminal exploitation is in part an extension of this understanding, and, again, is a response to a number of inquiries and reviews highlighting that what had once been constructed as criminality is in fact a form of abuse (Child Safeguarding Practice Review Panel, 2020). The challenge for those seeking to safeguard young people is to leverage public and policy attention in order to effect positive change, while resisting reactive or defensive responses that can often result from a focus on risk (Featherstone et al., 2018).

This book seeks to take a step back; to create space for reflection that is not reactive to a crisis or tragedy, but instead allows a more aspirational and evidence-informed reframing of the issues in hand. It aims to promote critical thinking, rather than offering simplistic solutions.

While seeking to engage with the diversity of young people's characteristics, it is important to note this book does not provide detailed consideration of the specific and nuanced needs that neuro-diverse young people or those with disabilities may have in terms of safeguarding, nor does it specifically detail key considerations for those supporting young people who identify as transgender.

This book is aimed at anyone seeking to improve the way in which young people are supported and safeguarded, whether as a practitioner, a leader or a policy maker. It is not a prescriptive practice manual, though it contains various concepts intended to be useful for those working directly with young people. Nor is it a step-by-step guide to producing new policy or designing new services, though it seeks to provoke thoughtfulness in those responsible for these important activities.

We have tried to use language carefully in this book. Language can serve, albeit unintentionally, to undermine the goal of creating a society in which young people are safe, happy, healthy and able to exercise their rights. As work by the Social Care Future movement illustrates, crisis-oriented or deficit-based language can contribute to a system response which is short-termist and exclusionary (Crowther, 2019). The framing of adolescent safeguarding is an important aspect of the response; crisis-led language arguably begets deficit-led solutions, and paternalistic or victim-blaming language begets paternalistic and punitive practice. It is somewhat telling, therefore, that current policy discourse is focused on 'youth violence' rather than 'youth safety', and that post-pandemic education initiatives have focused on 'behaviour' rather than wellbeing. Even well-intended phraseology illuminates our seeming inability to recognize the specificity of adolescents' experiences: terms such as 'vulnerable children' locate vulnerability in the individual rather than their context, phrases such as 'the child's voice' suggest that children's perspectives exist in isolation from their family system, and even the word 'child' can be problematic (as anyone who has tried to call a teenager 'a child' will know all too well). The various chapter authors use language that reflects the case they are making. As such, for some the word 'child' is used to emphasize the legal status of people under 18; for others, the term 'young people' is used to encompass young adults up to 25. We have focused our energies on creating coherent and intersecting narratives, rather than enforcing uniform terminology.

Risk, rights, relationships and resilience

The subtitle of this book is borne out of a sense that, in our efforts to address potential harm facing young people, there is a danger of focusing on risk without taking into account three other crucial factors relevant to a young person's sense of safety: their rights, their relationships and their resilience.

To focus on risk without considering a young person's rights is to undermine their citizenship. Within children's safeguarding much is made of the paramountcy of 'the welfare of the child', whereas in safeguarding adults, there is perhaps a clearer recognition that welfare is one aspect of wider wellbeing, and the right to safety must be considered in balance with other rights, such as privacy and freedom. As discussed in Chapter 10 by Cocker, Cooper and Holmes, within the sphere of safeguarding adults, the notion of balancing risk and rights is more explicitly established. There is an often-used quote from a case in the Court of Protection,[1] focused on the sexual relationship between two adults with care and support needs, wherein Sir James Munby as presiding judge stated:

> Physical health and safety can sometimes be bought at too high a price in happiness and emotional welfare. The emphasis must be on sensible risk appraisal, not striving to avoid all risk, whatever the price, but instead seeking a proper balance and being willing to tolerate manageable or acceptable risks as the price appropriately to be paid in order to achieve some other good – in particular to achieve the vital good of the elderly or vulnerable person's happiness. What good is it making someone safer if it merely makes them miserable?

Arguably, in the context of safeguarding young people, perhaps we are prepared to 'make them miserable' provided they are deemed to be physically safer. Furthermore, as discussed in both Chapter 5 by Wroe and Pearce and Chapter 6 by Davis and Marsh, a rights-based perspective requires us to engage with and actively seek to redress the structural disadvantages and discrimination facing many young people and their communities.

To focus on risk without considering young people's relational identities is to dislocate them from both protective and potentially harmful actors in their lives. Human beings do not exist in a vacuum; our families, our peers and indeed our relationship with the world all influence our safety and wellbeing. Relationships can be seen as both a source of harm and trauma for some young people, and are an important vehicle for repair and recovery within a trauma-informed practice paradigm, as explored in Chapter 8 by Hickle and Lefevre. As Beckett and Lloyd highlight in Chapter 4, young people may face harm within and outside

---

1   *Local Authority X v MM & Anor* (No. 1) [2007].

the family context – intra- and extra-familial harm are not mutually exclusive – and working with parents and carers as active partners is a key means of creating sustainable safety for those young people we are worried about. Developing a sense of relational identity is a key part of being a teenager, as Coleman and Hagell highlight in Chapter 3 on adolescent development. Peers, and sexual or romantic partners, often take on great significance and are likely to be highly influential for most young people irrespective of whether or not the adults in their life approve of these relationships. It is neither sufficient nor realistic to seek to sever all harmful or unhealthy relationships, nor can all relationships be categorized so neatly. Creating safeguarding responses that recognize the context in which young people can face harm – and understanding that a young person's relationships are a hugely influential factor of that context – requires us to adopt a systems-perspective, and this is not necessarily well supported by current legislative and policy frameworks, as Firmin and Knowles' Chapter 7 discusses.

To focus on risk without seeking to promote a young person's resilience is to undermine their emerging sense of agency and autonomy, and – at worst – can mirror the coercive dynamics of abuse and exploitation. As Hill and Warrington explore in Chapter 9, young people facing, and recovering from, harm need to be afforded as much choice and control as possible. This requires nuanced and thoughtful practice, which in turn requires nuanced and thoughtful local leadership and national policy. This work can be anxiety-provoking, complex and emotionally painful; it is understandable that professionals facing these challenges might seek to exert control, subtly or overtly. When we 'do to' a young person, rather than 'work with', we may inadvertently undermine their sense of self-efficacy, which in turn can destabilize their resilience. Language such as 'keeping young people safe' can suggest that young people are passive recipients of safeguarding activity, rather than central and active agents within their own lives. Importantly, and in keeping with the structural lens of this book, resilience must be understood as the galvanizing of internal and external resources (Pooley & Cohen, 2010); it is not a substitute for support.

An overview of the chapters

Each chapter tries to explore a different facet of safeguarding young people, offering food for thought and inviting reflection. Following this introductory chapter, the second chapter features reflections from two exceptionally wise young adults, Whitney Clark and Marley Hall, both of whom have experience of being supported by services as a result of the risks and harms they encountered in their lives. Their insights are offered verbatim and create a powerful narrative as to why the themes captured throughout the remaining chapters are so crucial to engage with.

Chapter 3, co-authored by John Coleman and Ann Hagell, provides an overview of adolescent development. This chapter contends that it is very difficult indeed to safeguard young people effectively without understanding this developmental life stage and the significant transition it represents. They offer an introductory analysis of the way in which puberty, an often-overlooked life change, can be a source of distress which in turn might heighten risks. They highlight how changes in the brain may leave some teenagers feeling confused, being drawn into exciting (unsafe) behaviour and experiences, and note research suggesting that the part of the brain that deals with feelings develops quicker than the bit of the brain that deals with logical thinking and rational decision-making. A further aspect of understanding the risk young people face is highlighted in research showing that many young people will experience mental health problems at some point between the age of 10 and 24. Coleman and Hagell assert that safeguarding professionals need to pay attention to the mental and physical health of young people, recognizing that these are connected aspects of overall wellbeing. Hearteningly, this chapter highlights that adolescence represents the optimum time to build healthy behaviours; if young people learn to eat healthily, exercise properly, develop safe sexual practices, and address drug and alcohol use at this age, then they have a good chance of being healthy adults for life. Despite the focus on young people's personal development, Coleman and Hagell emphasize the connection between individual development and structural factors influencing young people's health and development. This theme – of the individual and the structural being connected – is one that subsequent chapters build on.

Chapter 4, co-authored by Helen Beckett and Jenny Lloyd, offers a critical analysis of the way in which professionals have sought to address the harms facing many young people. The increasing recognition over the past decade or so of the range of harms that can affect young people has led to a variety of practice and policy responses. This chapter considers the complexity of this work, including in relation to peer-perpetrated harm and the dual identities that some young people hold as both victims and instigators of harm. Beckett and Lloyd acknowledge that while significant improvements have been made, efforts to address harm have in some instances been lacking, and a number of key challenges remain. They reflect on the way in which partial conceptualizations and problematic discourse around adolescent harm can sometimes elide the abusive nature of such experiences, and may even exacerbate the risks and harms young people encounter. In drawing attention to the unintended negative consequences of some practice and policy in this field, Beckett and Lloyd highlight the pervasive harm caused by victim-blaming narratives, and prompt us to recognize the systemic constraints that impede a young person-centred safeguarding response. The dominant discourse of child welfare can sometimes mean that professionals struggle to hold young people's autonomy and dependence in healthy tension. Furthermore, Beckett and Lloyd note that attention can sometimes be focused on one type of harm, or one particular group, in a way that distorts understanding – leading to disproportionate emphasis on one aspect of adolescent safeguarding at the expense of others. They argue that a more contextual and holistic approach could help to address these shortcomings and would better accommodate the complex realities of harm experienced in adolescence.

Chapter 5, authored by Lauren Wroe with Jenny Pearce, builds on this argument and makes a compelling case for a holistic and structurally informed framework for safeguarding young people that explicitly acknowledges the intersections between intra- and extra-familial harm. Wroe and Pearce provide a powerful argument for the importance of taking a structural perspective when seeking to understand and respond to young people facing risk and harm. In doing so, the authors emphasize the crucial importance of ensuring that professionals are able to recognize the structural factors – such as racism, classism, ableism, sexism and other forms of discrimination and oppression – and the way in which these create the conditions for harm. In particular, the role of poverty and inequality is highlighted as a key driver for harm and adversity, and one which can be overlooked to the detriment of young people's safety and wellbeing. Wroe and Pearce warn against safeguarding responses which are individualized to the extent that societal inequalities are obscured, as doing so can mean that responsibility is inappropriately placed on young people and their families, or on practitioners with limited ability to address the underlying adversities.

Chapter 6, co-authored by Jahnine Davis and Nicholas Marsh, takes this line of argument further and challenges the reader to recognize not only the intersectional and multifaceted nature of young people's identities, but also the role that professionals may inadvertently play in contributing to the marginalization of some groups. They highlight that ethnicity, gender, sexuality and class are all important aspects of a person's identity, and these aspects interact with each other in ways that can compound discrimination. A central argument of their chapter is that there is no such thing as a typical young person, nor a typical victim – and that recognizing this flawed logic is a vital starting point for developing an effective safeguarding response. Davis and Marsh introduce concepts such as 'adultification' to highlight the way in which professionals, and society more widely, can exacerbate young people's experience of harm through leaving biases unchallenged. The authors offer reflective exercises to support critical thinking. They also argue that some of the tools and theoretical frameworks that professionals use are based on out-of-date and Euro-centric constructs, which can mean that biases and blind-spots become absorbed and reinforced within practice. This chapter asserts that professionals need to recognize all the different ways a young person experiences discrimination, and the ways in which their practice can accidentally contribute to this. Importantly, the authors invite the reader to notice and 'lean in' to the discomfort that this chapter might evoke, and they challenge us all to reflect on the ways in which biases can permeate even the most well-intended efforts to safeguard young people.

Chapter 7, co-authored by Carlene Firmin and Rachel Knowles, explores a key aspect of the system in which professionals seek to safeguard young people from extra-familial harm – that is, the legal framework in which services in England and Wales operate. They note that young people ensnared in harm outside the family context have gradually been increasingly recognized as victims of abuse, and that England's child protection system has tried to mobilize over the past decade to protect children from harm, irrespective of its source. In analysing the child protection legislation and accordant policy and guidance, alongside the system requirements for safeguarding adolescents, Firmin and Knowles question the extent to which the legislative framework is fit for purpose. The authors draw on emergent evidence generated by the Contextual Safeguarding research programme, and look back to the original intentions of the Children Act 1989 to explore whether the distinction between children requiring protection from abuse and those whose behaviour was considered 'delinquent' still stands up to scrutiny. Specifically, Firmin and Knowles highlight the challenges of responding to extra-familial harm within a legislative and policy framework that foregrounds 'attribution'. In a system that was primarily designed to address harm to children that is attributable to parents' actions or inaction, how can professionals best support parents who are striving to keep their child safe in the face of sophisticated and deliberately undermining perpetrators? While recognizing the significant innovation with the practice of safeguarding young people from harm, Firmin and Knowles remind us that practice, whether good or poor, does not operate in a vacuum. True system reform for young people facing harm may require a redesign of the legal structures in which safeguarding practice occurs.

Chapter 8, co-authored by Kristi Hickle and Michelle Lefevre, offers a perspective that speaks closely to the passions of many professionals working with young people, that of adopting a trauma-informed approach. In this chapter, the authors draw a link between early attachment and later experiences of risk and harm, reminding the reader that adults do not always see what lies beneath young people's behaviour and social relationships, nor how they connect with young people's trauma and their unmet developmental needs. Hickle and Lefevre assert that viewing trauma through a developmental and relational – rather than a pathological – lens can enable us to make better sense of young people's worlds and the impact of their experiences. Young people can respond to traumatic experiences in ways that can result in behaviours that are challenging and sometimes harmful to themselves and others. The professional response to these behaviours – such as school exclusion – can potentially increase a young person's sense of trauma and may even exacerbate the risk of harm. Hickle and Lefevre emphasize that a trauma-informed, attachment-oriented approach can help young people form the foundations of resilience, develop a positive sense of self-worth and learn how to manage difficult emotions. They are clear, however, that nurturing caregiving cannot prevent a child from experiencing challenging, unexpected or oppressive circumstances such as illness, bereavement, poverty and racism. Warning against reductive thinking, and echoing the messages from Coleman and Hagell, Hickle and Lefevre firmly argue that 'foundations are not fate' and that neither attachment nor trauma are 'hard-wired'. They also emphasize that relationship-based, trauma-attuned practice requires practitioners to feel safe within their working context, and needs whole-organization commitment.

Chapter 9, co-authored by Nicky Hill and Camille Warrington, continues the discussion regarding trauma-informed responses, providing an overview of how participation and empowerment-focused approaches are an essential design feature of safeguarding young people. It builds on learning from research and emerging practice in interrelated disciplines such as youth and community work, social work, youth justice and adult safeguarding, and offers a thoughtful critique of the rhetoric and reality regarding participation. Chiming with Beckett and Lloyd's chapter, Hill and Warrington acknowledge the tension between protection and participation, and use young people's voices to make a powerful case for why these two seemingly opposing tenets must be better integrated if young people's safeguarding needs are to be addressed effectively and ethically. The authors assert that working *with* young people, treating them as experts and giving them as much voice, choice and power as possible, is essential within safeguarding practice and policy. The authors argue that this is especially important in the context of harm such as exploitation. Where young people have been controlled, manipulated and disempowered by those who seek to harm them, it is vital that professionals do not inadvertently mirror these coercive dynamics.

Chapter 10, co-authored by Christine Cocker, Adi Cooper and Dez Holmes, argues that a truly transformational approach to safeguarding adolescents requires us to rethink the boundaries of adolescence itself. While many parts of the wider system, for example services for young people with special educational needs and disabilities, have already established a more fluid and transitional approach, safeguarding is notable in retaining a binary notion of child/adulthood. Harm and its effects do not cease when a young person reaches 18, and recent evidence regarding adolescent development suggests that the brain doesn't stop developing until the mid-20s. Yet it remains that case that statutory safeguarding support ceases for many young people as they turn 18, arguably due to a preoccupation with eligibility thresholds at the expense of a needs-led and preventative approach. The authors draw on evidence regarding emerging adulthood as a distinct life stage to argue that this binary approach is ineffective and instead make a case for Transitional Safeguarding, within which a person-centred, needs-led and rights-based approach to safeguarding young people can be realized. The authors highlight the inconsistencies between safeguarding services for children and adults, and identify opportunities to draw on the respective strengths of children's and adults' safeguarding, to argue for a radical realignment of local and national safeguarding systems.

In summary

Taken together, these chapters offer a number of interwoven themes, the most striking of which is perhaps the importance of avoiding binary thinking. Effective safeguarding of young people requires us to hold a 'both/and' mindset: taking into account the structural or system-wide influences *as well as* ensuring a focus on the individual circumstances and wishes of the young person; recognizing the importance of early childhood or family influences *as well as* striving to engage parents and carers as partners; affording young people a degree of choice and control *as well as* being explicitly clear about our duty to protect them; recognizing that in terms of discrimination, professionals might be part of the problem *as well as* a key part of the solution; being bold enough to push for radical whole-system reform *as well as* taking responsibility for immediate change ourselves, however small that change might be.

The book aims to encourage critical thinking, and to acknowledge that complexity – even sometimes contradiction – is part of the context for this work. It draws on learning from research, practice wisdom and expertise from those with lived experience, recognizing that different sources of knowledge offer different emphases and there is no definitive 'answer' or 'fix'. Chapter authors were selected on the basis of their specific interest and expertise, and as such offer diverse perspectives. This book does not try to achieve consensus through a process of dilution or by enforcing uniformity between chapters, either in relation to terminology or approach. Some authors use case studies of young people, some use reflective questions for self-directed learning, others share promising initiatives from local areas. Some draw more heavily on academic evidence, others foreground lived experience or practice expertise. Rather like a 'team around a child', each chapter provides a particular contribution to the wider whole, and their diversity strengthens the collective impact. And, like a skilled practitioner working with a young person, we have tried to strike a balance between support and challenge. It should be possible for the reader to find at least one point they disagree with and, we hope, many more that affirm and inspire.

References

Association of Directors of Children's Services (ADCS) (2021). *Safeguarding Pressures Phase 7*. ADCS. https://adcs.org.uk/safeguarding/article/safeguarding-pressures-phase-7.

Child Safeguarding Practice Review Panel (2020). *It was Hard to Escape: Safeguarding Children at Risk from Criminal Exploitation*. Department for Education. www.gov.uk/government/publications/safeguarding-children-at-risk-from-criminal-exploitation.

Cohen, S. (1972). *Folk Devils and Moral Panics: The Creation of the Mods and Rockers*. London: Routledge.

Crowther, N. (2019). *Talking About a Brighter Social Care Future*. https://socialcarefuture.blog.

Featherstone, B., Gupta, A., Morris, K. & Warner, J. (2018). 'Let's stop feeding the risk monster: Towards a social model of "child protection". *Families, Relationships and Societies, 7*(1), 7–22.

HM Government (2020). *Working Together to Safeguard Children: A Guide to Inter-Agency Working to Safeguard and Promote the Welfare of Children*. London: HMSO. www.gov.uk/government/publications/working-together-to-safeguard-children--2.

Pooley, J. & Cohen, L. (2010). 'Resilience: A definition in context.' *Australian Community Psychologist, 22*, 30–37.

Webb, S.A. (2006). *Social Work in a Risk Society: Social and Political Perspectives*. London: Palgrave Macmillan.

Chapter 2

Our Voice, Our Experience

Whitney Clark and Marley Hall (with Dez Holmes)

This chapter was co-authored with two young adults, Whitney and Marley, who each bring lived experience of being supported by professionals during childhood and adolescence. Whitney and Marley also have more recent experience of supporting professional learning and development, and both now undertake a range of work with organizations to improve the way in which young people are supported.

In considering the key messages emerging from each chapter, Whitney and Marley reflect on how the research resonates with their own experiences and what this might mean for the professionals striving to support young people. Their professional experience affords them invaluable insights, and it is clear from their articulate and thoughtful reflections that they are no strangers to communicating with professionals.

Though foregrounding Marley and Whitney's expertise through lived experience, this chapter does not focus on the detail of their personal life stories. Those stories are for Marley and Whitney to share, in whatever way they choose – including writing their own books should they wish to.

Reflecting on adolescent development

The messages from Coleman and Hagell regarding adolescent development certainly strike a chord with Marley. He feels that understanding adolescent development should be a key aspect of any professional's expertise:

> I think there's still a lot we don't know to do with the brain, especially in adolescence. This is the time where our brain makes some of the

most important connections – connections that will define who we are as adults. Professionals who work with some of those most vulnerable adolescents really need to understand this.

Marley is also struck by the significance of puberty, wondering if professionals understand what a 'big deal' this is for many young people:

A big change happens for young people when they go through puberty; it can be a scary time! Minds and bodies changing and growing, judgement from peers, confusion with what you do. It's a very overwhelming time.

Marley also draws links between the messages about promoting healthy behaviours in Chapter 3 and the later messages in Chapters 8 and 9 regarding trusting relationships:

We need to think about what healthy behaviour is for an individual rather than use a blanket approach for all teenagers. And again, it's about trust. Once a relationship has been built between a young person and a professional then you begin to explore ways that their behaviours can be made safe.

Whitney reflects on the emotional and behavioural aspects of adolescent development and highlights the importance of allowing teenagers to negotiate boundaries as part of learning who they are:

We've reached that age where we all go through, like, a rebellion stage. And no matter how strict you [parents/carers] all are about how many boundaries you have, it's completely necessary in this stage of growing up. It teaches you who you are. It allows you to create an identity, within healthy relationships. It allows us to create a space to communicate both limitations and often will form a protection, and enables us to learn self-respect. Because as you get into your teenage years, that's when you start to find yourself a bit more.

Marley concurs:

Risk-taking, inappropriate behaviours and so on are all things that happen in adolescence. Risk-taking can also be positive, if it is done right with the correct support. It helps young people learn about the world and about themselves.

That said, Whitney also recognizes the importance of boundaries and sees these as an important aspect of caring for young people. She notes:

> I get the point [made by chapter authors] of having boundaries and having structure and having a routine. Because, once I got into that routine, and structure and I was placed in a foster placement that gave me that…I then started to realize who I was and where I was going. I was then able to create boundaries that didn't involve chaos, lack of routine, and I really then started to build my ambitions and goals. That made me reflect on who I was. And I don't think I would have ever been in that position if it wasn't for the love and structure that I got. I didn't realize that until I was 17.

Reflecting on structural, holistic and intersectional perspectives

Both Whitney and Marley recognize the crucial importance of seeing the whole young person: their relational eco-systems, their environment and their circumstances. They are passionate about the need for professionals to think holistically.

Whitney notes that professionals can sometimes focus on one aspect – often the presenting behaviour of a young person – and overlook the underpinning needs:

> Professionals sometimes just look at one component and it's actually other factors that are underlying that need to be looked at. The thing you're looking at isn't always necessarily the main factor, the behaviours for example. You've got to look at the whole thing: the first issue, the hidden problems, the environment, and the social issues. You've also got to try and think intergenerationally, because actually quite a lot of what we end up doing as young people is based on what we've learned from our parents or family.

Marley is blunter:

> Every young person is an individual – it's as simple as that. You've got to be personal about it, and see the whole picture, not just make assumptions or do what you're comfortable with.

In Chapter 4, Beckett and Lloyd highlight the perils of assuming that an issue, such as child sexual exploitation, has been 'dealt with' because it is afforded less media or policy attention. Whitney agrees and feels this faddishness is unhelpful:

> I think a lot of systems are doing 'what is hot'. Focusing on whatever is spoken about the most. People bring up child sexual exploitation and everyone's on to that now, or it's all about something else, so everyone jumps on to that, before the first issue has been resolved. It almost seems as though it's a trend. I think that's how systems are currently running – on a cycle of trends.

Wroe and Pearce, in Chapter 5, highlight the need to critique and reflect on policing powers, particularly in the context of some communities being disproportionately affected by law enforcement intervention. This also strikes a chord with Whitney:

> Police officers are just randomly allowed to stop and search people. As soon as you go into the custody suite, it's got to be done by the book, but on the street, you can just stop and search anyone. You [police] can do what you want, and young people feel that.

In exploring Davis and Marsh's discussion around intersectional identities, both Marley and Whitney immediately identify stereotyping as a key issue. Marley offers some challenging reflections on how these harmful attitudes can be reinforced within organizations that privilege experience over open-mindedness:

> I think there is too often an assumption that everyone is white and straight. People make a lot of assumptions. I don't want to stereotype, but sometimes professionals who are considered more experienced are also older, and this can sometimes mean that they aren't up to date with some of the changes in society or don't understand how young people now see the world. They can be a bit stuck in their ways. Sexuality and gender is a perfect example; the world has changed a lot in the past few years and professionals need to keep up or they can become part of the discrimination. The older or more experienced professionals also seem to be the ones that don't go on training – so how are they learning new ideas?

In terms of structural disadvantage, both Whitney and Marley highlight the way in which poverty affects families. Whitney emphasizes the need for professionals to raise this in ways that allow families to discuss it without feeling shamed, but she also notes that not raising it can be equally problematic:

> Poverty is a massive factor in our society. A lot of families where there's difficulty with the kids are also struggling in that way. I grew up using food banks and I saw that as a normal way of living because that was what I knew. We didn't question it and we never brought it up because nobody ever asked.

Families are a big part of young people's identity. An ability to understand families is understood to be a key part of working with a young person – even if they don't live with their families any more. Both Whitney and Marley draw connections between early childhood experiences and their family life and how they later experienced the world as teenagers. In addition, Whitney emphasizes the importance of helping people develop the skills and understanding that safe parenting requires:

> Parents are expected to know how to parent, but they're never actually taught how to parent. We are expected to know right from wrong – but as children, if you live in a chaotic household, you're never really taught right from wrong. So actually, what you think may be right may be wrong.

Reflecting on the arguments from Firmin and Knowles, and Wroe and Pearce, Marley and Whitney agree that whole-system change is necessary. They both argue that young people's safety and wellbeing is not simply an issue for children's social care, but also for health services, adult support services and the justice system. As Whitney explains:

> I don't feel like safeguarding can change on its own until you change things like the prison system, the housing system, mental health support… It's the whole system – everything is connected.

Reflecting on victim-blaming and labelling of young people

The importance of language is a theme that several chapters raise. Both Marley and Whitney can recall times when they have experienced negative labelling, and both feel that conscious efforts to avoid victim-blaming are an essential aspect of improving the safeguarding response for young people. Marley highlights that victim-blaming, however unintentional, can have damaging consequences for a young person's relationship with a professional:

> Victim-blaming really is a problem. Not only does it not actually help to resolve the problem, it hurts the relationship between the young person and the professional. It can also mean that any underlying issues are missed, because the professional is only seeing the bit that they think the young person is responsible for. Basically, this means as a professional you really haven't done your job.

Whitney takes a similar view, and is poignantly challenging in her assessment of why victim-blaming happens and its consequences:

> I guess there's some part of responsibility that you have to give the young person, some accountability and responsibility, I do get that. But I feel like it [victim-blaming] happens because it takes the onus off professionals and what they were meant to be doing. Saying 'It's because you put yourself in this position' is basically saying that it's your fault. Growing up, I was blamed all my life for stuff, and then blamed for being in the system that I never chose to be in. Actually, I didn't ask to be here. I'm here not because of me, but because of stuff that happened before, stuff that other people did.

Marley offers a similar perspective:

> Professionals need to take the time to explain – explain why I'm here, that it's not my fault. That I'm not at fault.

Marley and Whitney both feel that the language professionals use can contribute to a young person's vulnerabilities. Marley explains how labelling can leave a lasting impression on a young person:

> Being defined as a 'young offender', a 'problem child' or 'aggressive' or 'delinquent' – that stuff can stay with you for life.

Whitney highlights that labelling seems to be an approach designed to make young people fit into the system, rather than designing a system around young people:

> I feel like labels are sometimes used so that you fit somewhere; another tick-box exercise.

Echoing Beckett and Lloyd's warnings of how some risk assessment tools can serve to screen out some young people, Whitney describes how labelling young people as a means of categorizing them can also serve to exclude some young people from receiving support:

> I've been labelled quite a lot in my life, and actually half of them have stopped me accessing support – because by the time they come up with a new label, I'm 'too complex' for that service.

Whitney raises a further complexity regarding the labelling of young people, one that professionals may not be as alert to:

> To get treatment or a service, I have to be doing this thing that's got me a label. I feel that if you label someone in order to access support, you're saying to them, 'Well, you have to keep doing this so that you can continue to get help. If you stop this behaviour, you're no longer whatever label we said you were, so we're going to "step down" and leave you on your own.' Like, I've got a mate in prison at the moment; they've been in four times over the last two years. They've got nowhere to live, no support network, and all the help that they get is in prison. So, they've been institutionalized – they have to keep repeating the cycle, keep re-offending and end up back in the same place. That's going to damage them so much, but the fact is that they can't access support outside.

life cycle

Reflecting on behaviour, trauma and trust

Both Whitney and Marley have experienced educational exclusion as a result of their perceived behaviour. They each describe in different ways how, too often, professionals can focus on how a young person is demonstrating their anger, when in fact anger isn't the only (or even primary) emotion at play. As Marley puts it:

> I was scared, lost and anxious first – before I was angry. But the anger became the focus. That was what professionals saw in me. So it was what I showed them.

Whitney reflects on how school can feel like a safe space where children can express their feelings, but may soon learn that not all emotions are acceptable:

> At first, school can be a place away from the chaos. A place where you can express who you are...you might be the most angry kid you've ever

seen on the planet…but you're angry here because it feels safe enough to be angry here. Maybe it's not safe enough at home or in your community, but in school it is safe enough to express how angry you are. And then the response you get is: 'We don't have time or the resource to deal with you.' I was put in a pupil referral unit aged eight. It can feel like you don't matter at home and you don't matter in school. You can feel like this person who is just pushed around because nobody knows how to deal with you. In the most distressing times of my life I don't think it ever crossed people's minds the impact that adults' words and decisions would later have on my life.

Both Whitney and Marley articulate in different ways how some young people are better understood as victims, and others are seen as 'trouble'. Marley reflects on how some behaviours – such as crying – are seen as an acceptable response to trauma, whereas other equally rational behaviours – such as anger – seem less palatable to professionals.

The idea that anger is somehow a less acceptable response to trauma than other emotions displayed by young people has particular resonance in light of Davis and Marsh's chapter (Chapter 6). They highlight how Black and other minoritized young people can sometimes have attributes projected onto them, and can be seen by professionals as aggressive, rather than vulnerable. This bias may contribute, in part, to the disproportionate numbers of Black and minoritized young people within school exclusion and youth justice populations.

At the time of writing, news reports are circulating following the publication of a damning inspection report of a youth offending institution. Whitney reflects on this and articulates how these young people can be made invisible, and 'written off' by professionals and society:

It's about power. What's hidden behind closed doors and what people can't see doesn't matter. I feel like that's what happens with these young people – if you can't see it, well, it doesn't matter. I feel like that's how we roll as a society; we really don't believe in rehabilitation. It's just the 'naughty kids'. It's kind of like we don't invest in them.

Marley highlights that the investment needed for young people who are struggling is not only an issue of funding, but of emotional resource too:

The most important characteristics a professional can have from a perspective of the young person are to be open, honest, respectful and compassionate. I think if you can show a young person this, then they can see you care. All everyone wants is a sense of belonging, a bit of love.

The importance of giving young people a sense of autonomy or choice, as raised by Hickle and Lefevre, and Hill and Warrington, strongly resonates with both Whitney and Marley. They each reflect that this is particularly important in the context of trauma and suggest that, in an effort not to traumatize or re-traumatize young people, professionals can sometimes make the mistake of denying young people choice when, in fact, choice and control may be part of the healing process.

In relation to this, Whitney makes a powerful point regarding access to records, or indeed being given access to one's own life experiences:

> I've read my files...professionals sometimes don't want to re-open the wounds. Well, actually, sometimes we would much prefer you to ask us than just assume that we don't ever want to talk about those experiences again. By asking us, you give us a choice. Instead of just continuing what we are doing for many, many years... I ended up destroying my education, my relationships and, to some degree, my future.

Feeling let down or mistrustful of professionals is felt to be a powerful barrier to being able to establish a therapeutic relationship. Part of this, according to Marley, is about professionals needing to be honest about their limitations and constraints:

> Be straight up, explain that you won't be able to do everything a young person wants. Don't pretend you can do everything just to get me onside. I'm not a child, I'd rather you were honest upfront, otherwise we just feel lied to later. And that makes it more painful.

This is especially important in terms of confidentiality, something that Marley feels some professionals can struggle with in their efforts to have a positive relationship with a young person:

> It's important to be clear at all times that you are a professional, that if something dangerous is happening you will need to report it. There's a difference between being friendly as a professional, and trying to be our friend.

Whitney reflects on the need for relational repair, and the role that professionals have in not only creating relationships with the young person, but also helping the young person to develop skills in forming relationships with others:

> No one ever taught me how to make friendships. No one ever told me how to communicate in ways which people would understand. And it damaged every friendship that I had at school, and out in the community. I find it hard to trust, to believe people's empathy, and ultimately I never learned to trust and love myself.

In thinking about a trauma-informed approach to safeguarding practice, Marley and Whitney both comment on the distinction between sympathy and empathy. As Marley asserts:

> I don't want pity – I want respect.

Reflecting on resilience, participation, choice and control

The enduring themes of working with young people, of respecting their sense of agency and affording them a sense of choice and control resonate strongly with Whitney and Marley.

Whitney offers a valid challenge to the term resilience, explaining the potential dangers of applying it as a label which can limit young people:

> People say, 'Oh you're so resilient', but it's actually built something into me that hinders me quite a lot in life. Always knowing how to look like you're coping. I just act like I'm fine because that's what I'm meant to be doing. Because if I don't, then I'm not resilient…and if I'm not resilient then what am I?
>
> You have to be doing all right. And that I then feel like I can't ask for help. And I have a smile on my face 24/7 and I've got to be fine, and I'm not allowed to have a down day because I'm 'resilient'. And actually, what if one day I don't want to be okay? But I can't be because everybody else has this expectation of me.
>
> Resilience should be something you learn, not something that's forced, based on trauma.

Marley offers a further uncomfortable challenge, highlighting how sometimes the professional response to harm – however well intended – can serve to reinforce a young person's vulnerabilities and pain:

I felt like I lost all control and power as soon as I was being treated as someone with mental health problems – it definitely made things worse.

The messages from Hickle and Lefevre's chapter resonate with Marley and Whitney. Both feel strongly that working with young people in a way that affords them choice and control is a vital part of effective safeguarding. This includes being honest about the limitations of what you can offer, as Marley explains:

It is extremely important to give young people as much choice and control as possible. Professionals need to listen to what young people say and respond with respect – this includes explaining why you can't always do what they would like you to do.

Marley describes how this person-centred, participative approach to practice is particularly important for young people who have suffered harm and trauma:

Making a young person feel empowered and in control of their life can be a major part of recovery for many who have suffered abuse in any form – we need to trust that they [professionals] can make good decisions.

When a young person has been exploited, they've had so much control taken away from them already. They've had their self-worth damaged. You can't just make them feel like a failure, or like that [experience of exploitation] is the only thing you're interested in. You need to reinforce their strengths, not just focus on risks and concerns.

Whitney firmly agrees, and emphasizes the importance of working with young people as active partners in their own safeguarding. She explains what participative practice looks like and why it matters:

You're giving the young person power and control over the situation rather than telling them. We need to work together to be able to create something, create a solution to enable me to go on in life using the skills that I've now got because we've worked together. If you're just telling me, then I'm not going to listen. We need to understand why things are happening in order to understand them properly, because that's how we learn.

Whitney adds that working at the pace of a young person is part of a trauma-informed approach to safeguarding:

If you're not in the right space or you just don't feel comfortable, you're not going to care about how they're trying to keep you safe, because actually you don't care if you're safe. I was in that cycle for a very long time; I just didn't care what anyone said to me and I was going to do what I was going to do. No one could stop me and I was invincible. But eventually it changed. It took time to understand what people were saying to me. But it wasn't until somebody just sat there and listened and properly noticed.

The tensions between young people's need for autonomy and choice and their need for protection, acknowledged in Chapters 4 and 9 by Beckett and Lloyd, and Hill and Warrington, are understood by Whitney and Marley. Marley offers his thoughts on how professionals might navigate the path between being centred on the young person, but not colluding with their world view when their safety is at risk:

When there is a safeguarding issue or something a professional is worried about, you need to strike a balance. Start by being interested in a natural way: 'Oh, how did you meet this new boyfriend?' But rather than trying to make a young person think like you do about the risk, you've got to try and help them see it from a different perspective – maybe ask whether they'd be concerned if their younger sister had a boyfriend that much older. Help them to feel protective, rather than just trying to protect them without understanding their perspective. It's about being sensitive, helping a young person to reflect – not just telling them they are wrong.

Whitney and Marley recognize that the context of safeguarding practice, particularly the heightened anxiety facing practitioners, can act as a barrier to participative practice. As Marley explains:

Professionals sometimes panic when it comes to some issues – mental health or exploitation, for example. They sometimes can try to over-control the situation, maybe because they are worried that they can't control it at all. A young person needs to have their voice heard and be in as much control of their own life as possible, with as much support and compassion as you can offer as a professional.

Both Marley and Whitney are actively involved in supporting professionals and organizations and this affords them sophisticated insights into the pitfalls of participatory work. Part of true participation, they feel, is about respecting young people's expertise – and arguably that includes recognizing the limits of that expertise. Marley explains:

> Participation can be patronizing… You don't want to be responding to every idea as if it is brilliant – sometimes we have ideas that aren't doable, affordable or even sensible. A skilled professional with experience of doing participation well can challenge a young person, respectfully, explaining why a suggestion might not be a very useful one. Not dismissing, but explaining. We don't want to hear that we are right all the time – we aren't.

They also offer thought-provoking observations regarding the way in which young people are identified as 'good at this stuff' and so become relied on. This has benefits, but also some potential downsides.

Whitney reflects on one unintended consequence for young people who spend significant amounts of their time working with professionals. Rewarding though it is, it can leave some young people with few friends their own age:

> It can be like you don't really belong anywhere. You're not really in the professionals' group, but you're not like your peers either. It can be lonely sometimes.

Marley also articulates how specific young people can become the 'go-to' in their local area, and the issues this raises in terms of representation and equity of opportunity:

> As a care-experienced person, I do quite a lot of advisory work and consultation. I enjoy it – but I wonder what opportunities are available for other young people, those who are less articulate or who haven't learned to 'talk the talk' like me.

Reflecting on transition to adulthood

The messages from Chapter 10 by Cocker, Cooper and Holmes regarding Transitional Safeguarding resonate strongly with Whitney and Marley's experiences. They each have examples of support not being available or appropriate during their own transition to adulthood, and are adamant that greater alignment is needed between children's and adults' safeguarding systems.

Marley feels that co-working, even at its most basic, is not always in place for young people:

It's obvious! For young people under and over 18, there needs to be a plan between the young person and both sets of professionals – adult services and children's services. It's got to be clearly agreed what both sides will support so there is a sense of fluidity for the young person.

Whitney agrees that transitional support is a priority:

I feel like transition is a major issue from personal experience. I felt like I was dropped at 18 and left to fend for myself, not really knowing what to do – because lots of young people have never been taught how to be an adult. I mean, especially if you haven't got that parental support.

The current binary approach to safeguarding, whereby age and need are used in ways to 'gatekeep' services, resonates with both Whitney and Marley. It is not only the binary notion of child and adulthood that strikes them, but also the binary nature of support; they challenge the usefulness of a system that requires a young person to be either in need of formal support or not in need of support at all. Linked to this, they each highlight the need to think more broadly than statutory safeguarding intervention. As Whitney explains:

Lots of young adults need 'light-touch' support, the kind of everyday help you might need sometimes. But you can't get support unless you're already in a service, and you don't get a service until you need full-on support because things have got really bad for you.

Marley agrees and adds that there is a balancing act for professionals to strike when working with young people making the transition to adulthood:

Teenagers and young adults need a form of support that is more informal but still makes them feel cared for. Services need to be available to support young people to get to a positive place in their life, and whenever they're ready the support eases off. It's a balancing act though – you've got to support them with compassion and care, but not be condescending.

Marley and Whitney feel that the nature of the support offered to young people at this life stage is important. Whitney has good budget management skills. She is able to manage her money carefully and has plenty of practical skills. However, chiming with her earlier observation about the perils of labelling a young person as 'resilient', she recalls:

> I remember being thrown into my own property and being like, 'What if I mess up?' That's where it kind of went a bit wrong because I felt like I couldn't talk to anyone. I felt like I had to do alright. I felt like I couldn't voice my problems because I was meant to be able to look after myself and do everything right, and that got me in a lot of shit.

Whitney also highlights how important it is for transitional support to be emotional, not just practical. The issue of social isolation is particularly relevant for many young people:

> Loneliness is a massive thing in that transition period, especially when you're talking about people who come from families that aren't together. If somebody told me that it was going to be as lonely as it has been for the past four years, I would have been like, 'No thank you. Take it back.' And it can be a lonely world, especially when none of your friends or none of your peer group are in the same situation as you. It's almost as if you're doing it alone because you can't relate to anyone, your story is not relatable to anyone else's.

Reflecting on relationship-based aspirational practice

Whitney and Marley both emphasize the centrality of professionals truly knowing the young person they are working with. Whitney highlights the way that young people can sometimes present barriers to establishing an honest relationship, and how crucial it is that professionals enquire, are curious and tenacious in understanding the young person behind the behaviour:

> I was in the system so long, I knew how to play the system – how to manipulate it, and not in a good way. Actually, if I just owned up to how much I was struggling when I was younger, maybe I never would have gone to prison. But because I kind of kept to it and just went to my appointments and acted all like, you know, happy, I could hide it so well.

As Hickle and Lefevre illustrate in Chapter 8, for many young people, there is a need to repair and rebuild their sense of belief that others can and do care about them. As Whitney highlights:

If the people that surround you, I mean your core support network, couldn't support and protect you properly, then how can anyone else do it?

In reflecting on the case study in that chapter, in which we are shown the tenacity and perseverance of 'Anne' (a social worker seeking to practise in a trauma-informed way with a young man), Whitney describes her own positive experience of a determined professional:

She [my social worker] just sticks with it. I mean, she stuck by me for, like, everything. She always puts a smile on my face because I know that she knows me. That is not going to happen overnight, you've got to stick with it; once you get that trust and relationship, you kind of rebuild that faith. And when the next person comes, it's that much easier to trust them.

As Whitney says, building this kind of trusting relationship can take time. Equally, the benefits of such a relationship can endure for many years, as has been the case for Whitney:

My previous foster carer is still one of my biggest supporters nearly five years after I left her care. She's stuck by me, from 3am police station visits to countless court sittings, being a shoulder to cry on, someone to laugh with.

Marley strongly agrees. From his perspective, trust is the cornerstone of relationship-based practice with young people, and trust requires consistency:

You've got to create trust. Trust, respect and consistency. Once a young person knows that you are there for them – that you will be honest with them and you care…with a strong and consistent relationship, you can get an element of trust. Once there is trust and an open dialogue, that's when you can really make a difference.

One of the characteristics identified by Whitney and Marley as being central to relationship-based practice is the notion of professionals believing in young people, demonstrating their faith that a young person is capable, and holding space for them when they doubt themselves. As Whitney reflects:

A good professional will believe in me when I don't believe in myself, and support me when I'm making stupid decisions and impulsive decisions. My social worker was always there, bringing me back: 'No, let's talk it through'; 'Let's make a plan.' Just talking me through my brain, because sometimes it just doesn't know how to talk for itself, so somebody else has to be my brain for me. She's that person, who listens to my rants, cheers me on and is one of my biggest supporters. She's given me the consistency and stability, she's supported me through everything, she made a difference in how I see professionals who have failed me before.

The idea of aspiration is something that Whitney and Marley return to several times. They speak of the need for professionals to 'not just be kind' but to also have high expectations of young people and of themselves.

For Whitney, who uses her personal experiences to advise national government, and was recently appointed to the Child and Youth Advisory Group for the 2021 World Congress on Justice with Children, this sense of ambition is palpable. When reflecting on what she wants to do in future, she says:

> I want to change things. To make a difference to the lives of young people, to change systems that once failed me and to show people that you can achieve no matter your story; to give ambition to those who have lost all hope and to ultimately be the person I never had when I was younger.

Marley, whose work allows him to directly shape the recruitment and practice of professionals in his local area and beyond, is looking to apply to become a social worker. And he now has an added incentive to share his expertise:

> I can't wait for my baby daughter to grow up and see this book and think 'Wow, that's my dad!' I want her to see what I'm capable of – what we are all capable of.

Chapter 3

Understanding the Age of Adolescence

John Coleman and Ann Hagell

Introduction

Adolescence is a time of profound change. Major alterations in the biological, emotional and social spheres of human development occur during this stage. Many writers (e.g., Coleman, 2011; Hagell, 2012) see adolescence as a time of major transition, leading to growth and potential challenges in all aspects of life. In this chapter, we will explore the various dimensions of change, and argue that understanding the specific features of adolescent development is a key aspect of enabling a more effective safeguarding response for young people.

We suggest that the safeguarding of young people is different from the safeguarding of other age groups. This life stage has characteristics that distinguish it from other stages in the life cycle, leading to specific vulnerabilities (Coleman, 2019a). These may be to do with adverse experiences, the extent of change experienced, or the timing of such change.

When too much change occurs all at the same time, this will inevitably add to the burden of adaptation. However, we are keen to highlight that, in spite of the fact that this is often seen as a turbulent or stressful period, there are many ways in which young people demonstrate strengths and resilience, particularly when faced with adversity or disadvantage. In this chapter, we will briefly consider the concept of resilience, as well as showing how key elements of adolescence are significant for safeguarding practice. The chapter includes brief discussions of puberty, neurological development, changes in family structures, the digital world and mental health. It should be noted that there are particular considerations regarding those young people whose gender identity differs from their biological sex and we cannot do justice to that important and nuanced discussion here.

We are conscious that we are writing this chapter at a time of extreme national stress, as the Covid-19 pandemic has affected all aspects of our lives. Young people have, of course, been affected in a multitude of ways, not least because of interruptions to education and the possible long-term consequences for careers and future employment. While this is not a chapter about the pandemic, we will make reference to its impact.

Puberty and physical development

Puberty is not a topic that is usually included in social work training. Yet this aspect of adolescent development has a key role to play in the establishment of sexual identities and accordant professional responses to, for example, sexual abuse. It could be argued that puberty heralds the beginning of the adolescent period. It certainly involves some of the major changes and transitions that are key to understanding this stage of human development.

Young people experience significant physical, psychological and behavioural changes as they mature from children to adults. Apart from the early years of infancy, the physical changes of adolescence represent our second fastest period of development. The three or four years of pubertal development include a physical growth spurt, maturing of the reproductive organs, development of secondary sex characteristics and the start of periods (menarche) in girls. There is wide individual variation in the timing of the start and completion of puberty. Often, when people consider what puberty means, they think of girls beginning to menstruate or boys' voices deepening and 'breaking' (Coleman, 2011). But these are only two of the signs of a major process of change within the body that can take place at any time between the ages of approximately 9 and 14.

Puberty involves a lot more than the outward signs of sexual maturation. Change takes place in all organs of the body, including the lungs, the heart and the brain (Brady, 2016). The composition of the blood alters at this time, as does the hormone balance, a topic we will return to in the next section.

A good description of puberty can be found in Temple-Smith, Moore and Rosenthal (2016). Here are some basic facts about this phenomenon:

- The beginning of puberty is triggered primarily by the release of sex hormones – testosterone in the case of boys and oestrogen in the case of girls.

- The various changes associated with puberty last about two years.

- Puberty generally starts 12–18 months earlier for girls than it does for boys.

- In Britain today, the average age for a girl to start her periods is 11 years and 10 months old (Patton & Viner, 2007). However, one in five will start while still in primary school.

- Between 1900 and 1960, the average age at which children started puberty decreased, but it has not decreased further since then (Temple-Smith *et al.*, 2016).

- Muscle strength continues to develop in young men until their early 20s (Patton & Viner, 2007).

- Although physical changes are obvious and discernible, emotional changes can have a significant impact too.

It should be emphasized that the age at which young people start puberty is highly variable – it can happen as early as 9 years old or as late as age 14 (and indeed later for some). All this is to be expected, and has no implications for later sexual development. But 'fitting in' usually matters a great deal to most young people – few want to stand out from the crowd. Puberty can therefore be a painful process in this respect, with many young people worrying about pace of change (i.e., nothing is happening or it's all happening at once) and how it compares to the members of their peer group.

Starting puberty either extremely early or late can cause a lot of anxiety for young people, and for their parents or carers. It is important for parents and carers to know that none of these experiences will necessarily have lasting effects. What is critical is that adults know about the possible risks and are able to provide the necessary information and support for adolescents who experience puberty outside the expected age range.

Some research has shown that boys who mature very early usually do well, as they are stronger, taller and more developed than their peers. This often means they are good at sport, something that is associated with popularity. Conversely, boys who mature very much later than others are not necessarily popular and do not do so well in their school work (Coleman, 2011). As far as girls are concerned, both early and late development can be problematic (Coleman, Hendry & Kloep, 2007). Early puberty for girls has been linked to early sexual activity, often with older boys or young men, and so can raise the significant risk of abuse or exploitation. This is clearly of great importance where child protection and safeguarding issues are concerned. Practitioners should be aware of the pubertal status of any girl or young woman they are concerned about, since very early puberty is an important risk factor (Negriff & Susman, 2011; Temple-Smith *et al.*, 2016).

Very late pubertal development in young women has much the same impact as it does in boys, sometimes leading to poor social relationships and lower school attainment. The impact of early and late development is summarized in Temple-Smith *et al.* (2016, Chapter 3). A further illustration of how early puberty – or the perception of maturity – could influence a young person's safety can be found in Chapter 6. Here, Davis and Marsh explain how 'adultification' – where Black girls are presumed to be older or more mature than they are – can lead to children not being adequately safeguarded.

Puberty can be straightforward for some and complicated for others. For many, it is a time of anxiety and stress, while others pass through it with relative ease. One key feature is that it leads to emotional changes as well as to physical maturation. Puberty can have an impact on a young person's self-image and on their sense of self-worth (Ferrer-Wreder & Kroger, 2020).

We know from research that the self-concept of girls suffers around puberty, with nearly half feeling dissatisfied with their bodies (Coleman, 2011). The development of sexual feelings and behaviour is, of course, closely associated with puberty. For those who feel vulnerable at this time, sexuality can become a complicated aspect of life.

Understanding this feature of adolescence is clearly of importance for practitioners, since a significant proportion of safeguarding activity has links to sexual development. Where puberty does not run smoothly, where it occurs outside the usual age range or where there has been little or no preparation by those in caring roles, there may be additional risks for the young person.

For many young people, the arrival of puberty will not be straightforward. Those who have been exposed to abusive relationships in the home may find the occurrence of puberty problematic (Coleman, 2019b). Those who have been brought up in care (see Shaw & Frost, 2013) may not have had sufficient support to prepare themselves for this aspect of their development.

Practitioners may not prioritize the impact of puberty in their work, but as we have shown here, it may well pose a significant risk to development. It is therefore important that practitioners are sensitive to the significance of puberty for any young person that they are supporting, and are respectfully curious about what this life stage means for them.

The science of brain development

Adolescent brain development is another feature gradually coming into focus for practitioners, because research is beginning to demonstrate the significance during teenage years of neurological changes.

Knowledge of brain development can help adults to better understand adolescent behavioural problems like emotional dysregulation, confusion and uncertainty, sensitivity to rewards, what appears to be thoughtlessness, the search for sensation, and so on (Coleman, 2021). When considering neurological change at this time, it is also important to stress that the brain and the environment interact. Each affects the other enriching environments can really help brain development, while adverse circumstances may hold back or delay healthy change (Jensen, 2015). It is, however, important to note the caution offered by some researchers regarding the use of neuroscience in developing policy and practice. The 'dual use dilemma' (Walsh, 2010) noted in relation to youth justice, wherein neuroscience could be (mis)used in ways that are reductive and counterproductive, has parallels in relation to adolescent development. While such evidence regarding the adolescent brain can promote a better understanding of what lies beneath a young person's behaviour, conversely it could be used to undermine young people's self-efficacy, and its individualized focus could obscure the structural and interpersonal factors that are so important to a young person's safety.

In recent years, there has been a remarkable increase in knowledge of what happens in the brain during adolescence. Until 2000, it was widely believed that the brain stopped developing at the end of childhood (Coleman, 2021). We now know that not only does the brain continue to develop during teenage years, but it changes more at this time than any other stage in life, apart from the first three years of life (Coleman, 2021). There are also changes to the 'social brain', the part which governs interactions with others (Coleman, 2021). Evidence from MRI (magnetic resonance imaging) scans suggests that brain development continues up to age 25 (Galvan, 2017). Good descriptions of the developing teenage brain can be found in Jensen (2015) and in Blakemore (2019).

We now know many changes occur at this time. Here, we concentrate on some of the most important of these.

The first change to mention has to do with 'pruning'. This may seem an odd thing to be happening, but, in essence, the brain at the end of childhood produces far more neural connections than necessary. During adolescence, pruning takes place to ensure that effective connections are created and useless ones die away. What results is a lot of reorganization and restructuring, inevitably leading to a period of readjustment. This may have the effect of causing uncertainty, confusion and difficulty in making decisions (Jensen, 2015).

As part of the pruning process, new connections are formed that will enable new skills to develop – more complicated and sophisticated neural networks are created. A good example of this is the 'bridge' that connects the two halves of the brain, which develops rapidly during this stage. Although this bridge is active in childhood, it grows and becomes more important in adolescence, which allows the brain to use its different capacities in a more organized fashion (Blakemore, 2019).

As Coleman (2021) explains, the prefrontal cortex and the amygdala also develop rapidly during adolescence, though evidence shows that these two sites don't necessarily develop at the same pace. The amygdala, associated with emotion, sensation and arousal, may develop faster than the prefrontal cortex, which is associated with thinking, reasoning and problem-solving. It may therefore be the case that, for some young people, planning and thinking about consequences may come second to exploration and experimentation. This may also explain why some young people prefer living 'in the moment' to thinking about the future (Coleman, 2018).

New knowledge of the brain includes a new understanding of the role hormones play in adolescent development. It has long been understood that teenagers are affected by their hormones, which are often considered to be the cause of mood swings and irritability. What's new in our knowledge is that the balance of hormones seems to affect brain development. The alterations and fluctuations of hormones act on various parts of the brain that have already been mentioned, such as the prefrontal cortex and the amygdala (Jensen, 2015).

High levels of sex hormones, such as testosterone and progesterone, not only have an impact on the development of the sex organs and on sexual behaviour, but also lead to changes in behaviour more generally. Surges of these hormones may encourage young people to seek out emotionally charged experiences, or to look for novelty and excitement (Galvan, 2017).

It is also worth noting that levels of hormones like cortisol and serotonin fluctuate considerably during this stage. The release of cortisol is linked to experiences of anxiety, while serotonin helps to moderate that response. If these hormones are in flux, emotions may be difficult to manage. It is also important to mention dopamine, the hormone released by enjoyment and pleasure. The brain is particularly sensitive to dopamine during teenage years, which may explain risky or thrill-seeking behaviours (Jensen, 2015; Galvan, 2017).

Lastly there is melatonin, the hormone released at night that tells us it's time to sleep. We now know melatonin is released later in the day for adolescents, which means some young people may have more difficulty getting to sleep than other members of their family (Walker, 2018).

Sleep is very important for teenagers (Walker, 2018). If teenagers have to get up early for school they may miss hours of much-needed sleep. Research shows that sleep deficit (fewer than seven hours a night) has an impact on both learning and behaviour. Furthermore, research also shows that sleep is a time of memory consolidation. In other words, the information that has been learned during the day is stored and cemented during certain phases of sleep. With the help of caring adults, young people can overcome the effect of melatonin and get into good sleep routines (Coleman, 2018).

To conclude this section, it is important to state that the more adults understand adolescent brain development, the more they can work effectively with this age group. It is very easy to be critical of emotional, changeable, inconsistent or puzzling teenage behaviour. However, much of this behaviour has its roots in the changes and readjustments occurring in the brain, and – importantly – in the environment surrounding the young person.

Of course, early (especially adverse) experiences will also play their part, and may well lead to more troubled or troubling behaviours. Nonetheless, knowledge gained in recent years about brain development provides new insights which should help professional adults take a more sympathetic and informed approach in their work with young people. Other useful information about this topic can be found in Crone (2017) and Galvan (2017).

Adolescent health

In the context of safeguarding practice, the health of young people is another key consideration. The ways in which adolescents respond to difficult circumstances and adverse experiences will be affected not just by their own resources and the support structures around them, but by factors like their general health. For a review of the health of young people see Hagell and Shah (2019).

Adolescence is generally a healthy age period when compared to other age groups. Relatively few people die between the ages of 10 and 24, representing less than 1 per cent of all deaths each year (Office for National Statistics, 2020). The critical thing is that many of the causes of death for young people are described as 'external' – accidents, self-harm and assault – and are thus potentially preventable. Young men are particularly at risk. Those aged 15–24 are three times more likely than young women to die of accidents and almost four times more likely to die of intentional self-harm.

Mortality is an important issue when thinking about adolescent health, but this age period is also important for a range of other reasons, not least because lifelong behaviours are set in place at this time. In the long term, habits formed during adolescence may be related to cancer, heart disease, obesity and type 2 diabetes. Prevention and early intervention from parents and/or professionals offer lots of opportunities to change these trajectories, which makes stepping in critical during teenage years (Hagell & Rigby, 2015).

The key things to consider around adolescent health behaviours include physical activity, nutrition and obesity, smoking, drinking and drug use, sleep and sexual health. In terms of health conditions, there are a number with a peak age of diagnosis in adolescence, including asthma and type 1 diabetes. Headaches, abdominal pain, musculoskeletal disorders, allergies, skin disorders and acne, coughs and respiratory infections are some of the common physical health problems for which young people seek medical advice. On average, around 10 per cent of young people aged 10–24 have a disability of some kind that affects their ability to perform normal daily activities.

In addition, many young people will experience mental health problems at some point between the ages of 10 and 24 (Hagell & Shah, 2019). Estimates have suggested that 14 per cent of 11–16-year-olds experience mental health difficulties at any given time, although there is considerable variation by age and gender within these statistics (Sadler et al., 2018). Some of the most common difficulties during teenage years include anxiety and depression, eating disorders, conduct disorders (i.e., serious antisocial behaviour), and attention deficit hyperactivity disorder (ADHD). This phase of life will also witness the early emergence of rarer disorders such as bipolar disorder and schizophrenia. In fact, one half of all lifetime cases of psychiatric disorders start by the age of 14, and three-quarters begin by the age of 24 (Kessler et al., 2005).

Health is important in its own right across all the ages, but it is of particular relevance when thinking about supporting young people to navigate the challenges of adolescence. Understanding young people's health experiences and concerns is critical to helping them take control of their lives. Many young people who grow up in disadvantaged circumstances often suffer from poor health, and much has been written about health inequalities as they impact on the adolescent population (Currie et al., 2008; Pearce et al., 2019). It is also the case that access to health services is more irregular and uneven for those in care or living away from their birth families. Where safeguarding is concerned, attention to general health issues can be as important as concentrating on mental health or other vulnerabilities.

The changing nature of the family

When considering the safeguarding of adolescents, it will be clear that the family, or living circumstances of the individual, is critical for a full understanding of the situation. The great majority of the items in any list of adverse childhood experiences will have some connection to the family (Lacey & Minnis, 2020; Lacey et al., 2020). Furthermore, when considering resilience, it is instructive to note that the key factors in both the risk and protective categories concern the family (see Coleman & Hagell, 2007). This is also illustrated in Frydenberg's (2019) book on coping in adolescence, where she highlights the role of the family in contributing to a young person's ability to overcome adversity.

First, we consider some general points about family and young people. The majority of young people aged 10–19 live with their families. Family can mean a wide range of arrangements. Many will be living with step-parents, lone parents, or with their own partners. A smaller group – approximately 3 in 100 – are living in local authority care, hospitals, prisons, or as lodgers in other kinds of settings (Hagell & Shah, 2019).

The circumstances of those growing up in care are described in detail in Shaw and Frost (2013). Homelessness in young people is notoriously difficult to assess and respond to. Very few young people are registered as homeless in their own right, but an undetected sub-group live by 'sofa surfing' and do not show up in official statistics.

Second, to explore this in more detail, we will review three topics related to the family:

- Parenting approaches.

- The impact on adolescents of divorce and family breakdown.

- Recent work on support for the parents and carers of teenagers.

Looking first at parenting approaches, there has been a great deal of research on this subject over recent years (Abela & Walker, 2014; Misca & Smith, 2014). Broadly speaking, studies show that the 'authoritative' style of parenting is associated with the best outcomes for young people. This style is contrasted with the authoritarian, indulgent and indifferent styles of parenting. The authoritative parenting style includes warmth, the provision of structure, and the encouragement of age-appropriate autonomy (Smetana, 2013).

As far as divorce and family breakdown are concerned, it is evident that adolescents can be just as affected by these experiences as younger children. What is clear, however, is that it is not the divorce itself that is most significant, but what has happened in the family before that point, and what happens afterwards in terms of family relationships (Frydenberg, 2019). The most damaging experience for teenagers is to be 'caught in the middle' where there is continuing parental conflict following separation. By contrast, adolescents can do very well if they are able to maintain good relationships with the non-residential parent, and if their own needs are recognized (Boylan & Allan, 2013).

Having restricted access to one parent who is no longer living at home can also impact on the wellbeing of a young person, and the uncertainties that can come from a changing family may create additional stresses at a time of life where stable support is essential.

Increasing proportions of young people living at home with their families continue to do so into their early 20s and this is becoming the 'new normal' (Hagell & Shah, 2019). By 2017, the age by which 50 per cent had left home was 23, but we expect this to go up as economic crisis particularly hits the age group and access to independent income likely becomes more difficult following the impact of the Covid-19 pandemic.

To conclude this section, it is important to note that parents and carers of teenagers have a key role to play. They matter just as much as the parents and carers of younger children, but in different ways (Coleman, 2018). Research shows that the involvement of parents and carers during the adolescent years can make a major difference to outcomes, whether these are to do with educational achievement, health behaviours, the development of values, or future employment (Hagell, 2012). It is not uncommon for adults to believe the opposite, since young people may be sending the message that, at this stage, their friends are more important than their parents and carers. Practitioners can and should take every opportunity to explore this belief. Parents and carers have a central role to play during these years, and, as discussed in Chapter 4, where young people are at risk of harm outside the home, their parents and carers are crucial safeguarding partners. The more the importance of parents and carers is acknowledged, the better it will likely be for adolescent development (Coleman, 2018).

Key social changes affecting young people

One factor that has a profound influence on the type of transition experienced by the young person is the social context in which they grow up. The world that surrounds the teenager today is very different from the world as it was in, say, 1970, or even 1990. We should keep in mind that the teenager of today was born in the first decade of the 21st century, already very different from the 20th century. In this section, we will briefly explore some of the major changes that have occurred in the social world, which have an impact on the lives of young people.

We have mentioned changes to families. Other key social trends that affect young people's experiences include:

- The transition from education to employment.

- Increasing ethnic diversity.
- The impact of the digital world.

From education to employment

It should be noted that this has been written during the ongoing Covid-19 pandemic. While it is very difficult to say at this point how the lockdowns resulting from the virus will affect young people, they cannot be ignored as a factor that will influence their lives.

It is important to recognize the constant change that has occurred in secondary education in the 21st century. This includes the enormous impact that Covid-19 has had on the educational experiences of young people in 2020 and 2021, especially for adolescents who were expected to take examinations during these years.

On a more general note, young people are staying on longer at school with the increased participation agenda, and there have been numerous changes in the provisions for 16–18-year-olds. Furthermore, entry into the labour market has become more difficult, with major changes in employment opportunities for young adults. Writing today, it is important to note that higher youth unemployment will likely be one of the consequences of the pandemic. This fact, combined with the changes mentioned here, is going to impact on the life chances and development of teenagers growing up today.

Ethnic diversity

The increase in ethnic diversity is another factor that contributes to a changing social context. The circumstances of those from diverse ethnic backgrounds is something that has been at the forefront of social and political discussion in recent times. Unfortunately, prejudice and discrimination remain endemic in many walks of life.

Young people from a variety of different cultural and ethnic backgrounds play a full role in society in many ways. However, the fact remains that the chances for those from such backgrounds can still be far too limited. The experience of racism is damaging and distressing to those who have to live with this aspect of life in Britain (Owusu-Bempah, 2013). There is no doubt that the life chances of many Black and other minoritized people are negatively influenced or restricted by racial prejudice, as is discussed in Chapter 5 of this book. Higher rates of school exclusion (Department for Education, 2020), and clear disproportionality within the criminal justice system for young Black men (Bateman, 2017), are just two instances of the way these attitudes play out for certain young people.

Chapter 6 explores the particular implications of professional bias within safeguarding practice and policy. It is hoped that, with more recognition of systemic racism in society, opportunities and outcomes for all young Black and minoritized young people will improve.

The digital world

Finally in this section, we will say something about the digital world. Clearly this too has been significantly affected by the Covid-19 pandemic. Since the majority of young people spent 2020 attending school online, many of the things we might once have said about life in the 'virtual world' have changed, and this applies to adults as well.

The role played by social media in the lives of young people cannot be underestimated. The opportunities offered by the digital medium have changed the social context for teenagers growing up in this century (Goodyear & Armour, 2019). That said, there are two points to be made here. Adults spend as much time online as teenagers, so we have to be careful not to assume this is simply a teenage phenomenon. The second point is that the online and the offline world connect and interact. Both are important in their own right (Davies & Eynon, 2013). Young people still want to see their friends and take part in real-world activities. It is essential to remember that the virtual and physical worlds work together (Hayman & Coleman, 2016).

Many aspects of the digital world give rise to anxiety in adults. As readers will be well aware, the sources of this anxiety include grooming, pornography, gaming and the possibility of addiction, online bullying and other worrying facets of social media. It's important to ensure that young people are aware of and know how to navigate and minimize the risks. Conversely, the positive opportunities afforded by the digital world should also be acknowledged (Livingstone, Haddon & Gorzig, 2012).

The internet has changed so many aspects of life and has provided so many new avenues through which we can experience our social relationships. Life for a 21st-century teenager is unimaginable without being able to live in the virtual world just as easily as the physical one. Many teenagers would say this has created a richer life.

Understanding challenges to successfully navigating adolescence

Some young people have support to help them make these transitions with ease. Others find this a more challenging time, in which case they will need more support. Experiences of trauma or abuse can affect how young people manage this period of their lives. Awareness of their experiences can help professionals recognize what is happening and how best to help.

Identifying young people in particularly challenging situations

Without equal access to resources and support, significant proportions of today's young people are faced with disadvantages that affect how they experience adolescence (Hagell *et al.*, 2018). These disadvantages may be due to adverse events, or because the young people in question don't have access to the same levels of support as their peers. Such circumstances may set in motion inequalities that continue to play out across the rest of their lives. Being aware of these inequalities helps to shape our response to them.

Many factors play a part in contributing to adversity. Children in care tend to have more social, emotional and mental health problems than their peers. Young people with caring responsibilities are often hidden, but at increased risk of missing out on education and social opportunities. Black and other minoritized adolescents may be more likely to become victims of serious youth violence (Shaw & Frost, 2013). Young people who identify as LGBTQIA (lesbian, gay, bisexual, transgender, queer and/or questioning, intersex, asexual and/or ally) and are from a minoritized ethnic background may experience compounded discrimination – as explored in Chapter 6. Young people whose intersectional identities are not celebrated or recognized by those around them may find adolescence especially stressful.

What is 'normal adolescent behaviour' and what marks more serious problems?

Moodiness and irritability are of course typically described symptoms of adolescence. It is difficult for young people, parents, teachers and others to know when ordinary teenage ups and downs become mental health problems that need intervention (Hagell & Maughan, 2017).

There are no easy answers to that question, but there are some things to look out for that would suggest a problem is more than just transient moodiness:

- The problem is persistent – ongoing sadness, anxiety or irritability.
- There is a sense of hopelessness and not being able to enjoy regular activities, possibly with recurrent thoughts of death or suicidal ideation.
- The young person regularly expresses negative, distressing or unusual thoughts.
- Physical symptoms are also present – difficulties with sleeping (too much, or insomnia), changes to appetite or heart palpitations.
- An inability to do regular, daily things.
- Changes in performance at school, college or work.

If young people show several of these difficulties on most days, for two weeks or longer, it is likely that more support is needed.

Is mental health deteriorating?

There is much debate about whether today's generation of young people is more anxious, depressed and stressed than previous generations (Ogden & Hagen, 2019). The evidence suggests that there was a rise in emotional and behavioural problems over the last three or so decades of the 20th century up to 2000 (Collishaw *et al.*, 2004) but epidemiological data in the early 2000s suggested a levelling out (Maughan *et al.*, 2008).

The most recent nationally representative survey of child and adolescent mental health problems was published in 2018 after a long gap, which allowed us to look at trends from 1999 to 2017 (NHS Digital,

2018). The absolute rise in 11–15-year-olds was small – a couple of percentage points increase in mental health problems across these 18 years. Expressed as a proportional increase over the 1999 rates, however, the rise looks more dramatic, at 19 per cent for 11–15-year-olds compared with 13 per cent for younger children.

The group where we really suspect there has been a rise – the older teenagers – was not included in earlier surveys, so we cannot tell definitively what has been going on there. Even if good data are available, interpreting time trends is very difficult. Rises might just suggest that we diagnose more, or that our criteria for diagnosis have got wider, or that perceptions of 'normal' have changed. However, there are methodological checks and balances that can be brought to bear to make us more confident that what we see in the data is indeed what has happened. Thus, for example, in relation to the rises at the end of the 20th century, one study has shown that the strengths of associations between psychiatric symptoms and poor outcomes later in adulthood remained similar over time for three different birth cohorts from 1974 to 1999, suggesting that the results were not attributable to changes in the thresholds of what is counted as a problem (Collishaw *et al.*, 2004). Across that period at least, it seemed that the increasing time trends were not, for example, the result of an increasing tendency for parents to rate teenagers as having problems, but were instead the result of changes in frequency of problems.

Adolescent trauma and recovery: How plastic is the brain and what protective factors are needed to overcome early trauma?

It is understandable that those who work with young people who have experienced abuse or other traumatic events during their childhood want to know what effect these experiences will have on the teenage years (Hickle, 2019). In particular, they want to know whether trauma will continue to affect brain development and whether it is possible for teenagers to recover from earlier traumatic experiences (Danese, 2020).

Of course, these are not easy questions to answer. There is such a wide variety of possible traumas that can impact on a child's life that it is hard to construct studies that provide conclusive answers. Nonetheless many investigators have been studying this topic over the past decade or so. Researchers (McCrory, Gerin & Viding, 2017) carried out a review of numerous studies on this topic and concluded that there are significant differences in brain function of young people who have been exposed to childhood maltreatment.

These authors looked at evidence relating to four domains of brain function: threat processing, reward processing, emotion regulation and executive function. They reported that studies do illustrate differences in neural functioning in samples of young people who have experienced maltreatment in childhood. As far as threat processing is concerned, the evidence shows both heightened and depressed reactivity. This is thought to reflect either avoidance or hypervigilance.

Reward processing is seen to be blunted in comparison with other groups of young people, reflecting low expectations of positive experiences. Emotion regulation is significantly affected, with extra effort required to make sense of emotional stimuli. Finally, executive function is compromised, since this group finds it harder to recognize errors and to utilize effective inhibitory mechanisms.

The authors use the term 'latent vulnerability' to describe this overall picture of brain function. They explain this as a picture of brain activity which is adaptive in situations of trauma or maltreatment. The child develops a pattern of response that assists in dealing with the harmful environment. However, such a pattern of brain activity is not helpful as the individual moves away from the unsafe situation and is able to experience more nurturing and supportive relationships.

It should be noted that there are many challenges with this type of research. The great majority of studies have been carried out in the USA where definitions and criteria may be different from those we are used to in the UK. In addition, it is hard to find matched samples of children in order to draw sensible comparisons. As noted, there are so many different types of adverse experience that might be said to include maltreatment. Lastly, many children who have experienced maltreatment have histories which include multiple placements and disrupted lives, so that studying these groups poses particular problems (Nigg, 2017).

This leads on to the broader question of whether earlier trauma has a long-lasting impact on brain development. The simple answer to this is that we still do not know. However, there are some clues. It is the case that the human brain is amazingly plastic. This means that it has the capacity to repair itself. There are numerous examples of how, even after injury, the brain adapts and returns to normal functioning. There is also some useful information on this question from studies of fostering and adoption (McCrory et al., 2017; Shaw & Frost, 2013).

These studies show that the earlier the child is removed from the adverse environment, the more likely it is that the outcome will be a positive one. In addition, studies of resilience indicate that much will depend on the type of environment to which the child moves following maltreatment or trauma. The more supportive the environment, the more likely it is that the individual will overcome earlier adversity (see Coleman & Hagell, 2007; Hagell, 2012; Luthar, 2003).

There is much that we still do not know about the impact of childhood trauma. Nonetheless, there are some positive indications. The brain has a remarkable capacity to adjust and adapt. In addition, the environment plays a part. The more supportive the world is around the child or young person, the greater the chance of being able to overcome earlier adversity.

Promoting resilience: What should young people have in their 'toolbox'?

It is only too easy to concentrate on the problems and difficulties faced by young people in disadvantaged circumstances. Indeed, a portion of this chapter has been devoted to risk and vulnerability. Nonetheless, there has in recent years been a welcome move within social work and other disciplines to develop an approach which has more of a focus on the positive capabilities of the individual. This is sometimes known as a strengths-based approach, or the use of an asset model. This is linked to an increasing interest in young people's participation, and a growing recognition that adolescents can have a role to play in the development of policy and service planning (Tew, 2013), something explored further in Chapter 9.

These trends are closely associated with work on the promotion of resilience (Coleman & Hagell, 2007; Frydenberg, 2019). Such work identifies the protective factors that may be available for any individual young person, and attempts to reinforce these or harness them for the benefit of adolescent development.

One aspect of this work relates to the notion of agency mentioned at the beginning of this chapter (Hutchinson, 2013). The theory here is that, while adults believe that it is their influence which determines events, in reality it is the young person who is shaping and constructing their own environment. This is a central concept for any intervention. If professional adults are able to work collaboratively with the adolescent, there is a much greater chance of success.

It may seem a tall order to find ways of promoting resilience for young people facing serious adversities. Yet a number of commentators have suggested ways in which it might be possible to do this (Frydenberg, 2019). Sometimes this requires a different way of thinking about young people, with a focus on strengths and not 'weaknesses'. At other times, it demands an approach that concentrates on how to limit risk and promotes the available protective factors (Hutchinson, 2013).

Here are some suggestions:

- Reduce the young person's exposure to risk. This may involve disrupting a source of risk, changing the environment, finding safe spaces for the young person to live, work or study, or offering more contact with positive and protective role models.

- Interrupt the chain reaction that occurs after negative events. Key events such as bereavement, trauma, coming into contact with the police or a change in living circumstances may all lead to a downward spiral. Intervention at these times can make a significant difference.

- Offer the young person positive experiences that play to their strengths or enhance whatever protective factors are available.

- Remember the notion of agency. The young person will be hard at work constructing a life for themselves, even when facing adversity. The choices they make may not always be positive, but the goal should be to help them make safe and healthy ones regardless, rather than impose someone else's choices on them.

Conclusion

We started this chapter by arguing that there are particular aspects of adolescence that lead to the conclusion that safeguarding for this age group is different from the safeguarding of other age groups. This is partly to do with the major physical and emotional changes that characterize adolescence, and partly to do with the pressures and challenges that arise from the nature of the transition from childhood to maturity. In addition, particular events may occur that contribute to the challenges of this stage of life. In the present context, we refer especially to trauma, abuse and adverse childhood experiences.

In this chapter, we have explored topics including puberty,

neurological development, health, the role of parents and carers and the impact of social change. We have also noted some aspects of the work on resilience, pointing out that, even in seriously adverse circumstances, young people do have strengths and capabilities that can contribute to improved outcomes.

We believe it is important to underline the fact that the individual's own trajectory of development interacts with the environment in which they grow up. This is reflected particularly well in our understanding of brain development. We have learned that enriched environments foster healthy brain development, while restricted or damaging environments have the opposite effect. However, we have also seen that the brain is immensely plastic, so that under the right circumstances recovery is possible.

In our previous work (Coleman & Hagell, 2007), we have highlighted the balance between risk and protective factors in order to understand the outcomes for young people experiencing adverse events. The greater the risks, the more extensive the protective factors need to be for a positive outcome. As will be seen from what we have said about resilience, a strengths-based approach draws on the young person's capabilities and avoids an exclusive focus on the risks and problems.

Within this chapter, we have referred to the work relating to adverse childhood experiences. This chimes well with what has come to be known as trauma-informed approaches to abuse and exploitation. Here, the focus is on how earlier events in childhood impact adolescence. Such a view is pertinent to all the topics considered here. Nonetheless, we remain optimistic about the individual young person's capacity for adaptation and adjustment. The adolescent period is one of major changes in every aspect of development. Such change, given the right environment, can lead to the capacity to overcome adversity.

References

Abela, A. & Walker, J. (eds) (2014). *Contemporary Issues in Family Studies*. Chichester: Wiley-Blackwell.

Bateman, T. (2017). *The State of Youth Justice 2017: An Overview of Trends and Developments*. National Association of Youth Justice.

Blakemore, S-J. (2019). *Inventing Ourselves: The Secret Life of the Teenage Brain*. London: Transworld.

Boylan, J. & Allen, G. (2013). 'Family Disruption and Relationship Breakdown.' In M. Davies (ed.) *The Blackwell Companion to Social Work*. Chichester: Wiley-Blackwell.

Brady, M. (2016). *The Body in Adolescence*. London: Routledge.

Coleman, J. (2011). *The Nature of Adolescence* (fourth edition). London: Routledge.

Coleman, J. (2018). *Why Won't My Teenager Talk to Me?* (second edition). London: Routledge.

Coleman, J. (2019a). 'Understanding Adolescent Development in the Context of Child Sexual Exploitation.' In J. Pearce (ed.) *Child Sexual Exploitation: Why Theory Matters*. Bristol: Policy Press.

Coleman, J. (2019b). 'Helping teenagers in care flourish: What parenting research tells us about foster care.' *Child & Family Social Work, 24*(3), 354–359.

Coleman, J. (2021). *The Teacher and the Teenage Brain*. London: Routledge.

Coleman, J. & Hagell, A. (2007). *Adolescence: Risk and Resilience*. Chichester: Wiley-Blackwell.

Coleman, J., Hendry, L. & Kloep, M. (2007). *Adolescence and Health*. Chichester: Wiley-Blackwell.

Collishaw, S., Maughan, B., Goodman, R. & Pickles, A. (2004). 'Time trends in adolescent mental health.' *Journal of Child Psychology and Psychiatry, 45*, 1350–1362.

Crone, E. (2017). *The Adolescent Brain: Changes in Learning, Decision-Making and Social Relations*. London: Routledge.

Currie, C., Molcho, M., Boyce, W., Holstein, B., Torsheim, T. & Richter, M. (2008). 'Researching health inequalities in adolescents: The development of the Health Behaviour in School-Aged Children (HBSC) Family Affluence Scale.' *Social Science & Medicine, 66*(6), 1429–1436.

Danese, A. (2020). 'Rethinking childhood trauma: New research directions for measurement, study design and analytical strategies.' *Journal of Child Psychology and Psychiatry, 61*(3), 236–250.

Davies, C. & Eynon, R. (2013). *Teenagers and Technology*. London: Routledge.

Department for Education (2020). *Permanent and Fixed-Period Exclusions in England: Academic Year 2018 to 2019*. https://explore-education-statistics.service.gov.uk/find-statistics/permanent-and-fixed-period-exclusions-in-england.

Ferrer-Wreder, L. & Kroger, J. (2020). *Identity in Adolescence: The Balance Between Self and Other* (fourth edition). London: Routledge.

Frydenberg, E. (2019). *Adolescent Coping: Promoting Resilience and Well-Being*. London: Routledge.

Galvan, A. (2017). *The Neuroscience of Adolescence*. Cambridge: Cambridge University Press.

Goodyear, V. & Armour, K. (eds) (2019). *Young People, Social Media and Health*. London: Routledge.

Hagell, A. (ed.) (2012). *Changing Adolescence: Social Trends and Mental Health*. Bristol: Policy Press.

Hagell, A. & Maughan, B. (2017). 'Epidemiology: Are Mental Health Problems in Children and Young People Really a Big Issue?' In N. Midgley, J. Hayes & M. Cooper (eds) *Essential Research Findings in Child and Adolescent Counselling and Psychotherapy*. London: Sage/BACP.

Hagell, A. & Rigby, E. (2015). 'Looking at the effectiveness of prevention and early intervention.' *British Journal of School Nursing, 10*(1), 26–30.

Hagell, A. & Shah, R. (2019). *Key Data on Young People 2019*. London: Association for Young People's Health.

Hagell, A., Shah, R., Viner, R., Hargreaves, D., Varnes, L. & Heys, M. (2018). *The Social Determinants of Young People's Health: Identifying the Key Issues and Assessing How Young People Are Doing in the 2010s*. London: The Health Foundation.

Hayman, S. & Coleman, J. (2016). *Parents and Digital Technology*. London: Routledge.

Hickle, K. (2019). 'Understanding Trauma and its Relevance to Child Sexual Exploitation.' In J. Pearce (ed.) *Child Sexual Exploitation: Why Theory Matters*. Bristol: Policy Press.

Hutchinson, A. (2013). 'Strengths-Based/Resilience Theory.' In M. Davies (ed.) *The Blackwell Companion to Social Work*. Chichester: Wiley-Blackwell.

Jensen, F. (2015). *The Teenage Brain: A Neuroscientist's Survival Guide to Raising Adolescents and Young Adults*. New York, NY: Harper.

Kessler, R., Berglund, P., Demler, O., Jin, R., Merikangas, K. & Walters, E. (2005). 'Lifetime prevalence and age-of-onset distributions of DSM-IV disorders in the National Comorbidity Survey replication.' *Archives of General Psychiatry, 62*(6), 593–602.

Lacey, R., Howe, L., Kelly-Irving, M., Bartley, M. & Kelly, Y. (2020). 'The clustering of adverse childhood experiences in the Avon Longitudinal Study of Parents and Children: Are gender and poverty important?' *Journal of Interpersonal Violence*. https://journals.sagepub.com/doi/full/10.1177/0886260520935096.

Lacey, R. & Minnis, H. (2020). 'Practitioner review: Twenty years of research with adverse childhood experience scores – Advantages, disadvantages and applications to practice.' *Journal of Child Psychology & Psychiatry, 61*(2), 116–130.

Livingstone, S., Haddon, L. & Gorzig, A. (eds) (2012). *Children, Risk and Safety on the Internet.* Bristol: Policy Press.

Luthar, S. (2003). *Resilience and Vulnerability: Adaptation in the Context of Childhood Adversities.* Cambridge: Cambridge University Press.

Maughan, B., Collishaw, S., Meltzer, H. & Goodman, R. (2008). 'Recent trends in UK child and adolescent mental health.' *Social Psychiatry and Psychiatric Epidemiology, 43*(4), 305–310.

McCrory, E., Gerin, M. & Viding, E. (2017). 'Childhood maltreatment, latent vulnerability, and the shift to preventative psychiatry: The contribution of functional brain imaging.' *Journal of Child Psychology & Psychiatry, 58*(4), 338–357.

Misca, G. & Smith, J. (2014). 'Mothers, Fathers, Families and Child Development.' In A. Abela & J. Walker (eds) *Contemporary Issues in Family Studies.* Chichester: Wiley-Blackwell.

Negriff, S. & Susman, E. (2011). 'Pubertal timing, depression, and externalising problems: A framework, review and examination of gender differences.' *Journal of Research on Adolescence, 21*(3), 717–746.

NHS Digital (2018). *Mental Health of Children and Young People in England, 2017.* London: NHS Digital.

Nigg, J. (2017). 'On the relation among self-regulation, self-control, executive function, effortful control, risk-taking and inhibition for developmental psychopathology.' *Journal of Child Psychology & Psychiatry, 58*(4), 361–383.

Office for National Statistics (2020). *Dataset: Deaths Registered by Single Year of Age, UK.* www.ons.gov.uk/peoplepopulationandcommunity/birthsdeathsandmarriages/deaths/datasets/deathregistrationssummarytablesenglandandwalesdeathsbysingleyearofagetables.

Ogden, T. & Hagen, K.A. (2019). *Adolescent Mental Health: Prevention and Intervention.* London: Routledge.

Owusu-Bempah, K. (2013). 'Culture, Ethnicity and Identity.' In M. Davies (ed.) *The Blackwell Companion to Social Work* (fourth edition). Chichester: Wiley-Blackwell.

Patton, G. & Viner, R. (2007). 'Pubertal transitions in health.' *The Lancet, 369*, 1130–1139.

Pearce, A., Dundas, R., Whitehead, M. & Taylor-Robinson, D. (2019). 'Pathways to inequalities in child health.' *Archives of Disease in Childhood, 104*, 998–1003.

Sadler, K., Vizard, T., Ford, T., Goodman, A. & Goodman, R. (2018). *Mental Health of Children and Young People in England, 2017.* London: NHS Digital.

Shaw, J. & Frost, N. (2013). *Young People and the Care Experience.* London: Routledge.

Smetana, J. (2013). *Adolescents, Families and Social Development.* Chichester: Wiley-Blackwell.

Temple-Smith, M., Moore, S. & Rosenthal, D. (2016). *Sexuality in Adolescence: The Digital Generation.* London: Routledge.

Tew, J. (2013). 'Theories of Empowerment.' In M. Davies (ed.) *The Blackwell Companion to Social Work.* Chichester: Wiley-Blackwell.

Walker, M. (2018). *Why We Sleep: The New Science of Sleep and Dreams.* London: Penguin.

Walsh, C. (2010). 'Youth justice and neuro-science: A dual-use dilemma.' *British Journal of Criminology, 51*(1), 21–39.

Chapter 4

Growing Pains: Developing Safeguarding Responses to Adolescent Harm

Helen Beckett and Jenny Lloyd

Introduction

The last 15 years have seen increasing recognition of the range of harms that can be experienced during adolescence and the need for appropriate safeguarding responses to these. Realizing the provision of such responses has not, however, been unproblematic. A number of key challenges remain in terms of our understanding of, and responses to, such harm.

We begin by considering how partial conceptualizations and problematic narratives around adolescent harm can both obscure the abusive nature of such experiences and potentially compound, rather than alleviate, the associated risks and impacts. We explore how current systemic structures and associated practices may inhibit professional capacity to appropriately respond to such harms. We conclude with a consideration of how the application of a more contextual and holistic approach could help address these shortcomings and better accommodate the complex realities of the harm experienced in adolescence.

The critique presented within this chapter in no way seeks to undermine the commitment or contribution of the many dedicated professionals working hard to prevent and respond to adolescent harm. Nor is it intended to deny the observable progress in the field in recent years. Instead, it seeks to augment this progress and commitment by shedding light on some of the systemic constraints and inherited working practices that may conspire against it, and to consider how these might be better navigated or addressed.

Obscuring harm through partial and problematic narratives

The increasing recognition of potential harm in adolescence was initially driven by a focus on extra-familial child sexual exploitation (CSE), linked to high-profile cases such as those observed in Derby, Rotherham, Rochdale and Oxford. Such cases drew attention to the significant levels of sexual harm experienced by some adolescents and associated shortcomings in professional responses to such harm (Beckett, 2019a). More recently, potential harms associated with gang culture, county lines[1] and other forms of child criminal exploitation (CCE) are also receiving particular attention, although it is notable that recognition of these harms continues to be obscured by a focus on their links to potential criminality (Children's Commissioner, 2019; Maxwell et al., 2019; Wroe, 2019).

While it is undoubtedly positive that the existence of these, and other forms of adolescent harm, is more readily recognized, the narrative around them has not been without problems. The discourse around certain forms of harm has been at best partial, and at worst misleading, focusing only on subsets of people perpetrating and experiencing these. In the case of CSE, for example, the disproportionate focus on group-based face-to-face offending by Asian adult males against White girls has created a partial narrative around where risks of CSE lie. This has inadvertently obscured recognition of risks from single perpetrators, female perpetrators or those from other ethnic backgrounds. It has also obscured identification of CSE experienced by males, or those from Black, Asian and minority ethnic backgrounds (Ackerley & Latchford, 2018; Brandon et al., 2020; Cockbain, 2013; Gohir, 2013; McNaughton Nicholls et al., 2014; Rodger et al., 2020).

Discourse around CCE and youth violence has been similarly gendered and racialized, focusing primarily on risks to young males, and in particular young Black males (Firmin & Pearce, 2016; Williams & Clarke, 2016; Wroe, 2019). As with CSE, such partial discourses

---

1   Defined within Home Office 2018 guidance as the transportation of illegal drugs by gangs and organized criminal networks, using a dedicated phone line and involving the exploitation of children and vulnerable adults.

conspire against the identification of risks and harms experienced by others. Given the links between criminality and CCE, they also reinforce an unhelpful gendered and racialized narrative that problematizes the experiences and behaviours of young Black males, construing them as primarily causing, rather than experiencing, harm (Davis & Marsh, 2020).

A disproportionate focus on particular manifestations of harm has also unhelpfully directed attention and resources away from other forms of harm that adolescents can experience. The focus on CSE, for example – and its misinterpretation as only extra-familial in nature – has been argued to have negatively impacted on identification of, and responses to, other forms of sexual abuse. This includes sexual harm experienced within the home environment, which research continues to show is a significant issue of concern for adolescents (Beckett & Walker, 2018).

As illustrated in the following young person's reflections on police responses to her missing episodes, a singular focus on risks in extra-familial environments – and uncontested assumptions around the safety of the familial environment – can actually serve to undermine the self-protective actions of young people, and expose them to greater harm:

> 'It's weird because if you were running away from a problem at home, and you're running away because of that, and you…don't have anywhere safe to stay, the police will come and they go, "Oh you don't have anywhere safe to stay so we're going to have to take you home." They're putting you back in that position… So that young person may be going home at risk.' (17-year-old female, cited in Beckett *et al.*, 2016, p.56)

A further issue with narratives around adolescent harm, which can undermine young people's safety, is that much public discourse and preventative messaging focuses on harm perpetrated by adults. While this is, of course, a very real risk, evidence also documents a wide range of harms that young people can experience from their peers, including bullying, intimate partner violence, sexual harassment and assault, and gang-related physical violence (Firmin, 2017a). The evidence also documents the difficulties that young people can experience in identifying and navigating such harm, challenges often mirrored in professional responses to peer-on-peer harm (Barter *et al.*, 2009; Beckett & Warrington, 2015; Beckett *et al.*, 2019; Firmin, 2013, 2017a; Pearce, 2013). These include difficulties associated with:

- the absence of an age differential

- the role of peer influence

- a lack of clarity as to what constitutes abusive behaviour in peer relationships

- the normalization of harmful interactions between peers.

Responding to peer-on-peer harm is particularly challenging when a young person is both a 'victim' and a 'perpetrator' of harm (Firmin, 2017a; Lloyd, Walker & Bradbury, 2020). Such instances require us to hold in tandem their support needs around the harm they have experienced, while simultaneously responding to their role as an instigator of harm and ensuring others are protected from such harm. Managing these tensions requires a nuanced approach that moves beyond a binary victim/perpetrator conceptualization and prioritizes the child over the perpetration. It requires practitioners to recognize, for example, the impact of trauma on young people, or how the social contexts they are navigating – and the peer dynamics and power differentials within these – may influence their behaviour and experiences, and to take these into account in any response. However, as the following extract from an interview with a teacher, reflecting on a student who was sexually assaulted by another student in the school, illustrates, this is not straightforward within existing systems and cultures:

> 'She was counselled up. Absolutely, we threw everything at her… because she did experience an awful lot in the aftermath of [the sexual assault]… I dealt with her every single day because she would come to me and say, "Everyone's getting at me," and all this, that and the other. It culminated in, unfortunately, her receiving an exclusion for having a fight with someone because they had just pushed her buttons too much over a six, seven-week period.' (Lloyd *et al.*, 2020, p.16)

Compounding harm through blaming narratives

A wide body of literature, emanating from research, serious case reviews and inspections, documents how adolescents who have experienced serious harm have, at times, been thought of as being somehow responsible for that harm, and denied access to appropriate support services as a result (Beckett, Holmes & Walker, 2017; Davis & Marsh,

2020; Hallett, 2017; Maxwell *et al.*, 2019; Ofsted, 2016; Violence & Vulnerability Unit, 2018).

This is in part related to the nature of adolescence itself, and the way in which adolescence is conceptualized within western society. The increasing independence, exploration and choice associated with this life phase sits at odds with the dependence, innocence and passivity of childhood (Coleman, 2019; Hanson & Holmes, 2014). This tension is observable in the contradictory legislative positions around when children can understand and take responsibility for their actions. Most starkly, although clearly defined as a child until their 18th birthday in terms of safeguarding responsibilities, children are currently deemed to be criminally responsible from the age of ten in three of the four UK nations.

This tension between dependence and autonomy, and the inability to hold the concurrent presence of both in adolescence, is clearly played out in conceptualizations of adolescents who experience harm. On one hand, they are portrayed as entirely innocent, manipulated and controlled by another, and thus in need of rescuing. This is the acceptable face of victimhood, deserving of our support and intervention. On the other hand, those who fail to fit this passivity-driven understanding of victimhood are judged to be 'beyond control', 'putting themselves at risk' or 'making active lifestyle choices', with little consideration given to what may be driving these choices or to their continued need for protection and support (Beckett, 2019a; Brown, 2019; Hallett, 2017; Melrose, 2012; Pearce, 2013; Violence & Vulnerability Unit, 2018; Woodiwiss, 2018).

As one of the authors has explored with reference to CSE elsewhere (Beckett, 2019a), such a simplistic binary conceptualization is neither helpful nor reflective of the realities of many young people's experiences. It denies the potential for the concurrent existence of both agency and constraint, which is observable in many forms of adolescent harm. It inappropriately equates agency with culpability and blame, denying the 'still child' status of the adolescent, and (inadvertently) holding them to account for the harm that consequently ensues (Beckett, 2019a; Brandon *et al.*, 2020; Brown, 2019; Davis & Marsh, 2020; Hallett, 2017; Maxwell *et al.*, 2019; Sidebotham *et al.*, 2016). A 'gang-associated' young person, for example, wouldn't have been stabbed if they weren't in the gang. A young person who is sexually exploited wouldn't have been sexually assaulted if they hadn't gone to that party. A young person who is abused by a stranger online wouldn't have been, if they had had their privacy settings on as they had been advised.

Such judgements and blaming narratives are particularly observable in forms of harm, such as CSE or CCE, where the young person may be receiving something as part of the abuse, especially where they are the one who has initiated the exchange. They are also particularly apparent in relation to adolescents who (for many understandable reasons, as explored later) are resistant to service intervention (Beckett, 2019a; Ofsted *et al.*, 2018; Warrington, 2013b).

Alleviating or compounding harm through service responses?

While historically more focused on younger children's experiences of familial harm, recent years have seen adolescents' experiences of (extra-familial) harm increasingly, and more explicitly, drawn into child protection frameworks (see, for example, HM Government, 2018; Llywodraeth Cymru, 2019). Encompassing such harm, while positive, does however present some challenges in terms of the applicability (or lack thereof) of existing systems and structures. Systemic responses developed around the dependence and passivity of early childhood, for example, do not work well with the increasing exploration, independence and agency of adolescence. Similarly, responses formed around managing harm within the familial home, and assessing parental capacity to safeguard within an environment that is largely within their control, do not transfer well to non-familial environments where parents have little, if any, influence or control. This is a particularly pertinent issue during adolescence, when young people spend increasing time in non-familial environments, and when parental influence wanes and the views and actions of others take on increasing importance and prominence (Brandon *et al.*, 2020; Firmin, 2017a; Hill, 2018; Lloyd & Firmin, 2019; Maxwell *et al.*, 2019).

Evidence has highlighted a range of ways in which system responses to adolescent harm, though well intended, may actually increase risks or undermine safety. While beyond the scope of this chapter to provide an exhaustive critique, we highlight a range of issues that are illustrative of the challenges faced by, and the tensions at play for, professionals seeking to respond to adolescent harm.

Labelling harm

One of the early stages at which service responses can either alleviate or compound harm is when we seek to define and categorize the harm being experienced. This is a particular challenge in relation to adolescent harm, given the proliferation of labels and definitions that could be applied, and the lack of clarity as to the relationship between these (Beckett & Walker, 2018; Firmin, 2013; Firmin, Wroe & Lloyd, 2019; Maxwell *et al.*, 2019; Violence & Vulnerability Unit, 2018).

These decisions are more than conceptual. The labels applied to harm hold significant implications for the type of response a young person will receive. This is particularly important given the differential balance between safeguarding and punitive responses to different forms of adolescent harm. A label of trafficking or exploitation is, for example, more likely to receive a safeguarding response than a label of gang association or youth violence, which are more likely to be dealt with through criminal justice processes (Maxwell *et al.*, 2019; Violence & Vulnerability Unit, 2018). The conceptualization of harm is also important in terms of the legal recourse that it creates or denies access to, such as use of the National Referral Mechanism if recognized as modern slavery.

Assessing and managing risk

A proliferation of harm-specific screening tools, risk assessments and toolkits exist to assess the risk of CSE, CCE and other forms of adolescent harm, and – in doing so – determine what, if any, response is required. Serious concerns have, however, been documented around the basis of some of these tools in recent years (Beckett *et al.*, 2017; Brown *et al.*, 2016, 2018). Studies on CSE risk assessments, for example, have noted:

- their questionable evidential basis

- their construction around particular forms of harm (and exclusion of others)

- their confusion of risk and actuality, and the propensity to conflate actual harm with likely harm

- their deficit-based focus on the individual child and, relatedly, their failure to consider the inter-connected conditions of abuse.

Curiously, despite the fact that they have been shown to screen out cases where significant harm was occurring, CSE risk assessments (albeit in an adapted form) continue to be used to determine service need and response (Beckett, 2021; Brown *et al.*, 2016). Inexplicably, they have also served as the template for many more recently developed child (criminal) exploitation risk assessments, thereby increasing the number of young people who may have their harm obscured by, or inadequately responded to as a result of, flawed screening and assessment processes (Beckett, 2021).

Approaches to risk assessment and risk management in the field of adolescent harm have also resulted in documented concerns about an encroaching surveillance state that disproportionately disadvantages certain groups (Eubanks, 2018) and more generally undermines capacity for relational working. As Wroe and Lloyd (2020, p.3) observe, 'responses to extra-familial harm are ubiquitously accompanied by increases in surveillance practices and technologies'. These include, for example, the use of algorithms to identify 'at risk' groups, or the use of police powers (through dispersal orders or warning notices) to monitor and disrupt young people's friendship groups or limit their use of certain places. Such moves are justified by a need to safeguard young people, but sit in conflict with rights-based approaches to responding to such harm and may indeed potentially expose young people to greater harm by increasing othering and alienation (Wroe & Lloyd, 2020).

What response, for whom – and why?

It is clear that variations exist nationally in when and how harm is responded to and what the plan looks like (Firmin, Wroe & Skidmore, 2020; The Child Safeguarding Practice Review Panel, 2020). Concerns have been expressed as to the relationship between thresholds and the documented context of increasing referrals and diminished resources (All Party Parliamentary Group for Children, 2017). As Devaney (2019, p.260) concludes, 'the reality is that many organizations have experienced the setting of thresholds as a gate-keeping exercise to protect children's social care, rather than as a means of better meeting children's needs'. While resource management is understandable in the current climate, the failure to invest in early and preventative help is not only leaving young people exposed to risk and harm, but also increasing the likelihood for longer-term and resource-intensive interventions at a later date (All Party Parliamentary Group for Children, 2017; Violence & Vulnerability Unit, 2018).

Contextual Safeguarding[2] audits indicate that the decision as to what plan – for example, Child Protection, Child in Need, or Early Help – may also be less about the significance of the harm being experienced and more about the engagement, or lack of engagement, of parents. So, while, for some, placement on a child protection plan appears the most appropriate response, bringing with it statutory levers for partners, this is not always the case. Some social workers have reflected that the plans don't always work and can instead serve to further isolate and incriminate families, many of whom are doing everything they can (Lloyd & Firmin, 2019). Evidence shows that such negative parental experiences can directly undermine safeguarding efforts. Research with parents of adolescents who have experienced extra-familial CSE or CCE, for example, documents them feeling judged, excluded and disempowered in their efforts to protect their child. This undermines both their own protective efforts and their propensity to work in partnership with professionals to safeguard their child (Scott & McNeish, 2017; Shuker, 2017; The Child Safeguarding Practice Review Panel, 2020).

The assumptions and stereotypes around patterns of adolescent harm, explored earlier in the chapter, can also unhelpfully influence decisions around interventions and service pathways (Ackerley & Latchford, 2018; Bernard, 2019; Brandon *et al.*, 2020). This is in part a legacy of child protection systems developing in response to, as opposed to being pre-emptive of, high-profile incidents. This has, in turn, meant that elements of such cases – and the problematic narratives around these – are often embedded in the system design and practitioner psyche of who constitutes a victim and what response victims need. Such challenges are particularly evident for young people who do not fit preconceived ideas of victimhood:

> 'Trafficking her friends down to the county lines. That's how she came to our attention. She was never treated as a suspect for the murder. Why? Because of her gender, but if she was a young boy who was sent to be buying drugs off another boy and then he ended up getting killed, I'm sure she would've been on trial with the rest of them.' (Social worker, cited in unpublished MsUnderstood research on peer-on-peer abuse)

---

2   Contextual Safeguarding is an approach to child protection that responds to young people's experiences of harm outside the home (Contextual Safeguarding Network, 2020).

Ongoing Contextual Safeguarding audits of local authority responses to extra-familial harm across the UK demonstrate the frequency with which such a gendered response to adolescent harm can be observed. Multi-agency sexual exploitation (MASE) panels are often focused on girls, while their male peers are responded to via harmful sexual behaviour services, gangs panels or youth offending processes. This is despite the fact that both may have been involved in related incidents or demonstrated similar indicators of risk or harm.

As explored further in Chapter 6, such structural discrimination is compounded when viewed through an intersectional lens (Ackerley & Latchford, 2018; Bernard, 2019). When both ethnicity and gender are considered, for example, we see a disproportionate representation of Black male adolescents in gangs matrices (Williams & Clarke, 2016; Wroe, 2021) and a clear underrepresentation of the same in structures designed to respond to sexual harm (Bernard, 2019; Warrington *et al.*, 2017).

The risks of engagement

How young people experience our engagements with them also holds significant potential to either alleviate or compound harm. Professional working practices can often place system needs and priorities over those of the young person, and this can unhelpfully replicate the exploitative and oppressive power dynamics of their abuse (Children's Commissioner, 2013). As a young person in Beckett and Warrington's (2015, p.56) research reflected on her experience of engaging with the police following sexual exploitation, 'I was basically a puppet. When they wanted me, I had to do it. When they didn't want me, I heard nothing.'

We can also fail to recognize quite what we are asking of young people when we expect them to engage with our protective efforts and initiatives. Engaging with services, for example, can actually increase risk to a young person or undermine their safety in a range of ways. They may experience physical harm from a perpetrator who fears the implications of disclosure. They may experience condemnatory or dismissive reactions from professionals, or have their views and experiences invalidated in our efforts to help them recognize their victimhood. More positively, they may develop a healing relationship with a professional, but then have this disrupted due to staffing or service reconfigurations. Disruption of links with perpetrators may close down their access to something they need or want – drugs, money or a place to stay, for example – which may, in turn, increase risk as they seek other ways of having these needs met. These are very real risks, which can be heightened by siloed service interventions that fail to consider the young person's life as a whole and give space and recognition to their understandings, needs and wishes (Andell & Pitts, 2017; Beckett, 2011; Beckett *et al.*, 2013; Brown, 2019; Lefevre *et al.*, 2017; Warrington, 2013a).

Enhancing or disrupting safety?

In her work on CSE, Shuker (2013) identified three interconnected dimensions of young people's safety – physical, relational and psychological – all of which need to be concurrently present for a young person who has experienced harm to be truly safe. Service responses, however, often attend more to physical safety than the other critical dimensions, and in doing so may actually undermine a young person's wider sense of safety and wellbeing (Beckett, 2011; Beckett *et al.*, 2013; Ellis, 2018; Firmin *et al.*, 2020; Hickle & Roe-Sepowitz, 2018).

Placing a young person in secure accommodation or an out-of-area placement, for example, while helpful in terms of immediate physical safety and attempting to disrupt harmful relationships, can fracture positive supportive relationships. It can reinforce messages of culpability and blame ('hence you are being locked up') and indicate that professionals cannot keep a young person safe in their community – a message that does little to instil confidence in our protective capacity (Beckett, 2011, 2013; Beckett *et al.*, 2013; Firmin *et al.*, 2020).

As a practitioner in Firmin and colleagues' (2020, p.3) research into the use of relocation in response to extra-familial harm observed, 'everybody breathes a sigh of relief' when a child is placed out of area. Certainly, as the study also documents, there can be benefits associated with such approaches, but is the primary driver always what is best for the child? Might it be as much about the system's need to eliminate, rather than hold, risk, an approach which has been shown to result more in short-term enforced compliance rather than longer-term meaningful change (Beckett, 2011; Beckett *et al.*, 2017; Hickle & Hallett, 2015)?

Research also suggests that such care decisions, in a climate of limited resources, may be driven as much by availability as suitability

(Baginsky, Gorin & Sands, 2017; Brodie *et al.*, 2014). This appears particularly acute in relation to adolescents who are more likely to end up in residential care placements, and experience multiple placement moves and multiple personnel changes within a short time. The cumulative effect of these experiences is likely to compound, rather than alleviate, the harms they have already experienced (Beckett, 2013; Coy, 2009; Elliott, Staples & Scourfield, 2018; Hart, La Valle & Holmes, 2015; Hiller & St Clair, 2018).

What might a better response look like?

Having identified a number of ways in which current system responses can serve to obscure or compound harm rather than prevent or alleviate it, we turn now to consider some key principles that could underpin a more effective response to adolescent harm.

A more nuanced understanding of the complexities of harm in adolescence

While some adolescents' experiences of harm do fit the groomed, controlled and exploited model driving existing discourses around victimhood and harm, there are many others that do not. There are, for example, many young people who, finding themselves in less than ideal circumstances, choose – in the absence of any preferable option – to utilize the resources they have to meet a need or want and, in doing so, experience gain alongside harm (Beckett, 2019a). For example, staying in an abusive peer relationship in the absence of any other meaningful connections, initiating sexual activity in return for alcohol to block out the trauma of past abuse, or agreeing to transport drugs across the country to pay off an existing drug debt.

An ability to recognize and work with the concurrent presence of victimhood and agency, and harm and gain, observable in such scenarios is central to improving our responses to these young people. This is true both in terms of helping young people to understand the complex and varied ways that harm can manifest, and supporting professionals to identify experiences of harm which deviate from the dominant groomed and exploited victim model. It is also key to the development of a more appropriate service offer that recognizes the complex multifaceted dynamics at play in many instances of adolescent harm and works with, rather than denies, a young person's agency and understandings of their experiences of harm (Beckett, 2019a; Brown, 2019; Hallett, 2017; Warrington, 2013b).

The concept of constrained choice offers a helpful model in this regard (Beckett, 2004, 2019; Beckett *et al.*, 2017; Warrington, 2013a). It provides a framework for acknowledging and working with the agency of adolescence, while at the same time recognizing and responding to the constraints impinging on it. Understanding that choice can be both highly constrained and externally influenced allows us to see that a young person's seemingly irrational or self-destructive choices may actually be self-protective or adaptive, given the circumstances in which they find themselves. It also allows us to recognize that, if circumstances were different, a young person's choices may also have been different – a theme we see replicated throughout young people's accounts of their experiences of harm (Beckett, 2011; Beckett *et al.*, 2013; Hallett, 2017; Hanson & Holmes, 2014; Melrose, 2012; Warrington, 2013a).

This way of doing things moves us beyond pathologizing and judging an individual's actions, approaches which have been shown to alienate those we are seeking to help, invalidate their right to, and need for, support, and penalize them for the harm they have experienced (Beckett, 2019a; Warrington & Brodie, 2017). The concept of constrained choice also enables us to continue to pay necessary attention to the structural constraints and inequalities that can create the conditions for abuse and the associated assumptions and biases that can negatively influence systemic responses to such harm (Beckett, 2019; Bernard, 2019b; Melrose, 2012).

Problematizing and changing the contexts and drivers that allow adolescent harm to occur in this way, as opposed to problematizing the young people who experience it (or indeed the life stage of adolescence as a whole), is critical to moving beyond the alienating blaming narratives that have dominated responses to adolescent harm in the past.

At an individual case level

Considering first the identification and assessment of harm, we need to move beyond a deficit-based approach to assessing risk that focuses entirely on the vulnerabilities and behaviours of a young person. When considering why a young person may be at heightened risk of harm, it is important to remember that their vulnerability is not the reason they experience harm. As the interconnected conditions of abuse model (Beckett, 2011; Beckett *et al.*, 2017; Figure 4.1) posits, a young person's vulnerability is only an issue because there is someone who is willing to exploit this, and there are inadequate protective structures in place around them. Furthermore, young people with no known vulnerabilities can also experience harm, a fact occluded by risk assessments that focus solely on the vulnerability of a child.

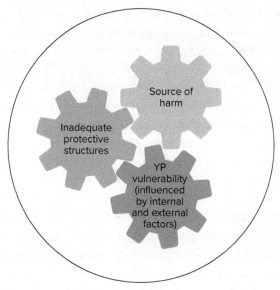

Figure 4.1: Beckett's interconnected conditions of abuse
(adapted from Beckett, 2011; Beckett et al., 2017)[3]

To truly assess and respond to adolescent harm, we need to consider not only the young person but also any potential sources of harm, and the absence or presence of protective structures that may mitigate against these, and invest in minimizing the potential for harm across all of these contexts. It is also important to view these interconnected conditions in light of the range of wider societal factors that can contribute to experiences of adolescent harm, and how these impinge on the contexts and manifestations of adolescent harm. This includes factors such as:

• harmful gendered norms

---

3   Text in the second cog changed from 'perpetrator risk' to 'source of harm', in work with Barnardo's (Beckett, 2019), to better encapsulate harm from peers.

- a potential normalization of sexual violence

- poverty and deprivation

- the decimation of youth work provision.

In terms of how we then respond to the individual experiencing harm, we need to invest in structures and practices that support a move towards long-term meaningful change rather than the short-term enforced compliance driver associated with many current responses. To do this, we need to identify and engage with the specific contextual drivers of harm, and work with young people (and their support networks) to address these. Simply shutting down avenues of contact with a perpetrator, or placing restrictions on a young person's liberty or agency without concurrently working to address the factors that increased their vulnerability or exposure to harm, offers only a short-term solution that does little to offer enhanced protection in the longer term (Beckett, 2011, 2013; Christie, 2018; Hickle, 2019).

As discussed in Chapter 9, we also need to move beyond a deficit-based approach to adolescence, and adopt a strengths-based lens and approach to working with young people, which focuses on and utilizes their strengths and resources rather than problematizing their actions and experiences. Adopting such an approach allows us to reframe young people's agency as a protective resource, rather than a vulnerability or liability. Strengths-based approaches support us to work with, rather than ignore, adolescent agency, to tread that difficult line of balancing a young person's need for protection alongside their need, desire and right to exercise control over their own life (Warrington, 2013a).

We need to actively engage adolescents in decisions about their care, in line with their increasing developmental capacity and Article 12 right (of the United Nations Convention on the Rights of the Child) to be consulted on matters which affect them. We need to work with them around their concerns and priorities (which may at times differ radically from those of 'the system'), and do so in their time and at their pace. As part of this, we need to recognize and respect that part of the exercise of agency, on the part of a young person, may be to reject service interventions, an understandable choice given the many risks and challenges that such engagement can represent, and the disconnect that can exist between what they need and want, and what we are able to offer (Beckett *et al.*, 2017; Warrington, 2013b).

One of the significant challenges that accommodating adolescent agency in this way presents is that it may mean holding risk while the young person reaches their own decisions about their circumstances, rather than forcibly eliminating it. As explored above, this sits at odds with the current systemic drivers to eliminate risk, both to the young person and to our services. It is not, however, a tension that can be ignored if we are to move beyond short-term risk management, enforced compliance and behavioural modification to longer-term safety, meaningful change and enhanced self-protective capacity (Beckett, 2011, 2019; Hickle, 2019; Hickle & Hallett, 2015; Warrington, 2013a; Wroe & Lloyd, 2020).

An enhanced case level response also needs to recognize the important role that non-abusing parents/carers can play in protective efforts around adolescent harm, and ensure that our responses improve, rather than undermine, their protective and supportive capacity. This requires better recognition of the strength and significance of influences at play in non-familial environments during the adolescent years, and the limited influence that a parent/carer – no matter how proactive – can have over these. It requires investment in parent–child relationships, and both their and their child's involvement in decision-making forums (Beckett *et al.*, 2017; Maxwell *et al.*, 2019; Scott & McNeish, 2017; Shuker, 2017).

An enhanced individual level case response also needs to consider how we can move beyond current siloed responses to different forms of harm, and engage with a holistic assessment of harms and their associated range of needs. It is, however, critical that we do so in a way that maintains a specificity on the nature of the harm(s) experienced, and what this means in terms of impacts and responses. Cases of CSE and CCE, for example, may share a number of common features, such as the potential role of grooming, the concurrent presence of harm and gain, and victims not recognizing the abusive nature of what they are experiencing as a result of these (Firmin *et al.*, 2019). The nature of the harm experienced and the contextual drivers at play can, however, vary considerably, as can the associated impacts and consequent support needs. We must attend to both these similarities and distinctions in progressing towards a more holistic response, attending to the possibility of concurrent experiences of different forms of harm, including those occurring both outside and within the family environment.

Extending the focus of our interventions

It is crucial to consider the context in which interventions are offered, in order to create the conditions required for effective practice. As Alexander Den Heijer is often quoted as saying, 'When a flower doesn't bloom you fix the environment in which it grows, not the flower.'

So what would it look like to fix the conditions in which adolescent harm can flourish? To move beyond an individual case level response to identify patterns of harm and intervene in the environments within which such harm is occurring?

While social work has a history of thinking systemically (Bronfenbrenner, 1979), these approaches have predominantly considered the wider ecologies of people's lives rather than promoted direct intervention in the contexts of harm. New approaches are, however, supporting professionals to identify opportunities to both assess and intervene in the social conditions of abuse. Contextual Safeguarding is one such approach, seeking to support child protection systems to engage with contexts – rather than just people – where extra-familial harm occurs (Firmin, 2017b).

Within this approach, if a young person is, for example, groomed to traffic drugs out of a takeaway shop, you could expect, alongside a social care and/or police referral for the young person, that there may also be an assessment and intervention with the takeaway shop itself (Contextual Safeguarding Network, 2020). Similarly, if a young person experiences sexual harassment from peers at school, interventions would focus on challenging the harmful peer culture at the school and changing any policies and systems which failed to identify and challenge that harm (Lloyd, 2019).

Such interventions not only respond to the individual incidents of harm (singular or plural) that may have occurred within the environment, but also decrease the likelihood of similar harms occurring to others within these environments. Furthermore, in drawing attention to the social conditions of abuse, such an approach helps challenge the unhelpful singular focus on the adolescent's actions and vulnerabilities, which has contributed to the harmful and alienating victim-blaming narratives explored earlier in the chapter.

Intervening in the contexts of abuse requires the engagement of new safeguarding partners. If a child is harmed in a park, a swimming pool or on the way to school, for example, we need to engage with the people and agencies that have reach into those contexts and hold responsibility for keeping those places safe, whether that be a park warden, a lifeguard or the transport police.

Engaging these partners is not without its challenges and raises important questions about training, information-sharing, consent and confidentiality and, ultimately, their interest in and willingness to become involved. Precedence does however exist. Working alongside social workers in London as part of a neighbourhood assessment, one of the authors of this chapter (Lloyd) and her colleagues met takeaway owners who had built relationships with local young people and developed their own techniques of managing harm, from contacting the school to giving away free chicken wings when tensions rose. Similarly, they met with supermarket workers whose investment in relationships with young people had meant they felt safe to come into the store when in need of help, as had been the case for a number of young people who had been stabbed (Contextual Safeguarding Network, 2020).

These and other examples suggest that it is not necessarily the willingness of others to help that is lacking, but a robust child protection framework in which to hold and support this. A number of initiatives have, however, been developed to begin to address this. Across England and Wales, for example, social care departments are beginning to implement the principles of Contextual Safeguarding. Such work includes allowing social care referrals for locations as opposed to just individuals. It involves locations such as schools, peer groups or neighbourhoods being subjected to 'context assessments' to consider the level of harm and protective factors in those locations, and the use of context conferences as a mechanism to develop plans and identify the partners needed to make change within those environments (Contextual Safeguarding Network, 2020). Such approaches support us to begin to understand and tackle patterns of adolescent harm, as opposed to just individual manifestations of the same, and in doing so, significantly extend our potential protective reach and preventative capacity.

Concluding comments

While the increasing recognition of adolescent harm witnessed over the last 15 years is certainly to be welcomed, it is clear that there is still some way to go in terms of refining our responses to such forms of harm and ensuring that all young people – irrespective of their biographies and the manifestations and contexts of harm – receive an appropriate and holistic response.

There are undoubtedly many tangible changes required in our systems and structures, and policies and practices, to enable us to 'do better' in this regard. Encouragingly, there are many tangible examples of these changes starting to take place. However, what is also ultimately required is a system-wide belief that such change is both possible and desirable. A belief that all contexts – home, school, parks, peer groups and online spaces – are capable of becoming safer environments for young people, both individually and collectively, and that young people deserve our efforts to bring about this change.

References

Ackerley, L. & Latchford, L. (2018). 'Applying an Intersectional Lens to Sexual Violence Research and Practice.' In H. Beckett & J. Pearce (eds) *Understanding and Responding to Child Sexual Exploitation* (pp.54–66). London: Routledge.

All Party Parliamentary Group for Children (2017). *No Good Options: Report of the Inquiry into Children's Social Care in England.* London: National Children's Bureau.

Andell, P. & Pitts, J. (2017). *Preventing the Violent and Sexual Victimisation of Vulnerable Gang-Involved and Gang-Affected Children and Young People in Ipswich.* Ipswich: University of Suffolk.

Baginsky, M., Gorin, S. & Sands, C. (2017). *The Fostering System in England: Evidence Review.* London: Department for Education.

Barter, C., McCarry, M., Berridge, D. & Evans, K. (2009). *Partner Exploitation and Violence in Teenage Intimate Relationships.* London: NSPCC.

Beckett, H. (2004). *An Ethnography of Youth Homelessness.* Doctoral thesis; Queen's University of Belfast.

Beckett, H. (2011). *Not a World Away. The Sexual Exploitation of Children and Young People in Northern Ireland.* Belfast: Barnardo's Northern Ireland.

Beckett, H. (2013). 'Looked After Young People and CSE: A View from Northern Ireland.' In M. Melrose & J. Pearce (eds) *Critical Perspectives on Child Sexual Exploitation and Related Trafficking* (pp.69–82). London: Palgrave Macmillan.

Beckett, H. (2019a). 'Moving Beyond Discourses of Agency, Gain and Blame: Reconceptualising Young People's Experiences of Sexual Exploitation.' In J. Pearce (ed.) *Child Sexual Exploitation: Why Theory Matters* (pp.23–42). Bristol: Policy Press.

Beckett, H. (2019b, 25 June) *Risk Assessment* [Presentation].

Beckett, H. (2021, 24 March) *Risk assessing child (sexual) exploitation* [Webinar]. Tackling Child Exploitation Support Programme. https://tce.researchinpractice.org.uk/risk-assessing-child-sexual-exploitation.

Beckett, H., Brodie, I., Factor, F., Melrose, M. *et al.* (2013). *'It's Wrong but You Get Used to It.' A Qualitative Study of Gang-Associated Sexual Violence towards, and Exploitation of, Young People in England.* London: Children's Commissioner for England.

Beckett, H., Holmes, D. & Walker, J. (2017). *Child Sexual Exploitation: Definition and Guide for Professionals.* London: Department for Education.

Beckett, H. & Walker, J. (2018). 'Words Matter: Reconceptualising the Conceptualisation of Child Sexual Exploitation.' In H. Beckett & J. Pearce (eds) *Understanding and Responding to Child Sexual Exploitation* (pp.9–23). London: Routledge.

Beckett, H. & Warrington, C. (2015). *Making Justice Work: Experiences of Criminal Justice for Children and Young People Affected by Sexual Exploitation as Victims and Witnesses.* Luton: University of Bedfordshire.

Beckett, H., Warrington, C., Ackerley, E. & Allnock, D. (2016). *Children's Voices Research Report. Children and Young People's Perspectives on the Police's Role in Safeguarding: A Report for Her Majesty's Inspectorate of Constabularies.* London: Her Majesty's Inspectorate of Constabulary.

Beckett, H. & Warrington, C. with Montgomery-Devlin, J. (2019). *Learning About Online Sexual Harm.* Independent Inquiry into Child Sexual Abuse.

Bernard, C. (2019). 'Child Sexual Exploitation of Black Adolescents.' In J. Pearce (ed.) *Child Sexual Exploitation: Why Theory Matters* (pp.193–208). Bristol: Policy Press.

Brandon, M., Belderson, P., Sorensen, P., Dickens, J. et al. (2020). *Complexity and Challenge: A Triennial Analysis of SCRs 2014–2017.* London: Department for Education.

Brodie, I., Christie, C., Cosis-Brown, H., Dance, C. & Prokop, J. (2014). *Out of Borough Placements for London's Looked After Children.* London Councils.

Bronfenbrenner, U. (1979). *The Ecology of Human Development: Experiments by Design and Nature.* Cambridge, MA: Harvard University Press.

Brown, K. (2019). 'Vulnerability and child sexual exploitation: Towards an approach grounded in life experiences.' *Critical Social Policy, 39*(4), 622–642. https://doi.org/10.1177/0261018318824480.

Brown, S., Brady, G., Franklin, A., Bradley, L., Kerrigan, N. & Sealey, C. (2016). *Child Sexual Abuse and Exploitation: Understanding Risk and Vulnerability.* London: Early Intervention Foundation.

Brown, S., Brady, G., Franklin, A. & Crookes, R. (2018). *The Use of Tools and Checklists to Assess Risk of Child Sexual Exploitation: An Exploratory Study.* Centre of Expertise Child Sexual Abuse.

Children's Commissioner (2013). *'If Only Someone Had Listened.' Office of the Children's Commissioner's Inquiry into Child Sexual Exploitation in Gangs and Groups Final Report.* London: Children's Commissioner for England.

Children's Commissioner (2019). *Keeping Kids Safe. Improving Safeguarding Responses to Gang Violence and Criminal Exploitation.* London: Children's Commissioner for England.

Christie, C. (2018). *A Trauma-Informed Health and Care Approach for Responding to Child Sexual Abuse and Exploitation. Current Knowledge Report.* London: Department of Health and Social Care.

Cockbain, E. (2013). 'Grooming and the "Asian sex gang predator": The construction of a racial crime threat.' *Race & Class, 54*(4), 22–32. https://doi.org/10.1177%2F0306396813475983.

Coleman, J. (2019). 'Understanding Adolescent Development in the Context of Child Sexual Exploitation.' In J. Pearce (ed.) *Child Sexual Exploitation: Why Theory Matters* (pp.117–132). Bristol: Policy Press.

Contextual Safeguarding Network (2020). *Neighbourhood Assessment Toolkit.* www.csnetwork.org.uk/en/toolkit/assessment/neighbourhood-assessment-toolkit.

Coy, M. (2009). 'Moved around like bags of rubbish nobody wants: How multiple placement moves can make young women vulnerable to sexual exploitation.' *Child Abuse Review, 18*(4), 254–266. https://doi.org/10.1002/car.1064.

Davis, J. & Marsh, N. (2020). 'Boys to men: The cost of "adultification" in safeguarding responses to Black boys.' *Critical and Radical Social Work, 8*(2), 255–259. https://doi.org/10.1332/204986020X15945756023543.

Devaney, J. (2019). 'The trouble with thresholds: Rationing as a rational choice in child and family social work.' *Child & Family Social Work, 24*(4), 458–466. https://doi.org/10.1111/cfs.12625.

Elliott, M., Staples, E. & Scourfield, J. (2018). 'The characteristics of children and young people in residential care in Wales.' *Child Care in Practice, 24*(3), 317–330. https://doi.org/10.1080/13575279.2017.1319798.

Ellis, K. (2018). 'Contested vulnerability: A case study of girls in secure care in Children and Youth Services.' *Review, 88,* 156–163. https://doi.org/10.1016/j.childyouth.2018.02.047.

Eubanks, V. (2018). *Automating Inequality: How High Tech Tools Profile, Police and Punish the Poor.* New York, NY: St Martin's Press.

Firmin, C. (2013). 'Something Old or Something New: Do Pre-Existing Conceptualisations of Abuse Enable a Sufficient Response to Abuse in Young People's Relationships and Peer Groups?' In M. Melrose & J. Pearce (eds) *Critical Perspectives on Child Sexual Exploitation and Related Trafficking* (pp.38–51). London: Palgrave Macmillan.

Firmin, C. (2017a). *Abuse Between Young People: A Contextual Account*. London: Routledge.

Firmin, C. (2017b). *Contextual Safeguarding: An Overview of the Operational, Strategic and Conceptual Framework*. Luton: University of Bedfordshire.

Firmin, C. & Pearce, J. (2016). 'Living in Gang Affected Neighbourhoods.' In C. Bernard & P. Harris (eds) *Safeguarding Black Children: Good Practice in Child Protection* (pp.76–91). London: Jessica Kingsley Publishers.

Firmin, C., Wroe, L. & Lloyd, J. (2019). *Safeguarding and Exploitation – Complex, Contextual and Holistic Approaches: Strategic Briefing*. Totnes: Research in Practice.

Firmin, C., Wroe, L. & Skidmore, P. (2020). *A Sigh of Relief: A Summary of the Phase One Results from the Securing Safety Study*. Luton: University of Bedfordshire.

Gohir, S. (2013). *Unheard Voices. The Sexual Exploitation of Asian Girls and Young Women*. Birmingham: Muslim Women's Network UK.

Hallett, S. (2017). *Making Sense of Child Sexual Exploitation. Exchange, Abuse and Young People*. Bristol: Policy Press.

Hanson, E. & Holmes, D. (2014). *That Difficult Age: Developing a More Effective Response to Risks in Adolescence. Evidence Scope*. Totnes: Research in Practice.

Hart, D., La Valle, I. & Holmes, L. (2015). *The Place of Residential Care in the English Child Welfare System: Research Report*. London: Department for Education.

Hickle, K. (2019). 'Understanding Trauma and its Relevance to Child Sexual Exploitation.' In J. Pearce (ed.) *Child Sexual Exploitation: Why Theory Matters* (pp.151–172). Bristol: Policy Press.

Hickle, K. & Hallett, S. (2015). 'Mitigating harm: Considering harm reduction principles in work with sexually exploited young people.' *Children and Society, 30*(4), 302–313. https://doi.org/10.1111/chso.1215.

Hickle, K. & Roe-Sepowitz, D. (2018). 'Adversity and intervention needs among girls in residential care with experiences of commercial sexual exploitation.' *Children and Youth Services Review, 93*, 17–23. https://doi.org/10.1016/j.childyouth.2018.06.043.

Hill, N. (2018). *Serious Case Review – Chris*. London: Newham Safeguarding Children Board.

Hiller, R. & St Clair, M. (2018). 'The emotional and behavioural symptom trajectories of children in long-term out-of-home care in an English local authority.' *Child Abuse & Neglect, 81*, 106–117. https://doi.org/10.1016/j.chiabu.2018.04.017.

HM Government (2018). *Working Together to Safeguard Children*. London: HMSO.

Home Office (2018). *Criminal Exploitation of Children and Vulnerable Adults: County Lines Guidance*. London: HMSO. www.gov.uk/government/publications/criminal-exploitation-of-children-and-vulnerable-adults-county-lines.

Lefevre, M., Hickle, K., Luckock, B. & Ruch, G. (2017). 'Building trust with children and young people at risk of child sexual exploitation: The professional challenge.' *The British Journal of Social Work, 47*(8), 2456–2473. https://doi.org/10.1093/bjsw/bcw181.

Lloyd, J. (2019). 'Response and interventions into harmful sexual behaviour in schools.' *Child Abuse & Neglect, 94*, 104037. https://doi.org/10.1016/j.chiabu.2019.104037.

Lloyd, J. & Firmin, C. (2019). 'No further action: Contextualising social care decisions for children victimised in extra-familial settings.' *Youth Justice, 20*(3), 79–92. https://doi.org/10.1177%2F1473225419893789.

Lloyd, J., Walker, J. & Bradbury, V. (2020). *Beyond Referrals. Harmful Sexual Behaviour in Schools: A Briefing on the Findings, Implications and Resources for Schools and Multi-Agency Partners*. Luton: University of Bedfordshire.

Llywodraeth Cymru (2019). *National Action Plan Preventing and Responding to Child Sexual Abuse. Working Together to Safeguard People*. Welsh Government.

Maxwell, N., Wallace, C., Cummings, A., Bayfield, H. & Morgan, H. (2019). *A Systematic Map and Synthesis Review of Child Criminal Exploitation*. Cardiff: Cardiff University.

McNaughton Nicholls, C., Cockbain, E., Brayley, H., Harvey, S. *et al.* (2014). *Research on the Sexual Exploitation of Boys and Young Men. A UK Scoping Study. Summary of Findings*. London: Barnardo's.

Melrose, M. (2012). 'Twenty-first century party people: Young people and sexual exploitation in the new millennium.' *Child Abuse Review, 22*(3), 155–168. https://doi.org/10.1002/car.2238.

Ofsted (2016). *Time to Listen. A Joined up Response to Child Sexual Exploitation and Missing Children.* London: Ofsted.

Ofsted, Care Quality Commission, Her Majesty's Inspectorate of Constabulary & Fire & Rescue Services, & Her Majesty's Inspectorate of Probation (2018). *Protecting Children from Criminal Exploitation, Human Trafficking and Modern Slavery: An Addendum.* London: Ofsted.

Pearce, J. (2013). 'A Social Model of "Abused Consent".' In M. Melrose & J. Pearce (eds) *Critical Perspectives on Child Sexual Exploitation and Related Trafficking* (pp.52–68). London: Palgrave Macmillan.

Rodger, H., Hurcombe, R., Redmond, T. & George, R. (2020). *'People Don't Talk About It': Child Sexual Abuse in Ethnic Minority Communities.* Independent Inquiry into Child Sexual Abuse.

Scott, S. & McNeish, D. (2017). *Supporting Parents of Sexually Exploited Young People. An Evidence Review.* CSA Centre.

Shuker, L. (2013). 'Constructs of Safety for Children in Care Affected by Sexual Exploitation.' In M. Melrose & J. Pearce (eds) *Critical Perspectives on Child Sexual Exploitation and Related Trafficking* (pp.125–138). London: Palgrave Macmillan.

Shuker, L. (2017). *Virtuous Circles. Theorising the Impact of Parents Against Child Sexual Exploitation (Pace) Discussion Paper.* Luton: University of Bedfordshire.

Sidebotham, P., Brandon, M., Bailey, S., Belderson, P. *et al.* (2016). *Pathways to Harm, Pathways to Protection: A Triennial Analysis of SCRs 2011–2014.* London: Department for Education.

The Child Safeguarding Practice Review Panel (2020). *It Was Hard to Escape. Safeguarding Children at Risk of Criminal Exploitation.* London: HM Government.

Violence & Vulnerability Unit (2018). *County Lines: A National Summary and Emerging Best Practice.* London: Home Office.

Warrington, C. (2013a). *Helping Me Find My Own Way. Sexually Exploited Young People's Involvement in Decision-Making about their Care.* Doctoral thesis. University of Bedfordshire.

Warrington, C. (2013b). 'Partners in Care? Sexually Exploited Young People's Inclusion and Exclusion from Decision Making about Safeguarding.' In M. Melrose & J. Pearce (eds) *Critical Perspectives on Child Sexual Exploitation and Related Trafficking* (pp.110–124). London: Palgrave Macmillan.

Warrington, C., with Beckett, H., Ackerley, E., Walker, M. & Allnock, D. (2017). *Making Noise: Children's Voices for Positive Change After Sexual Abuse.* Luton: University of Bedfordshire.

Warrington, C. & Brodie, I. (2017). 'Developing Participatory Practice and Culture in CSE Services.' In H. Beckett & J. Pearce (eds) *Understanding and Responding to Child Sexual Exploitation* (pp.121–133). London: Routledge.

Williams, P. & Clarke, B. (2016). *Dangerous Associations: Joint Enterprise, Gangs and Racism. An Analysis of the Processes of Criminalisation of Black, Asian and Minority Ethnic Individuals.* London: Centre for Crime and Justice Studies.

Woodiwiss, J. (2018). 'From one girl to "three girls": The importance of separating agency from blame (and harm from wrongfulness) in narratives of childhood sexual abuse and exploitation.' *Pastoral Care in Education, 36*(2), 154–166. https://doi.org/10.1080/02643944.2018.1464593.

Wroe, L. (2019). *Contextual Safeguarding and County Lines.* Luton: University of Bedfordshire.

Wroe, L. (2021). 'Young people and "county lines": A contextual and social account.' *Journal of Children's Services, 16*(1), 39–55. https://doi.org/10.1108/JCS-10-2020-0063.

Wroe, L. & Lloyd, J. (2020). 'Watching over or working with? Understanding social work innovation in response to extra-familial harm.' *Social Sciences, 9*(4), 37. https://doi.org/10.3390/socsci9040037.

Chapter 5

Young People Negotiating Intra- and Extra-Familial Harm and Safety: Social and Holistic Approaches

Lauren Wroe with Jenny Pearce

Introduction

In this chapter, we propose a holistic and structurally informed framework for understanding the intersections between intra-familial and extra-familial harm, and the intersecting and overlapping characteristics of extra-familial forms of harm, in adolescence. We will reference academic and grey literature that seeks to explain experiences of neglect and harm both behind and beyond young people's front doors. Drawing on this literature, and experiences from our research and practice in the sector, we propose that contextual, social and structural understandings of child harm provide a useful framework for interpreting and responding to young people's experiences of multiple forms of harms in their families and beyond. We will focus on harm that is recognized as neglectful or abusive by child protection systems in England and Wales, exploring where current theories of harm fall short, resulting in responses that are individualized and siloed. Building on poverty aware (Krumer-Nevo, 2020), contextual (Firmin, 2020) and 'social models' (Featherstone *et al.*, 2018) of social work, we consider the need for holistic service responses that acknowledge and alleviate the structural pressures on families and young people, as a means of tackling both intra- and extra-familial experiences of child harm, and the intersecting drivers of extra-familial harm in adolescence.

We present an overview of the harms and risks adolescents face and the complex ways in which these harms interact, and consider the ways in which intra-familial harm (e.g., neglect in childhood) might also interact with these risks.

For us, this demands a holistic account of a range of harms experienced by all children, irrespective of their age, in the context of their families, their friendships, their schools and their neighbourhoods. It also requires a critical engagement with what is considered harm, and by whom, and how child protection services and their partners currently go about addressing it. Individualized responses to child harm are arguably the dominant paradigm through which children's social work interventions, including interventions with adolescents, are understood, designed and delivered. We present this as a limiting tendency.

Individualized responses to child harm are limited in a number of ways, often asking individuals to change their behaviour when this behaviour has been adapted in order to cope in the complex contexts of their daily lives. When discussing these limitations for the purposes of this chapter, we reflected on Lauren's experience as a student social worker in a child protection team where she encountered numerous families who were subject to child protection referrals, having left their young children at home while they went out to work. Constrained by inflexible working arrangements and expensive childcare (the same challenges facing the primarily female social workers), parents had to make a choice: leave their children at home, or stay at home without a wage. Both would have had a significant impact on the welfare of their children. Lauren reflected that parents were caught 'between a rock and a hard place', and that she, too, had felt compromised as a trainee social worker, working with the frameworks and tools available to her.

Individualized responses to child harm also have a tendency to foreground discrete experiences of harm that are recognized as an act of abuse or criminal activity, while ignoring sources of sorrow and distress such as the shame of poverty or experiences of racism. For example, Lauren was recently contacted by a child advocate about a young person who had been referred to a child protection conference due to cannabis use, missing episodes, and a recent arrest. This resulted in the young person being placed on a child protection plan where interventions were put in place around his behaviour, and it was documented that he posed a risk to his siblings due to suspected involvement in 'county lines'. The young person was left conscious that the 'work' to be done was solely about his behaviour rather than him needing help and support to understand and address his experiences of racism in school and police harassment in his neighbourhood. The advocate attending the meeting with him was concerned at this seemingly unfounded escalation that had left the young person confused and worried.

To advance our understanding of the ways in which multiple harms play out for children and young people, we look to the contexts and conditions that predicate harm, echoing an emerging acknowledgement that context matters in how we understand and respond to child harm (Featherstone *et al.*, 2018; Firmin, 2020; Krumer-Nevo, 2020; Nayak, 2020). However, rather than understanding this focus on context as a new voice in the room, we might consider it an echo, as Nayak does, drawing on holistic and relational perspectives from Black feminist scholarship, where she outlines how context might be utilized in social work:

> The logic of context recognises context as instrumental in the production of the issues, pathologies and impairments that become fastened to individuals, communities and societies. In the logic of context, the attention of social work shifts from casework with individuals and families to casework with contexts: the context of poverty; patriarchy; class; racism; capitalism and oppressive constructions. (Nayak, 2020, p.45)

This chapter is an invitation to consider how we might understand the trajectories and intersections of child harm, both intra- and extra-familial, through the lens of such contexts.

A child welfare system in crisis?

First, let's consider how the child welfare system is currently responding to children's experiences of harm within and beyond their families. The number of children and young people entering the care system in the UK is rising (Department for Education, 2019), with some local variability (see also Bennet *et al.*, 2020). While these statistics could signal that children and young people in the UK are facing an increasing array of abuses (as some would propose, particularly in the context of the Covid-19 pandemic: see National Youth Agency, 2020; Pitts, 2020), they may also indicate troubles with the internal logic and operations of the child welfare system.

In their work promoting a 'social model' of child protection,

Featherstone and colleagues (2018) highlight a steady increase in children and families subject to child protection investigations from an early age, with little evidence of such investigation resulting in offers of support, or indeed uncovering actual harm or abuse (see also Bilson, Featherstone & Martin, 2017). In 2016, James Munby, President of the Family Division of the High Court, named it: 'We are facing a crisis and, truth be told, we have no very clear strategy for meeting the crisis. What is to be done?' (Munby, 2016).

Exploring these troubling observations and unpacking what exactly might need to 'be done', the Care Crisis Review (2018) concluded that young people, families and professionals often felt that the child protection system was in crisis, that services were stretched and under-resourced and that familial deprivation, austerity and a lack of early help were making it difficult for families, and the system, to cope. Resonating with these findings, a review of 'children looked after' figures and corresponding inequalities across local authorities in England between 2004 and 2019 noted a steep rise in 'children looked after' in line with widening inequalities brought about by rising child poverty and disinvestment from children and youth services (Bennet et al., 2020).

The number of older young people referred to children's social care for the first time during adolescence has also risen (Association of Directors of Children's Services, 2018, 2021). At the end of 2019, the Children's Commissioner reported a 21 per cent increase in 'teenagers in care', with one in four children in care (23%) being over 16, and 39 per cent aged 10–15 (Children's Commissioner, 2019). This rise was attributed to a range of harms these young people had experienced beyond their family homes. In research exploring 'children looked after' and inequalities data, an increase in 16–17-year-olds entering the care system was also identified, with a widening gap between deprived and affluent areas (Bennet et al., 2020).

While child protection services have traditionally been concerned with intra-familial harm between parents and their young children, extra-familial forms of harm have recently garnered increased policy attention. This is reflected in changes to *Working Together to Safeguard Children*, which stipulates that multi-agency child safeguarding partnerships are required to 'understand the level of need and risk in, or faced by, a family from the child's perspective' (HM Government, 2018, p.28), outlining that assessments and interventions should be able to address extra-familial contexts and harms. Bennet and colleagues (2020) query whether the rise in 16–17-year-olds entering the care system might be attributable to this policy turn with regard to adolescent harm, and increased buy-in to 'Contextual Safeguarding', while noting that this does not account for the disproportionate 'children looked after rates' in more deprived areas. Indeed, a study conducted by Firmin, Wroe and Skidmore in 2020 spoke to this trend. Exploring the use of out-of-area care placements for adolescents impacted by extra-familial forms of harm, they established that across 13 local authorities in England and Wales, between 1 and 19 per cent of all young people for whom children's services teams had an open case (early help through to children in care teams) were open due to extra-familial harms, and between 0 and 25 per cent of these young people were in out-of-area care placements due to this harm. Risk, in the form of physical harm, was the major driver of these care placements, with *routes to safety* for young people beyond their placement often overlooked (Firmin *et al.*, 2020).

This paints a messy picture. While we are witnessing a rise in young people entering care for the first time during adolescence due to a range of extra-familial harms, there is also evidence that referrals to children's social care teams for adolescents impacted by extra-familial harm are often not progressed (Lloyd & Firmin, 2019), and that when they are, in some areas of England and Wales, they routinely result in disruptive interventions such as the removal of children from their families and home towns (Firmin *et al.*, 2020). This reflects the conclusions of Munby and others (Bennet *et al.*, 2020; Care Crisis Review, 2018; Featherstone *et al.*, 2018) that the child welfare system is both under-resourced, particularly at a preventative level, ineffective in addressing universal drivers of harm, and, reflecting a shift in spending towards 'acute' services, often punitive and disruptive when it does intervene.

The child protection system's engagement with contextual and structural causes of harm

There is emerging evidence, then, that child protective services in the UK, while disproportionately investigating families living in poverty, are unable to engage with the contextual and structural drivers of a range of universal and specific harm types in childhood and adolescence (Bilson *et al.*, 2017; Lloyd & Firmin, 2019; NSPCC, 2014). Reactions oscillate between 'no further action' or escalation to 'last resort' interventions such as removal, to safeguard young people from harm in their families and beyond. A mounting set of voices, including academics (Saar-Heiman & Gupta, 2020), professional organizations (British Association of Social Workers[1]), young people (Reclaim, 2020) and campaign groups (ATD Fourth World;[2] Parents, Families & Allies Network;[3] Family Rights Group[4]), have, albeit in different ways, spoken to the need for child welfare services to engage with the complex contexts of young people's lives. They call for support through relational, local, collaborative and properly resourced practices. We are compelled to frame our understanding of the relationship between intra- and extra-familial harm, and between varying forms of extra-familial harm, through this contextual, holistic and structural lens. Citing data that demonstrates a relationship between deprivation and children being looked after by the state, Featherstone and colleagues (2018) query why family troubles are not positioned as socially determined in such a way as physical or mental health concerns commonly are. They conclude:

> Because of the individualistic focus in child protection…there are no mechanisms for understanding or engaging with the links between differing health and welfare outcomes in particular contexts. Because we lack knowledge about particular social and economic contexts, we are deprived of important understandings about the ecology of children's lives. (Featherstone *et al.*, 2018, p.5)

Early childhood neglect and adolescent extra-familial harm

There is evidence to suggest that some adolescents experiencing abuse or exploitation may have been subjected to one or more forms of abuse as children within the family home. While there can never be a pre-determined, causal link between experiences of abuse in early childhood and subsequent experiences of abuse in adolescence, child sexual abuse within the home has been shown to be a 'risk factor' of later adolescent experiences of sexual violence (Berelowitz *et al.*, 2013; Davidson & Bifulco, 2019; Fisher *et al.*, 2017). While we cannot assume that abuse in the home will lead to continued extra-familial harm,

---

1   www.basw.co.uk/what-we-do/policy-and-research/anti-poverty-practice-guide-social-work.
2   https://atd-uk.org/projects-campaigns/social-work-training-programme.
3   www.pfan.uk/parental-rights-and-parent-advocacy-andy-bilson.
4   www.frg.org.uk.

neither should adolescents' experiences of sexual violence and harm be seen as disconnected from previous experiences in childhood. Taking this point, it is important to try to identify and address overlapping drivers of intra- and extra-familial harm in order to inform our work in creating better childhoods for young people. We propose that there is an opportunity to engage in this debate by considering the social and structural contexts that shape experiences of harm at home, and the contexts that shape experiences of harm in friendship circles, schools and neighbourhoods.

Bailey and Brake (1975) explored this question in their seminal text *Radical Social Work*, asking child welfare professionals to assess their role when intervening with families who have experienced long-term poverty. Their argument was that much of the abuse taking place within families who have experienced long-term poverty is an implosion of harm, a consequence of long-term deprivation and disadvantage. They questioned whether the role of the social worker is to apply a sticking plaster, helping the family to be better equipped to manage the harm and abuse caused by this long-term poverty, or whether the worker's role is to help families understand the injustice caused by poverty and to link them with others in the community to try to address these harms. This argument was picked up in the 1990s by Langham and Lee (1989) in their text *Radical Social Work Today* and again in more recent work quoted above by Featherstone and colleagues (2018), and by the inspiring text *Radical Help* (Cottam, 2018). This strand of work is asking social work to move beyond seeing just the symptom (violence imploding within the home) to engage with addressing the cause (social inequality and injustice). It relates to work on community activism and political engagement.

Other work asks questions about the impact of the environment, of discrimination and particularly of racism on families' capacities to create safe spaces within and outside the home, when discrimination and structural disadvantage have already created an environment of attack and abuse. Bernard's work on social work with Black families, for example, highlights a lack of awareness among social workers about the impact of racism on families who come to the attention of welfare agencies (Bernard, 2019; Bernard & Harris, 2016). Bernard and others argue that social work can only be effective if it considers questions of power as experienced by families, through engagement with community activities and radical approaches to creating social change.

Critics of this work may argue that it is idealistic, and that such radical interventions do not acknowledge that some individuals are harmful to others, and that harm and abuse of children can be experienced across all social classes and economic divides. This latter critique is important if we are to avoid the pathologization of poverty and child harm.

Other important work argues that the social work lens is targeted at 'the poor', who are disproportionately from Black, Asian and minoritized ethnic communities, rather than extending its lens to reveal the extent of harm and abuse within wealthy, privileged and economically powerful families. It notes that poor and Black, Asian and minoritized ethnic families are subject to a range of structural oppressions which have become increasingly embedded as austerity impacts on the day-to-day life of families and communities (Bernard, 2018).

Although research is in the early stages to track trajectories from intra-familial through to experiences of extra-familial harm, studies that have taken place suggest a correlation between children's experience of social deprivation and personal harm in the home and continued harm within extra-familial contexts (Pitts, 2008, 2020). Pitts' work shows how childhood inequality and familial poverty can severely constrain families' abilities to create contexts in which children can thrive, and how inequality and poverty have also been located as major drivers of harm in adolescence, including serious youth violence and criminal exploitation. Although it cannot be assumed, it is possible, therefore, that the social conditions that mediate harm in families also mediate harm experienced by adolescents outside their homes.

Taking these points into consideration, we propose that a structural and contextual account of child harm can inform the debate about the relationship between intra-familial violence experienced by children in the home and (sometimes the same) children's experiences of extra-familial violence. In doing so, we note the need for child welfare services to be able to engage with the impact of disadvantage and discrimination both within the home and within and across communities (Flood & Holmes, 2016).

Social work and other welfare agencies need to be able to engage with individuals, families and communities to share experiences and create a collective voice for action. This may reach beyond economic boundaries and move into critical assessments of the harm caused by over-privileged and unquestioned power. In short, children's experiences of harm are shaped by the contexts of their lives and there is an emerging body of evidence that suggests that contexts of intra- and extra-familial harm share some defining characteristics, both in how inequalities configure experiences of harm and in how statutory services respond to them.

Holistic features of extra-familial harm

This chapter's major focus is on extra-familial harms. Yet it is important that we address the question of the intersection between intra-familial and extra-familial harm. As we have discussed, the experience (and identification) of intra-familial forms of harm is shaped by complex and intersecting social, economic and relational contexts. The jury is out regarding the strength or generalizability of any relationship (and indeed casuality) between experiences of violence at home and experiences of violence outside the home. However, voices from the sector suggest that child welfare agencies are struggling to address both, and emerging practice frameworks such as the 'social model' of child protection, 'poverty-aware practice' and 'contextual safeguarding' appear to agree that child welfare systems are focused on individual behaviours and are de-contextualized from the environments in which people live their lives.

When young people are abused by others outside their family homes, the contexts in which this abuse happens can be complex, often characterized and informed by multiple locations and relationships. The complexity of responding to harm that takes place outside the family home is not a challenge that has traditionally sat with child protection services. Young people who were harmed in contexts outside their homes were traditionally diverted into youth justice services, or overlooked by family-focused child protection systems, until significant cultural, policy and practice changes in the last two decades (focused largely on work to challenge child sexual exploitation: Beckett & Pearce, 2017; Pearce, 2009, 2019) brought issues of extra-familial harm under the lens of child welfare. There is still significant work to do.

Amendments to *Working Together* include reference to extra-familial harm, noting that multi-agency partnerships are required to assess and intervene in issues faced by (as well as within) families (HM Government, 2018). This has placed a requirement on local safeguarding partnerships to be able to identify where children and young people are coming to harm outside their families, to have mechanisms in place to assess risk, to create safety in extra-familial contexts, and to be able to monitor the outcome of interventions to ensure that young people are safeguarded. However, there is no national framework overseeing a strategic approach to safeguarding adolescents, and a recent study by Firmin and colleagues (2020) indicates a lack of oversight as to how many young people are impacted by extra-familial forms of harm, and in what circumstances. As such, local areas are developing their own responses. For some, this has involved expanding their CSE (child sexual exploitation) services, which many local areas have established in the last decade, integrating their child protection, youth justice and community safety partnerships into exploitation panels, or embedding 'contextual' safeguarding responses drawing on the work of Firmin and others at the University of Bedfordshire (Association of London Directors of Children's Services, 2018; Firmin & Knowles, 2020).

However, local areas are facing a number of challenges in responding to extra-familial harm. A 2019 study by Lloyd and Firmin explored how referrals to children's services for extra-familial forms of harm were progressed. They found that, despite young people having experienced severe violence outside their homes, the majority of referrals were closed, and frequently referred to youth offending services that may be equipped to respond to offending behaviour but not necessarily to working with the core contexts that promote that behaviour. This case closure and referral onward took place despite the availability of the Section 17 provision for 'children in need' affording support around extra-familial harm, and this being required in light of changes to *Working Together* (HM Government, 2018).

Referrals for extra-familial harm were closed despite the significance of the harm faced, in some cases because parenting capacity could not be implicated in the reason for the harm occurring or persisting. Furthermore, the welcomed attempts to decriminalize a range of child harms, from sexual exploitation through to criminal exploitation, cannot simply mean the surveillance and monitoring of children by child protection rather than criminal justice agencies. Reproducing these approaches in turn perpetuates – rather than challenges – class-based, racialized and gendered biases (Wrennall, 2010; Wroe & Lloyd, 2020). Alongside ambiguity in the legislative frameworks for responding to extra-familial harm, there remains an individualized (Wroe, 2019) and siloed response to harm types that fails to address the conditions that drive multiple forms of harm young people might experience. As the Association of Directors of Children's Services states:

> Tackling the root causes of harm as well as the societal conditions that allow abuse and exploitation to flourish requires a radical shift in both policy, practice and funding. Several government departments lead on different aspects of related policy resulting in separate strategies and funding streams being developed for complex and overlapping risks including child sexual exploitation, criminal exploitation, modern slavery, offending behaviours, serious violence and radicalization. The best way to make headway with these interrelated issues is to take a holistic and integrated approach. (Association of Directors of Children's Services, 2019, p.3)

While identifying and responding to extra-familial forms of harm presents challenges at both policy and practice levels, we suggest that there are some deeper conceptual and societal issues at play that determine what is recognized as harm in extra-familial contexts, how this harm is defined and what resource is mobilized to attend to it. Extra-familial forms of harm are defined in *Working Together* (HM Government, 2018) as including sexual exploitation, criminal exploitation, trafficking, online abuse and 'extremism'.[5] We know that young people in the UK are impacted by a far broader and insidious range of extra-familial harms, including the direct impact of poverty on health and life outcomes (Cooper & Stewart, 2020), the significant and at times fatal impact of bullying and mental ill-health, and experiences of institutionalized harms including violence (Taylor, 2016), sexism and racism (Joseph-Salisbury, 2020; Women and Equalities Committee, 2016) in spaces that are meant to keep them safe.

There is also evidence of inaccuracies in how harm types are attributed and that the very process of labelling young people as associated to a particular harm type can have a stigmatizing and lasting impact. A 2018 report by Williams described the experiences of policing by young Black British boys who were deemed to be 'gang'

---

5   'Extremism' and 'radicalization' are categories of child harm that, while prioritized by the UK Government and Home Office, are implicated in the disproportionate surveillance and monitoring of Muslim children, families and communities with evidenced human rights implications. For a critique of the UK's counter-radicalization agenda and its impact on young people, see: www.justiceinitiative.org/publications/eroding-trust-uk-s-prevent-counter-extremism-strategy-health-and-education and www.cage.ngo/product/separating-families-how-prevent-seeks-the-removal-of-children-report.

affiliated. The report revealed the misidentification of young people as 'gang affected', the stigmatizing consequences of this labelling resulting in over-policing and exclusion from welfare and educational provision, and the criminogenic impact of being labelled as 'gang affected' (Williams, 2018). The adverse consequences of misrepresentation and over-focusing on 'gangs', particularly in relation to policy regarding youth violence, include the perpetuation of racialized stereotypes and distracting attention from deeper structural drivers of violence such as inequality, oppression and exploitation (Irwin-Rogers & Fraser, 2021).

There is arguably a valorization of particular categories of harm that reflect policy (and political) objectives, rather than the lived experience and needs of young people. The question of what drives the sector's understanding of the types of extra-familial harm impacting young people and where resource and attention should be focused were raised in the 2020 study by Firmin, Wroe and Skidmore (2020, p.10):

> 'I think other local authorities as well have become too probably focused on "in vogue" areas of concern and maybe media hype, and to the detriment then of other things like, for example, your serious youth violence and peer-on-peer abuse, which probably hadn't had that kind of attention that your CSE has had, for right reasons of course, but not necessarily helpful in this world, which seems to be quite knee-jerk in terms of how it responds to trends and patterns.' (Interview with a local authority children's social care team manager)

The issues with this are two-fold. First, there is a valorization and, arguably, a politicization of certain harm types that inform funding and commissioning (see Wroe, 2019, for an account of how 'county lines' emerge from the Government's anti-'gangs' agenda). Second, this can negatively impact young people through over-identification to some harm types (as above) and under-identification of others (such as racism in schools; Joseph-Salisbury, 2020).

Evidence suggests that when we move away from these specific labels and consider the ways in which children experience harm in contexts outside their families, they are often characterized by shared definitions, characteristics, methods and situations of harm (Firmin, Wroe & Lloyd, 2019). Firmin and colleagues (2019) note that definitions of child sexual exploitation, child criminal exploitation and human trafficking and modern slavery are all structured around the pillars of power, exchange and consent.

These forms of child harm also often:

- involve similar methods of accessing and controlling young people

- are facilitated by features of extra-familial contexts including school cultures, community guardianship and friendships (Ashurst & McAlinden, 2015; Barter, 2009; Firmin, 2017; Smallbone, Rayment-McHugh & Smith, 2013)

- feature aspects of threat or coercion (McNaughton Nicholls *et al.*, 2014; Pearce, 2013)

- can result in multiple relocations – placements/school moves (Hudek, 2018; Ofsted, 2018; Shuker, 2013)

- persist into adulthood (Coy, 2009; Holmes & Smale, 2018; Young, Fitzgibbon & Silverstone, 2013).

While these studies suggest overlapping features and circumstances of extra-familial harm, there is, as noted above, also emerging evidence that the overlapping characteristics of extra-familial harm interact with social and economic conditions, including poverty, sexism and racism and so on (Davis & Marsh, 2020; Grimshaw & Ford, 2018; Temple, 2020; Wroe, 2021). Indeed, the critical youth work literature names this blindness to the social and economic nature of young people's lives as 'context minimization error' (Lavie-Ajayi & Krumer-Nevo, 2013), where enduring structural factors are minimized despite their clearly evident impact on young lives (Reclaim, 2020).

Sexual exploitation, class and consent

Retrospective inquiries into the sexual exploitation of young people in Rotherham, Rochdale and other UK towns in the early to mid-1990s shone a light on the ways in which class, race(ism) and poverty created vulnerabilities to harm, while also distorting how policy makers, the media and the child welfare sector responded to the issue (Jay, 2014; Melrose, 2013; Wood, 2020). Notwithstanding the outdated policy environment, which until 2009 still used the term 'child prostitution' to describe the serious violence inflicted on young people, it is clear that classist, gendered and racialized ideas about victimhood led policy makers and practitioners to overlook many instances of CSE

(Beckett & Pearce, 2017). Subsequently, a similarly racialized, gendered and classist narrative has resulted in the under-identification of boys and Black and Asian girls and a disproportionate (and inaccurate) focus on Asian 'gangs' as perpetrators of CSE (Cockbain & Tufail, 2020).

Brown (2019) notes that before the Department of Health defined CSE as a form of child abuse in 2000 (while still referring to it as 'child prostitution'), poverty and disadvantage had shaped policy and practice discussions, arguably because the label 'prostitution' signalled an economic relationship through the selling of sex. While class and poverty have dominated media coverage of high-profile cases of CSE in the last decade (Melrose & Pearce, 2013), the move in 2009 from the language of child prostitution to child sexual exploitation saw the issue framed firmly as a child protection issue (Brown, 2019; Pearce, 2013). Policy makers and practitioners turned away from the socioeconomic circumstances of child exploitation (where local authorities might have been required and resourced to address issues such as unemployment, access to benefits and housing) and towards a simplistic and individualized focus on predatory men and vulnerable girls. Brown notes:

> Attempts to stress that 'anyone' can be a victim are driven by a desire to avoid pathologization, but these narratives can obscure profound disproportionalities in vulnerability which have been evident for some time. (Brown, 2019, p.625)

Brown reveals the ways in which vulnerability is constructed around idealized notions of childhood innocence that can exclude working class and Black, Asian and minoritized ethnic children, who, we know, are less likely to be identified and recognized as victims (Berelowitz, 2013; Davis & Marsh, 2020). This finding is echoed by Davis and Marsh in Chapter 6 of this book. Despite the prevailing discourse insisting that children and young people who have experienced CSE are victims, Brown documents the ways in which young people are expected to perform a predetermined demonstration of vulnerability that aligns with perceived notions of victim authenticity as a condition for receiving support. This has meant them needing to demonstrate their victimhood, innocence and lack of agency in order to 'fit' into accepted binary notions of 'innocent victim' or 'evil perpetrator'. Moving away from individualized notions of vulnerability and risk, Brown uses participatory research and accounts from young people, evidencing the need for services to attend to the material needs of young people through the distribution of resources, not just services.

The social model of consent provides a framework for considering the impact of poverty on experiences of CSE. The social model moves away from a medicalized understanding of consent grounded in Gillick competencies and Fraser guidelines[6] and towards thinking about and understanding the social processes and structures that impact on young people's choices (Pearce, 2013). Presenting four categories of 'abused consent', Pearce provides for a poverty-informed account of young people's restricted choices and agency in the context of CSE. 'Survival' consent 'recognizes the impact that poverty may have on young women and men's decisions to swap, sell or exchange sex for some form of reward, gift or money' (Pearce, 2013, p.64).

'Survival' consent allows for the recognition that young people may be making informed decisions about receiving payment for sexual activity as a means of generating an income or providing for themselves, while still recognizing this as a form of abused consent and thus as child abuse/exploitation. This model accounts, in part, for the complex contexts in which sexual exploitation can happen, opens up the possibility for intervention to move beyond individual decision-making and choice, and requires child welfare systems to consider the social and economic conditions that young people are navigating. If a 'social model' of consent is applied with an intersectional lens, it also allows for consideration of how gender, (dis)ability, race and class inform 'survival' consent. In this sense, a social model of consent in the context of childhood sexual exploitation aligns with calls from adult sex worker campaigns to address the social and economic conditions that can make consensual *adult* sex work precarious (Smith & Mac, 2018).

Child criminal exploitation, racism and poverty

A national review conducted by the Child Safeguarding Practice Review Panel (2020) into UK responses to child criminal exploitation (CCE) evidenced a disproportionate representation of young Black boys in affected cohorts of young people. However, despite this being noted as a 'serious concern', no recommendations were made as to how policy or

---

6   For an overview of both see: https://learning.nspcc.org.uk/child-protection-system/gillick-competence-fraser-guidelines#heading-top.

interventions might consider issues of race, or racism, when it comes to 'tackling' CCE.

A Serious Case Review (SCR) was undertaken by Waltham Forest Safeguarding Children Board in 2020, following the murder of 'Child C', a 14-year-old Black British boy who was criminally exploited and murdered in Waltham Forest in 2019. The Review details his mother's concerns that, at a young age, he was subject to racist discrimination in school. Child C's mother decided to home school him in order to avoid what she predicted would be an inevitable exclusion. This began a lengthy process in which she struggled to get her son back into an appropriate school place. The report concludes that there was no evidence that 'racial stereotyping came into play in the judgements made by the various professionals' (2019, p.50), noting that many professionals were themselves Black or from minority ethnic backgrounds. The SCR concludes with no recommendations as to how the role of race, or racism, in the events that led to Child C's tragic death could inform future prevention or intervention planning.

While both reviews discuss the significance of school exclusions, neither reviews fully or addresses the broader social and economic contexts of the lives of many Black boys in the UK, wherein Black Caribbean and mixed White and Black Caribbean children are three times more likely than White pupils to be permanently excluded from school (UK Government, 2020). This is despite school exclusion being cited as a major and most consistent risk factor for criminal exploitation identified by the Child Safeguarding Practice Review Panel in 2020 (see also Temple, 2020).

The reason for the disproportionate representation of Black boys in 'county lines' and CCE cohorts has not to date received proper investigation. However, critical race research in sociology and criminology points to a number of potential explanations. This over-representation could be explained as a result of the re-purposing of 'gangs' strategies to respond to 'county lines'-affected cohorts of young people (Wroe, 2021) – strategies that disproportionately (and often inaccurately) target young Black boys and men (Amnesty International, 2018; Williams & Clarke, 2016). Compounding this, the control of the distribution of illegal drugs has a long history centred on the policing of Black people (Koram, 2019), despite lower levels of reported drug use from Black communities (Shiner et al., 2019), requiring us to turn our attention to the processes that drive over-identification and surveillance

(Williams, 2018; Wroe, 2021). Yet we also know that young Black people live in low-income households at a higher rate than the national average and face higher rates of unemployment (Office for National Statistics, 2020), are permanently excluded from school at a higher rate than their White peers (UK Government, 2020) and that Black Caribbean 16–17-year-olds are three times as likely to be placed by child protection systems into out-of-home placements than White peers (Bywaters *et al.*, 2017), all of which are considered as vulnerabilities to exploitation (The Children's Society, 2019). Young Black people, then, find themselves *structurally* marginalized and simultaneously subject to hyper-surveillance by state services.

There is an accepted wisdom that children are drawn into 'gangs' seeking a 'sense of belonging' (Antrobus, 2009) due to a developmental desire to fit in with peers, compounded for some by neglectful or absent families. The Children's Society has this to say about 'child criminal exploitation':

> A lot of these children are targeted by criminal gangs because they haven't got a family, or security, or love. Likely to be trapped in poverty, they are picked off the street, having nowhere else to go, and are made to feel part of a family. (The Children's Society, 2020)

The language of 'criminal gangs' is drawn from a long history of racialized policing of working class and Black communities in the UK (Williams, 2015). When we consider the evidence, and adopt a more holistic lens, if children are growing up in poor communities, experiencing structural racism, disproportionate monitoring and surveillance by the state and disruptive child protection interventions (out-of-home care), then perhaps it is pertinent to turn our attention away from individual families and towards the systems and structures that push young people to the margins, over-identify them in criminal cohorts and under-identify them in child welfare cohorts (Berelowitz, 2013). Might this be giving them the impression that they do not belong? The notion of belonging and 'mattering' is highlighted in research regarding violence between young people (Billingham & Irwin-Rogers, 2021). Chiming with the core argument of this chapter, the authors emphasize the connection between young people's personal sense of belonging and the wider socioeconomic and political contexts in which they arguably are *not* treated as though they matter.

Speaking to a Serious Violence Home Affairs select committee in

April 2019, a youth work consultant highlighted a consensus among his co-witnesses: 'My personal opinion is that the root of this all is poverty' (Home Affairs Committee witness, 2019[7]).

Responding to the Children's Commissioner's report on CCE, the Chair of the Association of Directors of Children's Services Families, Communities and Young People Policy Committee echoed this:

> The impact of austerity, cuts to youth services and the availability of early support and positive activities for young people within their communities cannot be understated, neither can the cuts to community policing. Add to this, a rising number of children living in poverty and being excluded from school it's easy to see how children can become vulnerable to exploitation by gangs. (Association of Directors of Children's Services, 2019[8])

'County lines' is hailed as a major driver of 'serious youth violence' and, as such, is a key strategic priority in the government's 2019 Serious Youth Violence Strategy. The 2020 Youth Violence Commission report states that 'increasing rates of child poverty and growing levels of inequality are fundamental drivers of serious violence' (Irwin-Rogers, Muthoo & Billingham, 2020, p.1), pointing to the detrimental impact of childhood poverty on early developmental outcomes and the relationship between precarious housing, work and finances, and vulnerability to violence. Indeed, childhood poverty is named here as a form of violence. And yet the 'County Lines Action Plan' appended to the 2019 Serious Youth Violence Strategy has no actions that relate to the alleviation of poverty, but does feature 12 actions for policing, prosecution and the criminal justice system (a system in which young Black boys, those we are ostensibly seeking to safeguard, are significantly over-represented).

Given the mounting evidence that poverty and institutionalized racism in schooling (Joseph-Salisbury, 2020) and over-policing (Williams, 2018) characterize the contexts of these children's lives, there is a need for prevention and response strategies to address issues of deprivation, classism, racism and the harms inherent in school, policing and drug policies that centre monitoring and surveillance of racialized and classed communities. This calls for turning attention away from

---

7   https://data.parliament.uk/writtenevidence/committeeevidence.svc/evidencedocument/home-affairs-committee/serious-violence/oral/101992.html.

8   https://adcs.org.uk/safeguarding/article/Childrens-Commissioner-report-on-the-criminal-exploitation-of-children.

'intervening' in communities and towards considering how multi-agency processes (of over-policing and monitoring), and government social policy, might result in the (over)representation of young people in such cohorts (Williams, 2018; Wroe, 2021).

What does this mean for child welfare services?

Some have already begun to consider the ways in which responses to extra-familial harm might address the systems and structures that create vulnerabilities for whole populations of young people, and specific vulnerabilities for those few who experience significant harm. Beckett (2011, cited in Beckett, Holmes & Walker, 2017) outlines the 'interconnected conditions for CSE', noting that the vulnerability of an individual child alone cannot explain why CSE happens. Adopting an ecological approach, Beckett describes a process in which perpetrator risk (that is, the presence of a perpetrator), a young person's vulnerability (which is influenced by internal *and* external factors) and inadequate protective structures intersect to create the conditions for harm to happen. Similarly, Contextual Safeguarding, an approach to safeguarding adolescents from extra-familial forms of harm (Firmin, 2020), is grounded in Bourdieusian sociological theory, focusing on the 'rules at play' in young people's social contexts and the 'capital' they have to navigate harmful rules. Both approaches account for the contexts of young people's lives to explain adolescent abuse.

Others have taken this further, accounting not only for the people and places that characterize abusive contexts, but the ways in which the very structural conditions and histories of our societies create the conditions for adolescent exploitation. Speaking to the relationship between intersecting forms of structural oppression (namely poverty, racism, patriarchy and ableism) and child sexual abuse, Generation Five, a child sexual abuse transformative justice collective, points out:

> We are living within social, economic, and political systems that fundamentally operate on a premise of 'power-over.' By power-over, we mean that our world gets divided into those individuals or groups who are considered valid, real, worthy, and human and those that are considered less valuable, unimportant, or not-fully-human based on race, class, gender, sexual orientation, nationality, dis/ability, religion, and age.

> For many children, sexual abuse is part of our process of socialization into a power-over worldview. (Generation Five, 2017, p.21)

So how do we address these holistic contexts of extra-familial forms of harm? Poverty, racism and patriarchy can seem like abstract or politicized issues but, as we have seen, they have a direct impact on young people's experiences of harm within their families and beyond and are often issues that young people and families say are affecting them (Reclaim, 2020). If society is serious about preventing adolescent abuse, then professional agencies together with communities must begin to tackle the conditions that allow it to flourish, and be adequately equipped and resourced to do so. Some have begun to do this work.

Critical youth work refers back to some of the principles explored by the radical social work tradition explained earlier in this chapter. It takes to task the idea of 'youth at risk' and the individualized case-management model (Lavie-Ajayi & Krumer-Nevo, 2013) and engages with young people in the spaces in which they spend their time. It builds relationships of trust not for the purpose of engagement in formal/statutory processes or for building 'intelligence' about an issue, but to create 'close symmetrical relationships of empathy, love and authenticity' (Lavie-Ajayi & Krumer-Nevo, 2013, p.1699). It works to increase the social capital of adolescents, to challenge deficit narratives about young people, to help young people understand and challenge their low or marginalized status and to create, and facilitate access to, resources. This includes work with young people who have harmed or been harmed by others:

> The narrative of worth should not ignore the aspects of their behavior that damage both themselves and others, but rather seek to incorporate these in a complex story using a new and contextualized perspective. (Lavie-Ajayi & Krumer-Nevo, 2013, p.1701)

Evaluated youth work projects that have sought to work in, and address, the contexts of young people's experiences of violence and harm speak to the need for sustainably funded, strengths-based, trauma-informed and relational models of engagement. Such engagement could support young people to name the ways in which they lack power, or have had power taken away from them, whether through poverty, racism, or abuse by institutions or individuals. Finally, the approach can be participatory, supporting young people to lead responses, while youth workers, social workers, teachers and other professionals utilize their amassed social and economic capital to levy resources (both material and social) to help scaffold young people's safety (Evans, Dillon & Wroe, 2021; Harden *et al.*, 2014; Lavie-Ajayi & Krumer-Nevo, 2013; Spolander, Englebrecht & Sansfacon, 2016).

At a commissioning level, community engagement and collaborative work across sectors has revealed innovative responses to preventing extra-familial harm. Sheffield Council, in collaboration with local universities, schools, youth services, voluntary and community sector (VCS) organizations and counselling organizations, held a symposium on youth violence in the city. They noted that young people living in highly deprived areas are the most affected by serious youth violence and decreases to protective services due to austerity, and are least represented in the design of violence reduction strategies. Social exclusion (including institutional racism in educational settings), mental health and community voice, and investment emerged as the major themes of the symposium. The following recommendations were put forward:

- Mapping local VCS provision and ensuring core funding for projects and trauma-informed training.

- The convening of a paid group of adults and young people to collaborate on the design of violence reduction programmes.

- The provision of benefits advice and income maximization support via VCS organizations.

- Commitment to reducing school exclusions through an inclusion strategy involving a scrutiny committee of young people and parents in high exclusion schools. (Mason *et al.*, 2019)

Such collaborations are a welcome step in the direction proposed by the array of voices convened in this chapter.

This chapter and the voices contained within it contend that, in order to safeguard children and young people from specific and generalized forms of harm, we need to consider the structural and contextual dynamics of children's lives. In 2019, Firmin, Wroe and Lloyd presented a holistic model for understanding the intersecting conditions of adolescent extra-familial harm. They proposed five fundamental issues that child welfare services with a statutory duty to protect children, and wider multi-agency partners, need to be able to address in order to prevent extra-familial harm in adolescence (see Figure 5.1).

Working with relationships and adolescent agency, addressing the contexts of grooming and coercion, considering the impact of debt on young people's decisions and behaviour, and exploring a meaningful and safe counter-offer are each understood within the context of young people's lives and the social and economic conditions that characterize them.

Understood in a structural sense, a counter-offer would need to extend beyond a trip to McDonald's to consistent relationships that elevate young people's social capital and status in society, and advocate and broker for secure housing, employment opportunities, and access to education and local youth services.

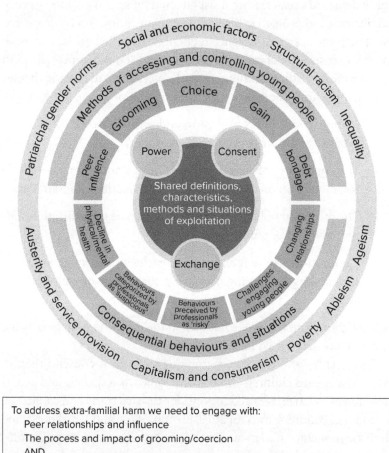

To address extra-familial harm we need to engage with:
    Peer relationships and influence
    The process and impact of grooming/coercion
    AND
    Work *with* young people's sense of agency and desire to make choices
    Make an offer – counteract the gain
    Mitigate the risks of 'debt'

Figure 5.1: 'Ways in which forms of exploitation can inter-connect' from Firmin, Wroe & Lloyd (2019)

Conclusion

This chapter has considered the relationship between young people's experiences of harm in their families, and beyond their front doors. We have shown that while some argue that intra-familial harms such as childhood neglect are invariably linked to experiences of exploitation outside the home, others question a simplistic assumption of causation, criticizing this as deterministic and stigmatizing. Furthermore, we have argued that the exploitation or abuse of young people in extra-familial contexts can be unhelpfully siloed, and we ask instead for a holistic understanding of the interconnected conditions for exploitation.

Examining these debates, we propose that when we are considering intra- or extra-familial harm, and the various manifestations of harm in children's extra-familial contexts, there is evidence that child protection systems are falling short in comparable ways: failure to engage in the contexts of children's lives, limited acknowledgement of the ways in which these contexts are defined by inequalities, and a vast and under-resourced middle ground between no further action and the removal of children from their homes. In doing so, we aim to open up a discussion about the intersecting contexts of child harm that are structural, thereby encompassing factors beyond the individual.

Rather than *blaming* individuals, we advocate approaches that are *naming* of a range of social harms and oppressions. We have begun to discuss and propose ways in which child welfare systems might organize themselves to begin to meaningfully engage with the complexity of these contexts.

References

Amnesty International (2018). *Trapped in the Matrix: Secrecy, Stigma and Bias in the Met's Gangs Database*. London: Amnesty International UK.

Antrobus, S. (2009). *Dying to Belong: An In-Depth Review of Street Gangs in Britain*. London: The Centre for Social Justice.

Ashurst, L. & McAlinden, A. (2015). 'Young people, peer-to-peer grooming and sexual offending: Understanding and responding to harmful sexual behaviour within a social media society.' *Probation Journal, 62*(4), 374–388.

Association of Directors of Children's Services (ADCS) (2018). *Safeguarding Pressures Phase 6.* Manchester: ADCS.

Association of Directors of Children's Services (ADCS) (2019). *ADCS Discussion Paper: Serious Youth Violence and Knife Crime.* Manchester: ADCS.

Association of Directors of Children's Services (ADCS) (2021). *Safeguarding Pressures Phase 7.* Manchester: ADCS.

Association of London Directors of Children's Services (ALDCS) (2018). *The Response of London Children's Services to Serious Youth Violence and Knife Crime.* London: ALDCS.

Bailey, R. & Brake, M. (1975). *Radical Social Work*. London: Random House Publishers.

Barter, C. (2009). 'In the name of love: Partner abuse and violence in teenage relationships.' *The British Journal of Social Work, 39*(2), 211–233.

Beckett, H., Holmes, D. & Walker, J. (2017). *Child Sexual Exploitation: Definition and Guide for Professionals*. London: Department for Education.

Beckett, H. & Pearce, J. (2017). *Understanding and Responding to Child Sexual Exploitation*. London: Routledge.

Bennet, D.L., Mason, K.E., Schluter, D.K., Wickham, S. *et al.* (2020). 'Trends in inequalities in Children Looked After in England between 2004 and 2019: A local area ecological analysis.' *British Medical Journal, 10*. https://bmjopen.bmj.com/content/10/11/e041774.

Berelowitz, S., Clifton, J., Firmin, C., Gulyurtlu, S. & Edwards, G. (2013). *If Only Someone Had Listened: Office of the Children's Commissioner's Inquiry into Child Sexual Exploitation in Gangs and Groups*. London: Office of the Children's Commissioner.

Bernard, C. (2018). *An Exploration of How Social Workers Engage Neglectful Parents from Affluent Backgrounds in the Child Protection System*. Goldsmiths, University of London.

Bernard, C. (2019). 'Using an Intersectional Lens to Examine the Child Sexual Exploitation of Black Adolescents.' In J. Pearce (ed.) *Child Sexual Exploitation: Why Theory Matters* (pp.193–209). Bristol: Policy Press.

Bernard, C. & Harris, P. (2016). *Safeguarding Black Children: Good Practice in Child Protection*. London: Jessica Kingsley Publishers.

Billingham, L. & Irwin-Rogers, K. (2021). 'The terrifying abyss of insignificance: Marginalisation, mattering and violence between young people.' *Oñati Socio-Legal Series*.

Bilson, A., Featherstone, B. & Martin, K. (2017). 'How child protection's "investigative turn" impacts on poor and deprived communities.' *Family Law, 47*, 316–319.

Brown, K. (2019). 'Vulnerability and child sexual exploitation: Towards an approach grounded in life experiences.' *Critical Social Policy, 39*(4), 622–642.

Bywaters, P., Kwhali, J., Brady, G., Sparks, T. & Bos, E. (2017). 'Out of sight, out of mind: Ethnic inequalities in child protection and out-of-home care intervention rates.' *The British Journal of Social Work, 47*, 1884–1902.

Care Crisis Review (2018). *Care Crisis Review: Options for Change*. London: Family Rights Group.

Children's Commissioner (2019). *The Stability Index 2019*. London: HM Government.

Children's Society, The (2020). 'The frontline of child exploitation.' *The Children's Society Blog*. https://www.childrenssociety.org.uk/what-we-do/blogs/working-on-the-frontline-of-child-exploitation.

Child Safeguarding Practice Review Panel (2020). *It was Hard to Escape. Safeguarding Children at Risk from Criminal Exploitation*. London: HM Government.

Cockbain, E. & Tufail, W. (2020). 'Failing victims, fuelling hate: Challenging the harms of the "Muslim grooming gangs" narrative.' *Race and Class, 61*(3), 3–32.

Cooper, K. & Stewart, K. (2020). 'Does household income affect children's outcomes? A systematic review of the evidence.' *Child Indicators Research*, 981–1005. https://doi.org/10.1007/s12187-020-09782-0.

Cottam, H. (2018). *Radical Help. How We Can Remake the Relationships Between Us and Revolutionize the Welfare State*. London: Little, Brown Book Group.

Coy, M. (2009). '"Moved around like bags of rubbish nobody wants": How multiple placement moves can make young women vulnerable to sexual exploitation.' *Child Abuse Review, 18*(4), 254–266.

Davidson, J. & Bifulco, A. (2019). *Child Abuse and Protection: Contemporary Issues in Research, Policy and Practice*. London: Routledge.

Davis, J. & Marsh, N. (2020). 'Boys to men: The cost of adultification in safeguarding responses to Black boys.' *Critical and Radical Social Work, 8*(2), 255–259.

Department for Education (2019). *Children Looked After in England Including Adoption: 2018 to 2019*. London: Department for Education. www.gov.uk/government/statistics/children-looked-after-in-england-including-adoption-2018-to-2019.

Evans, F., Dillon, J. & Wroe, L.E. (2021). 'Covid-19: Changing fields of social work practice with children and young people.' *Critical and Radical Social Work*. https://doi.org/10.1332/20498 6021X16109919842882.

Featherstone, B., Gupta, A., Morris, K. & White, S. (2018). *Protecting Children: A Social Model*. Bristol: Policy Press.

Firmin, C. (2017). *Abuse Between Young People: A Contextual Account* (first edition). London: Routledge.

Firmin, C. (2020). *Contextual Safeguarding and Child Protection: Rewriting the Rules*. London: Routledge.

Firmin, C. & Knowles, R. (2020). *The Legal and Policy Framework for Contextual Safeguarding Approaches*. Luton: Contextual Safeguarding.

Firmin, C., Wroe, L.E. & Lloyd, J. (2019). *Safeguarding and Exploitation – Complex, Contextual and Holistic Approaches. Strategic Briefing*. Totnes: Research in Practice.

Firmin, C., Wroe, L.E. & Skidmore, P. (2020). *'A Sigh of Relief': A Summary of the Phase One Results from the Securing Safety Study*. Luton: Contextual Safeguarding.

Fisher, C., Goldsmith, A., Hurcombe, R. & Soares, C. (2017). *The Impacts of Child Sexual Abuse*. London: The Independent Inquiry into Child Sexual Abuse.

Flood, S. & Holmes, D. (2016). *Child Neglect and its Relationship to Other Forms of Harm – Responding Effectively to Children's Needs: Evidence Scopes*. NSPCC, Research in Practice and Action for Children.

Generation Five (2017). *Ending Child Sexual Abuse: Transformative Justice Handbook*. Generation Five.

Grimshaw, R. & Ford, M. (2018). *Young People, Violence and Knives – Revisiting the Evidence and Policy Discussions*. Centre for Crime and Justice Studies.

Harden, T., Kenemore, T., Mann, K., Edwards, M., List, C. & Martinson, K.J. (2014). 'The Truth N' Trauma Project: Addressing community violence through a youth-led, trauma-informed and restorative framework.' *Child and Adolescent Social Work Journal, 32*(1), 65–79.

HM Government (2018, revised 2020). *Working Together to Safeguard Children: A Guide to Inter-Agency Working to Safeguard and Promote the Welfare of Children*. London: HMSO.

Holmes, D. & Smale, E. (2018). *Strategic Briefing: Transitional Safeguarding – Adolescence to Adulthood*. Totnes: Research in Practice and Research in Practice for Adults.

Hudek, J. (2018). *County Lines: Scoping Report*. London: British Association of Social Workers. www.basw.co.uk/resources/county-lines-scoping-report-may-2018.

Irwin-Rogers, K. & Fraser, A. (2021). *A Public Health Approach to Violence Reduction: Strategic Briefing*. Totnes: Research in Practice.

Irwin-Rogers, K., Muthoo, A. & Billingham, L. (2020). *Youth Violence Commission Final Report*. Youth Violence Commission.

Jay, A. (2014). *Independent Inquiry into Child Sexual Exploitation in Rotherham (1997–2013)*. Rotherham: LSCB.

Joseph-Salisbury, R. (2020). *Race and Racism in English Secondary Schools*. London: Runnymede.

Koram, K. (2019). *The War on Drugs and the Global Colour Line*. London: Pluto Press.

Krumer-Nevo, M. (2020). *Radical Hope: Poverty-Aware Practice for Social Work*. Bristol: Policy Press.

Langham, M. & Lee, P. (1989). *Radical Social Work Today*. London: Routledge.

Lavie-Ajayi, M. & Krumer-Nevo, M. (2013). 'In a different mindset: Critical youth work with marginalized youth.' *Children and Youth Services Review, 35*(10), 1698–1704.

Lloyd, J. & Firmin, C. (2019). 'No further action: Contextualising social care decisions for children victimised in extra-familial settings.' *Youth Justice, 20*(1/2), 79–92.

Mason, W., Brasab, S., Stone, B., Soutar, J., Mohamed, A. & Mwale, T. (2019). *Youth Violence, Masculinity and Mental Health: Learning from Communities Most Affected*. Sheffield: University of Sheffield.

McNaughton Nicholls, C., Cockbain, E., Brayley, H., Harvey, S., Fox, C. & Paskell, C. (2014). *Research on the Sexual Exploitation of Boys and Young Men: A UK Scoping Study, Summary of the Findings*. London: Barnardo's.

Melrose, M. (2013). 'Young People and Sexual Exploitation: A Critical Discourse Analysis.' In M. Melrose & J. Pearce. *Critical Perspectives on Child Sexual Exploitation and Related Trafficking* (pp.9–22). London: Palgrave Macmillan.

Melrose, M. & Pearce, J. (2013). *Critical Perspectives on Child Sexual Exploitation and Related Trafficking*. London: Palgrave Macmillan.

Munby, J. (2016). *15th View from the President's Chambers. Care Cases: The Looming Crisis.* Family Law. www.familylaw.co.uk/news_and_comment/15th-view-from-the-president-s-chambers-care-cases-the-looming-crisis.

National Youth Agency (2020). *Hidden in Plain Sight. Gangs and Exploitation: A Youth Work Response to COVID-19.* Leicester: NYA. https://nya.org.uk/resource/hidden-in-plain-sight-gangs-and-exploitation.

Nayak, S. (2020). 'Black Feminist Diaspora Spaces of Social Work Critical Reflexivity.' In L. Wroe, R. Larkin & R.A. Maglajlic (eds) *Social Work with Refugees, Asylum Seekers and Migrants: Theory and Skills for Practice* (pp.41–55). London: Jessica Kingsley Publishers.

NSPCC (2014). *Teenagers: Learning from Case Reviews.* London: NSPCC Learning.

Office for National Statistics (ONS) (2020). *Child Poverty and Education Outcomes by Ethnicity.* London: ONS.

Ofsted (2018). *Growing Up Neglected: A Multi-Agency Response to Older Children.* London: Ofsted.

Pearce, J. (2009). *Child Sexual Exploitation: It's Not Hidden, You Just Aren't Looking.* London: Routledge.

Pearce, J. (2013). 'A Social Model of "Abused Consent".' In M. Melrose & J. Pearce. *Critical Perspectives on Child Sexual Exploitation and Related Trafficking* (pp.52–68). London: Palgrave Macmillan.

Pearce, J. (ed.) (2019). *Child Sexual Exploitation: Why Theory Matters.* Bristol: Policy Press.

Pitts, J. (2008). *Reluctant Gangster: The Changing Face of Youth Crime.* London: Routledge.

Pitts, J. (2020). 'Covid-19, county lines and the seriously "left behind".' *Journal of Children's Services, 15*(4), 209–213.

Reclaim (2020). *Listening to the Experts: Getting Behind the Headlines to Hear What Young People Want and Need to Stay Safe from Violent Crime.* Manchester: Reclaim.

Saar-Heiman, Y. & Gupta, A. (2020). 'The poverty-aware paradigm for child protection: A critical framework for policy and practice.' *The British Journal of Social Work, 50*(4), 1167–1184.

Shiner, M., Carre, Z., Delsol, R. & Eastwood, N. (2019). *The Colour of Injustice: 'Race', Drugs and Law Enforcement in England and Wales.* London: Stopwatch & Release.

Shuker, L. (2013). 'Constructs of Safety for Children in Care Affected by Sexual Exploitation.' In M. Melrose & J. Pearce. *Critical Perspectives on Child Sexual Exploitation and Related Trafficking* (pp.125–138). London: Palgrave Macmillan.

Smallbone, S., Rayment-McHugh, S. & Smith, D. (2013). 'Youth sexual offending: Context, good-enough lives, and engaging with a wider prevention agenda.' *International Journal of Behavioural Consultation and Therapy, 8*(3–4), 49–54.

Smith, P. & Mac, J. (2018). *Revolting Prostitutes: The Fight for Sex Workers' Rights.* London: Verso.

Spolander, G., Englebrecht, L. & Sansfacon, A.P. (2016). 'Social work and macro-economic neoliberalism: Beyond the social justice rhetoric.' *European Journal of Social Work, 19*(5), 634–649.

Taylor, C. (2016). *Review of the Youth Justice System in England and Wales.* London: Ministry of Justice.

Temple, A. (2020). *Excluded, Exploited, Forgotten: Childhood Criminal Exploitation and School Exclusions.* London: Just for Kids Law.

UK Government (2020). 'Temporary exclusion.' www.ethnicity-facts-figures.service.gov.uk/education-skills-and-training/absence-and-exclusions/pupil-exclusions/latest.

Waltham Forest Safeguarding Children Board (2020). *Serious Case Review: Child C: A 14-Year-Old Boy.* London: WFSCB.

Williams, P. (2015). 'Criminalising the other: Challenging the race-gang nexus.' *Race & Class, 56*(3), 18–35.

Williams, P. (2018). *Being Matrixed: The (Over) Policing of Gang Suspects in London.* London: Stopwatch.

Williams, P. & Clarke, B. (2016). *Dangerous Associations: Joint Enterprise, Gangs and Racism: An Analysis of the Process of Criminalisation of Black, Asian and Minority Ethnic Individuals.* London: Centre for Crime and Justice Studies.

Women and Equalities Committee (2016). *Sexual Harassment and Sexual Violence in Schools.* London: UK Parliament.

Wood, H. (2020). 'Three (working-class) girls: Social realism, the "at-risk" girl and alternative classed subjectivities.' *Journal of British Cinema and Television, 17*(1), 70–90.

Wrennall, L. (2010). 'Surveillance and child protection: De-mystifying the Trojan Horse.' *Surveillance & Society, 7*(30), 4–24.

Wroe, L.E. (2019). *Contextual Safeguarding and 'County Lines'.* Luton: Contextual Safeguarding.

Wroe, L.E. (2021). 'Young people and "county lines": A contextual and social account.' *Journal of Children's Services.* https://doi.org/10.1108/JCS-10-2020-0063.

Wroe, L.E. & Lloyd, J. (2020). 'Watching over or working with? Understanding social work innovation in response to extra-familial harm.' *Social Sciences, 9*(4), 37.

Young, T., Fitzgibbon, W. & Silverstone, D. (2013). *The Role of the Family in Facilitating Gang Membership, Criminality and Exit: A Report Prepared for Catch 22.* London: Catch 22.

Chapter 6

The Myth of the Universal Child

Jahnine Davis and Nicholas Marsh

Introduction: The pursuit of the 'universal child'

This chapter is written with a focus on improving safeguarding and child protection responses, specifically for those young people who fall out of sight when we consider their needs and experiences through a universal lens. One of the core arguments of our chapter is the concept of adultification, where Black children in particular are at a greater risk of being perceived as older and in less need of protection. Therefore, we are deliberately using the terms child/children as a reminder that it is fundamental for professionals to consider the ways in which they view this group of children, even more so when they are more likely to be ascribed adult characteristics.

The use of the term 'universal' is applied throughout this chapter in reference to the hypothetical 'universal child'[1] and their assumed normative development and lived experiences. The universal child and their supposed family act as an ever-present measuring rod and are understood as abstract from context, time, history and culture (Taylor, 2007), yet the norms they assume and project into practice and policy settings are undoubtedly of a western ideology. Children, young people and families who don't 'measure up' or conform to these standards are frequently misunderstood and treated with suspicion (Bernard, 2020; Bernard & Harris, 2019; Davis & Marsh, 2020; Flynn, 2019; Taylor, 2007). An example of this may include: when safeguarding professionals

---

1   The use of the word child is to re-emphasize that we are talking about children and who by definition and status are the victims or beneficiaries of adult actions (Cunningham, 2006).

and services interact with Black[2] and minoritized[3] families, they are viewed through the lens and assumptions that White western traditions, standards and approaches are the apex (Barn, 2007). The consequence of a 'white apex' is that everything that falls outside these standards is pathologized and seen as a deficit (Barn, 2007).

In this chapter, we argue that professionals, the systems they work within, and society at large, whether consciously or otherwise, often work from the basis that everyone is White-European, heterosexual and able-bodied. This is in part due to the research and theories that influence and underpin safeguarding practice, which largely excludes children from marginalized and minoritized backgrounds. These underpinnings are deeply ingrained in our professional psyche and have influenced practice for almost 60 years, observable in psychological development theories (of which child development is one). This includes Erik Erikson's life cycle (1959), which has been critiqued for being gendered, Eurocentric[4] and ableist (Davis, 1997; Gilligan, 1982). Additionally, it is argued that Bowlby's attachment theory (1969) is also Eurocentric and based on the promotion of the nuclear family as the normative approach to how healthy childhood relationships are formed (Choate et al., 2020). Both Erikson and Bowlby's influences are still present today and can be detected in the language we use, whether it is the cycle and phases of child development (Erikson, 1959) or references to 'attachment styles' between a child and their caregiver (Bowlby, 1969).

Therefore, this chapter starts on the footing that many of our systems, tools and processes are underpinned and informed by Eurocentric, heteronormative and ableist standards and norms, and that our training and practice does not go far enough to recognize the pervasive and alienating effect this can have on the services we provide to children (Dwivedi, 2002; Hicks, 2008; Hollinrake et al., 2019; Taylor, 2007).

---

2   Black is capitalized throughout this chapter to recognize it is 'a specific cultural group that requires use of a proper noun', as argued by Ferdinand Lee Barnett in his 1878 editorial 'Spell it with a Capital B'. Ferdinand Lee Barnett was an attorney, writer, lecturer, and the editor and founder of Chicago's first black newspaper, The Chicago Conservator. He is often remembered today as the husband of anti-lynching crusader Ida B. Wells.

3   Gunaratnam (2003) suggests the term 'minoritized' as it conceptualizes the process of becoming a minority and what that means.

4   Eurocentric emphasizes the values, histories and perspectives of the European tradition (Webster's New World College Dictionary, Fourth Edition, 1999).

It starts with you

Theories, research and policies only tell part of the story, as it is us – individuals and groups – who enact these theories, research and policies, and put them into operation as we go about our daily tasks. Therefore, if change is going to take place, we all have a duty to critically reflect on our own biases, beliefs and attitudes. We all bear individual and collective responsibility. We have to start by first acknowledging our own obligations in regards to adopting and enacting inclusive and equitable practice, which includes the use of critical reflection, to strengthen individual and organizational responses to children and their families.

As such, this chapter takes the position that racism and discrimination do exist and are undoubtedly experienced by some children receiving safeguarding interventions. Of course, this is not to say that all practitioners are necessarily racist or discriminatory, but to recognize that, in the main, our default approach does not have sufficient nuance and flex in it to accommodate difference. This is particularly true, as we shall discover, for children.

As discussed in Chapter 5, poverty and inequality have been found to have a significant impact on child welfare intervention rates, and poverty intersects with ethnicity in ways that can compound families' experiences of inequality (Bywaters *et al.*, 2017). While this chapter explores intersectionality in its widest application, there is an intentional focus on the interactions between race, ethnicity, gender and age. This is in acknowledgement of the lack of literature exploring young Black people's safeguarding experiences, though the content in this chapter can be transferred to other children's experiences.

We hope that you find this chapter engaging and challenging, and if you feel uncomfortable when reading, embrace this feeling, as it means you are involved in the content. We hope that by the end of this chapter you feel more confident and better equipped to understand and support all children, and may have even dispelled a few closely held assumptions of your own.

Understanding the child's universe

To not take action and accept the status quo is an act of endorsement – the endorsement of the comfortable and routinely compliant relationship practitioners and policy makers have with the aforementioned child development theories, research and practice standards and tools. Doing nothing inadvertently serves to silence the experiences of marginalized and minoritized children and validates the standards and measures of the universal child. It achieves this by diluting the importance of the political, historical, cultural and familial experiences and events in some children's lives (Taylor, 2007).

By principally focusing on the use of an intersectional[5] lens (Crenshaw, 1989), this chapter places children firmly in their individual and communal contexts. Crenshaw identified that a person's interactions with the world are not just solely based on one aspect of their identity, but are rather layered and multifaceted interactions in which racism, sexism, ableism, classism, homophobia (and so forth) are experienced simultaneously.

Recognizing a child's intersectional identities acknowledges their own and their family's recent and intergenerational and historical experiences. This is important if we are serious about providing supportive and inclusive safeguarding services to all children.

Discussion point

- Practitioners generally recognize the need to consider the impact of trauma, such as bereavement or a form of abuse, in their work with children.

- When working with a child from a marginalized or minoritized background, are we curious enough about their possible experiences of discrimination and societal and systemic inequalities?

- Do we take in to account the impact this can have on a child's emotional wellbeing and sense of self?

- Do we acknowledge the intergenerational experiences of discrimination and social injustices that may have occurred outside a child's direct experiences?

---

5   Crenshaw describes intersectionality as a metaphor or as a prism to understand social advocacy and multiple oppressions.

Concepts and theories

The use of concepts and theories in child protection and safeguarding is one of many crucial elements which develop practitioners' thinking and practice. They influence and inform various approaches, helping us to identify, respond and effectively support children and families. However, as previously identified, even some of the most well-meaning approaches may not go far enough to understand those children who are seldom heard and are under-represented, particularly children from marginalized and minoritized backgrounds.

This chapter argues that safeguarding professionals, services and organizations must accept that a one-size-fits-all approach is narrow and limits the opportunities to effectively support all children. As such, the application of intersectionality is fundamental in developing safeguarding practice and extending our own learning – recognizing that these may previously have unintentionally universalized children's experiences.

The theory of intersectionality

Although the application of intersectionality is a relatively new concept within child protection and safeguarding, its application to practice is over 40 years old, with its origins founded in Black feminist activism.

Intersectionality provides safeguarding professionals with an opportunity to extend their curiosity and consider how various forms of inequality and discrimination operate together and compound one another. By exploring a child's intersectional identity, we can better appreciate the combined experiences of oppression rather than understanding them in isolation from one another.

> Intersectionality is a lens through which you can see where power comes and collides, where it interlocks and intersects. It's not simply that there's a race problem here, a gender problem here, and a class or LBGTQ problem there. Many times, that framework erases what happens to people who are subject to all these things. (Crenshaw, 2018)

As illustrated by Figure 6.1, a child experiences life through the prism of all of their characteristics simultaneously. Even in spaces that are organized to be shared and inclusive, individuals may still experience discrimination.

While intersectionality has been expanded to accommodate wider experiences of oppressions and injustices, it is important that services and professionals recognize and understand its initial purpose. As such, there must be a commitment that anyone applying intersectionality to practice, policy or research acknowledges that it was originally formed to bring attention to the social inequalities Black women and girls encountered and who still bear the brunt of sexist, racist and classist oppression (hooks, 1989). Therefore, while professionals should be encouraged to apply intersectionality as a universal tool, we have a responsibility to not erase its history as to do so perversely contributes to further neglecting the experiences of Black women and girls.

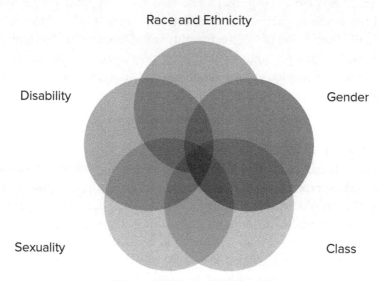

Figure 6.1: Intersecting identities

Intersectionality in practice

To demonstrate intersectionality in practice and to honour its origins, let us initially focus on the experience of Black girls who come in to contact with services. How often do our current approaches and assessments sufficiently acknowledge and understand risks to Black girls, while also guarding against any professional or personal biases?

Reflective exercise

Using the case study below, consider how you would apply intersectionality to understand and provide support to Amina.

> Amina is a 14-year-old Nigerian girl. Amina moved to the UK from Nigeria four years ago with her mum and younger sister. The school reports Amina's first two years at school were without incident. She previously played for the school football team, she had a steady group of friends (also Nigerian) and did well in her studies. However, recently Amina has been arriving at school late, she frequently smells of cannabis and she has lots of new clothes, bags, trainers and phones. The school also reports that she is being picked up in an unknown car most Fridays. The school has shared the licence plate number with the police. The school has referred Amina to social care, who have completed a child exploitation risk assessment (used for child sexual and criminal exploitation) on the information provided by the school, her mum and the school nurse. Amina has been identified as 'high risk' and as such she has been referred to the new County Lines team 'My Future'. This team has been established in partnership with social care, youth offending services and the police as a prevention and intervention service.
>
> 1. What assumptions are being made about Amina's presentation and behaviours?
>
> 2. How might theories, systems, structures, tools and policies reinforce these assumptions?
>
> 3. How might adopting an intersectional lens provide a deeper understanding of Amina's experiences?
>
> 4. Is there anything you would do differently?

In Bernard and Harris' (2019) review of 14 Serious Case Reviews (SCRs) on the 'lived experience of Black children', they identified a persistent failure of professionals to appreciate the 'risks to and vulnerability of older Black children'. The review stated that assumptions and racialized gendered narratives associated with Black children resulted in their needs for protection and safeguarding being overlooked.

Reflective exercise

A Black girl from a working class background will experience gendered racism and classism together. This would be a different experience to that of a Black boy who identifies as gay, for example. Both may experience racism and discrimination, but how they experience it will differ, as do the preconceived ideas and notions related to their other intersecting characteristics.

1. Reflecting on what you have just read, can you think of ways in which an intersectional approach may enhance your work with children?

2. Spend a couple of moments reflecting on a child you have worked with where race, ethnicity, gender, class, age, sexuality and/or (dis)ability was a feature. How did you explore the overlaps between these intersections?

3. Would the application of an intersectional lens alter the questions you asked, your reflections or your understanding of their experiences?

Intersectionality and social graces

As touched on above and throughout this book, the use of theories and concepts in safeguarding has long been established. Crenshaw's theory on intersectionality (1989), though not originally conceived with child safeguarding in mind, is highly relevant; as a 'systems' approach it lends itself to illuminating children's lived experiences and realities. Systems and systemic approaches are not a particularly new or radical concept in child safeguarding practice. Indeed, Munro's review of the child protection system (Munro, 2011a, 2011b), whose central question was to explore 'what helps professionals make the best judgements they can to protect a vulnerable child' (Munro, 2011b, p.6), advocates for systemic approaches to improving child protection practices. Systemic approaches provide practitioners with tools and ideas to help make sense of the connectedness of everything around us: our relationships, the environments and society we live and operate within and everything else in between (Campbell, 2000). How these compounding factors interconnect can influence a child's lived experiences, and encourages us to take a structural and holistic approach to safeguarding, as discussed in Chapters 4 and 5.

One such tool that can support our understanding of how a child may experience the world is Burnham's (1992, 1993) and Roper-Hall's (1998) Social Graces (Social GGRRAAACCEEESSS). This is a well-known systemic tool that practitioners and policy makers may find useful in identifying and exploring implicit and explicit biases.[6] As a tool, Social Graces provides a user-friendly framework which allows practitioners to pause, reflect and compare how their own social graces interact and differ from the child they are working with. This enables the practitioner to acknowledge that, when interacting with children, all of their intersectional experiences, perceptions and interactions with professional agencies will also be present, as will the practitioner's perceptions and experiences. Being alert to these can only serve to improve our responses.

Understanding how a child's individual characteristics influence their everyday experiences (including the response they receive from professionals and services) is important. Crenshaw (1991) called these biological and social traits 'intersections'; Burnham (1992, 1993) and Roper-Hall (1998) describe them as social graces. Burnham (2011) prefers the more 'eccentric' spelling of 'GGRRAAACCEEESSS' as it draws attention to the particular purpose of the tool.

Social GGRRAAACCEEESSS (Burnham, 2011) may include:

G: Gender
G: Geography
R: Race
R: Religion
A: Age
A: Ability
A: Appearance
C: Class
C: Culture
E: Education
E: Ethnicity
E: Employment
S: Spirituality

---

6   The term implicit and explicit biases is used to indicate that biases may not always be unconscious and at times biases are reinforced by known external factors.

S: Sexuality

S: Sexual orientation.

Intersectionality and social graces have multiple touchpoints. Both draw attention to the interconnected nature of an individual's biological and personal traits, their lived experiences, and the environment and structures in which they live and operate. This is an important consideration for practitioners when working with children, in particular those at risk of extra-familial harm, where characteristics such as ethnicity, age, gender and disability may influence the response of institutions and professionals. Examples of this include the more frequent rates of 'off-rolling'[7] children with special educational needs and some 'minority ethnic groups' (Long & Danechi, 2019). This is of significance in the context of extra-familial harm, not only because exclusion from school is increasingly considered to be a risk factor in terms of exploitation (Child Safeguarding Practice Review Panel, 2020), but also because being 'off-rolled' outside mainstream education can also lead to overall 'poorer' outcomes (Long & Danechi, 2019).

With regards to safeguarding, it is important that we do not consider a child's social graces as independent from one another, as the mnemonic suggests. As practitioners, it is incumbent on us to recognize the intersecting and compounding nature of a child's characteristics. The consequences of not fully grasping a child's intersecting characteristics and subsequent experiences can possibly be observed in the over-representation of Black boys and boys from ethnic minoritized communities reported to be caught-up in criminal exploitation (Child Safeguarding Practice Review Panel, 2020) or the absence of Black girls within child sexual abuse services (Davis, 2019). In both examples, it appears as though the system and practitioners struggled to identify signs of abuse, trauma and exploitation early enough – or in some cases at all.

Adopting an intersectional approach to social graces challenges the notion of the universal child when safeguarding children, providing practitioners, managers and policy makers with an opportunity to explore biases and any potential gaps in knowledge and service provision. The lack of recognition or consideration of a child's identity can also be seen in the exclusionary indicators used in child sexual

---

7   There is no legal definition of 'off-rolling'. However, Ofsted defines it as: 'The practice of removing a pupil from the school roll without a formal, permanent exclusion or by encouraging a parent to remove their child from the school roll, when the removal is primarily in the interests of the school rather than in the best interests of the pupil' (Long & Danechi, 2019, p.11).

exploitation risk assessment tools, which do not sufficiently consider gender (boys), ethnicity, sexuality or disabilities (Brown *et al.*, 2017; Franklin, Brown & Brady, 2018), or indeed children who may represent several or all of these identities. Though the limitations of these tools have been well documented for a number of years, such tools and assessments are still widely used by safeguarding practitioners in child exploitation-related services. This highlights the multi-agency and systemic shift required to move away from a reliance on a universal lens and towards developing inclusive tools and practices.

Team activity: Social graces

As a team, use an intersectional approach to applying social graces and reflect on the types of social graces you have as a team, and which social graces and experiences are perhaps missing.

1. How do your team's collective intersectional experiences possibly influence the interventions you provide, the assessments and supervision within your service and which children access your service?

2. How can social graces encourage team conversations about discrimination and celebrating diversity?

3. Following this activity, consider ways in which you can either build on or develop your team's practice to be more inclusive.

Adultification

As discussed, the application of intersectionality and social graces encourages us as professionals to actively engage in critical reflective discussions on how our own personal and professional experiences and biases may unintentionally influence how we safeguard and support children. This requires an organizational culture which represents continued learning, non-blaming environments and safer spaces to encourage and hold uncomfortable and courageous conversations. It is important that we look inwards as professionals, services and wider institutions to contemplate how our individual and systemic biases can affect safeguarding practice.

'Adultification' is a concept that is highly relevant to safeguarding children and provides a means of exploring potential biases. Adultification is the notion that some children are more likely to be ascribed adult-like characteristics, diminishing the perceived vulnerability of these children (Davis, 2019; Davis & Marsh, 2020; Epstein, Blake & Gonzalez, 2017; Goff *et al.*, 2014). It is a term that has been applied to child safeguarding literature over the past two decades. However, this phenomenon has been applied more broadly in child protection-related research in North America, with an emerging body of research developing in the UK (Davis, 2019).

Figure 6.2 provides a definition of adultification bias.

The concept of adultification is where notions of innocence and vulnerability are not afforded to certain children. This is determined by people and institutions who hold power over children. When adultification occurs outside of the home, it is always founded within discrimination and bias.

There are various definitions of adultification, all related to a child's personal characteristics, socioeconomic influences and their lived experiences. Regardless of the context in which adultification takes place, the impact results in children's rights being either diminished or not being upheld.

Figure 6.2: Adultification bias

This definition provides examples of how adultification can impact children differently, depending on their personal characteristics, social backgrounds and wider lived experiences. This includes children who witness domestic abuse, who assume, or are expected to assume, an adult role, for example they may feel an increased sense of responsibility to look after their siblings or mother (Stephens, 1999). Similarly, children living in socioeconomic deprivation may be given additional responsibilities to support the family income (Burton, 2007). However, adultification should not be conflated with the appropriate development of life skills. More recently, it has also been applied to transgender girls, who are 'presented as adult-like; framed as "immutably gendered, confused and sexual predators"' (Stone, 2017, p.1). Here, researchers have argued that transgender girls are adultified and sexualized, perpetuating cisgender oppressions and biases (Stone, 2017). We believe adultification bias can also be identified by the language used to describe children, such as 'streetwise', 'resilient', 'mature' and making 'lifestyle choices'.

However, the opposite could be said of 'children' with learning disabilities who experience, or are at risk of, child sexual exploitation. Research indicates that 'children' with learning disabilities are more likely to be infantilized[8] by professionals (Franklin, Raws & Smeaton, 2015). That said, we suggest that not all children with learning disabilities will experience being infantilized. This is due to their intersecting identities and experiences, which can influence how children are perceived and interacted with. For example, in the Serious Case Review of Chris, a 14-year-old Black British Caribbean boy who was being criminally exploited, Chris was diagnosed with attention deficit hyperactivity disorder and conduct disorder. However, the review indicated 'that there was little evidence that his SEND (special education needs or disabilities) needs were fully understood or met...' (Hill, 2018, p.5). Instead, the framing of Chris was that he was a risk to others (Davis & Marsh, 2020). This suggests that some children with learning needs and disabilities may still experience adultification, arguably because other aspects of their identities are perceived by professionals in ways that undermine their vulnerabilities and identified needs.

Adultification and Black children

While adultification can impact all children, studies suggest Black children are at a heightened risk of experiencing this form of bias (Davis, 2019; Davis & Marsh, 2020; Epstein *et al.*, 2017; Goff *et al.*, 2014). Racism and racialized stereotypes are the compounding factors which can influence how professionals, services and wider institutions may perceive the needs and risks of harm facing Black children (Davis, 2019; Davis & Marsh, 2020; Epstein *et al.*, 2017; Goff *et al.*, 2014).

Findings from North America identified that, from the age of five, African American girls were assumed to be more adult-like than White girls across all aspects of their childhood (Epstein *et al.*, 2017). Furthermore, the study found that professionals held racialized stereotypes of African American girls, such as them being 'strong' and 'aggressive', leading to assumptions that they were in less need of support, protection and nurture (Epstein *et al.*, 2017). When comparing this to findings in the UK, Davis (2019) identified that Black girls falling victim to child sexual abuse were less likely to have their safeguarding needs met due to

---

8   Infantilization means to treat someone as if they are still a small child.

similar professional biases, particularly the notion of 'the strong Black woman' and harmful assumptions of Black girls being innately sexual.

The consequences of these stereotypes are illustrated in the quotes below from Davis' (2019) research study exploring the absence of Black girls in child sexual abuse research and services.

> 'When you try to speak out you're seen as aggressive or you don't want to engage. No! it's because I was raped! A 14-year-old and I had no one to speak to, I think they just think, well, Black girls are quite sexual anyway and not worth the bother.' Makeda. (Davis, 2019, p.67)

> 'No one cares about us, or our experiences, do you think anyone cares about Black girls? People think we are strong.' Candice. (Davis, 2019, p.54)

In the context of child criminal exploitation, we argue that the hallmarks of adultification bias featured in two separate safeguarding case reviews published two years apart. Both case reviews involved two 14-year-old Black British Caribbean boys who were murdered as a consequence of child criminal exploitation (Davis & Marsh, 2020). Our analysis found that in both cases, each child received criminal justice responses when a child welfare response was required. We also identified that adultification occurred across all the settings the children encountered, from education and social care to police and housing. In the case of these two boys, the innate vulnerability of all children was not afforded to them, resulting in an erasure of their rights to be treated as children and provided with adequate care, protection and support.

In our analysis, we concluded:

> To ensure that lessons are learnt, and we provide effective welfare responses to Black children vulnerable to exploitation, we must consider adopting an intersectional approach. Using such an approach provides a framework for professionals to better understand the oppressions Black children may experience. It may also support a cultural shift in safeguarding practice, where Black boys are treated with care rather than suspicion. (Davis & Marsh, 2020, p.258)

Therefore, it is incumbent on all safeguarding professionals and services to reflect on and consider how bias may affect, or even predetermine, safeguarding responses to Black children (Davis, 2019; Davis & Marsh, 2020).

Team activity

As a team, reflect on the following questions:

1. As a team, how often do you hold courageous conversations and reflect on personal biases?

2. To what extent do you consider how your own biases may influence your decision-making and professional curiosity?

3. How does your service or organization promote continued discussions about bias and discrimination?

4. 'Strong', 'angry' and 'intimidating' are words often used to frame Black children. How might such a stereotype influence safeguarding responses?

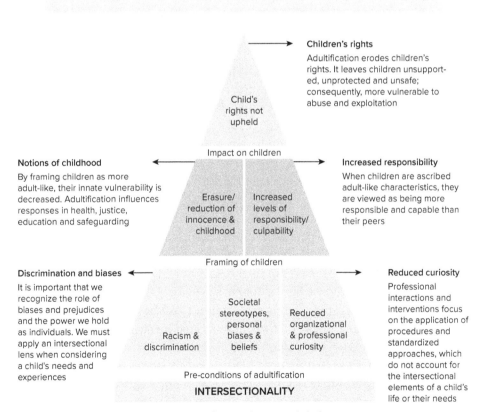

Figure 6.3: Professional Inter-Adultification

The above diagram (Figure 6.3) illustrates the pre-conditions of adultification bias and how it can reduce safeguarding responses if not identified, understood and challenged. The model is called Professional Inter-Adultification (PIA), as it refers to the adultification of children by professionals, services, organizations and institutions. It also highlights the importance of understanding adultification through the lens of intersectionality. This is because adultification manifests differently depending on a child's personal intersecting characteristics and wider lived experiences.

Uncomfortable conversations and conclusions

At the beginning of this chapter, we invited you to become comfortable with uncomfortable and challenging conversations, including reflecting on your own biases and assumptions relating to children and how this can impact on safeguarding practice. We hope that by providing theoretical frameworks, reflective questions and illustrative case studies, this has energized your commitment to challenging the myth of the universal child.

For the professional and the system response to be close to what children need, we must apply an intersectional lens to research, practice and policy. This includes holding challenging conversations within our teams and organizations about the discrimination and biases we personally hold and those within our systems and processes. If we do not centre our safeguarding approaches within equitable practice, we must question if this leads to a dereliction of our safeguarding duties to protect all children from harm.

Once we are able to accept that racism and wider discrimination are present within safeguarding responses we offer to children, we can move past the 'good intentions' of professional and service interventions and instead focus on the impact racism and discrimination can have on the children we have a duty to safeguard and protect.

Our role as safeguarding professionals is to acknowledge the whole of a child and to understand their multifaceted identity, their position in society and how this may have affected them. This involves understanding and interrogating our perceptions of them, recognizing that this also shapes our response. We have to remind ourselves that all children, regardless of age, gender, ethnicity, sexuality and disability, are innately vulnerable due to their status in society.

The myth of the universal child is just that – a myth; there is no such thing as a universal child.

References

Barn, R. (2007). '"Race", ethnicity and child welfare: A fine balancing act.' *The British Journal of Social Work, 37*(8), 1425–1434.

Bernard, C. (2020). 'Using an Intersectional Lens to Examine the Child Sexual Exploitation of Black Adolescents.' In J. Pearce (ed.) *Child Sexual Exploitation: Why Theory Matters* (pp.193–209). Bristol: Policy Press.

Bernard, C. & Harris, P. (2019). 'Serious case reviews: The lived experiences of Black children.' *Child & Family Social Work, 24*, 256–263.

Bowlby, J. (1969). *Attachment and Loss v. 3 (Vol. 1)*. London: Random House.

Brown, S., Brady, G., Franklin, A. & Crookes, R. (2017). *The Use of Tools and Checklists to Assess Risk of Child Sexual Exploitation: An Exploratory Study*. Centre of Expertise in Child Sexual Abuse.

Burnham, J. (1992). 'Approach, method, technique.' *Human Systems, 3*(10), 3–26.

Burnham, J. (1993). 'Systemic supervision: The evolution of reflexivity in the context of supervisory relationships.' *Human Systems, 4*(3–4), 349–381.

Burnham, J. (2011). 'Developments in Social GGRRAAACCEEESSS: Visible-invisible and Voiced-unvoiced.' In B. Krause (ed.) *Mutual Perspectives: Culture and Reflexivity in Systemic Psychotherapy* (pp.139–160). London: Karnac Books.

Burton, L. (2007). 'Childhood adultification in economically disadvantaged families: A conceptual model.' *Family Relations, 56*, 329–334.

Bywaters, P., Kwhali, J., Brady, G., Sparks, T. & Bos, E. (2017). 'Out of sight, out of mind: Ethnic inequalities in child protection and out-of-home care intervention rates.' *The British Journal of Social Work, 47*(7), 1884–1902.

Campbell, D. (2000). *The Socially Constructed Organization*. London: Karnac Books.

Child Safeguarding Practice Review Panel (2020). *It was Hard to Escape. Safeguarding Children at Risk from Criminal Exploitation*. London: HM Government.

Choate, P., CrazyBull, B., Lindstrom, D. & Lindstrom, G. (2020). 'Where do we go from here? Ongoing colonialism from Attachment Theory.' *Aotearoa New Zealand Social Work, 32*(1), 32–44.

Crenshaw, K. (1989). 'Demarginalising the intersection of race and sex: A Black feminist critique of antidiscrimination doctrine, feminist theory and antiracist politics.' *University of Chicago Legal Forum, 14*, 538–554.

Crenshaw, K. (1991). 'Mapping the margins: Intersectionality, identity politics, and violence against women of color.' *Stanford Law Review, 43*, 1241–1299.

Crenshaw, K. (2018). *Reach Everyone on the Planet*. Heinrich-Böll-Stiftung. www.gwi-boell.de/sites/default/files/endf_crenshaw_web_gesamt_en_0.pdf.

Cunningham, H. (2006). *The Invention of Childhood*. London: BBC Books.

Davis, J. (2019). Where are the Black Girls? Racialised Sexualisation and the Under-Identification of Child Sexual Abuse Among Black Girls in the UK. Unpublished master's dissertation. London Metropolitan University.

Davis, J. & Marsh, N. (2020). 'Boys to men: The cost of adultification in safeguarding responses to Black boys.' *Critical and Radical Social Work, 8*(2), 255–259.

Davis, L.J. (1997). 'Constructing Normalcy: The Bell Curve, the Novel and the Invention of the Disabled Body in the Nineteenth Century.' In L.J. Davis (ed.) *The Disability Studies Reader* (pp.9–28). London: Routledge.

Dwivedi, K. (2002). *Meeting the Needs of Ethnic Minority Children: Including Refugee, Black, and Mixed Parentage Children*. London: Jessica Kingsley Publishers.

Epstein, R., Blake, J. & Gonzalez, T. (2017). *Girlhood Interrupted: The Erasure of Black Girls' Childhood*. Washington, DC: The Georgetown Law Center on Poverty and Inequality.

Erikson, E. (1959). 'Identity and the life cycle.' *Psychological Issues, 1,* 18–164.

Flynn, K. (2019). 'Social work reframed? The experiences of social workers applying systemic ideas in child protection.' *Journal of Family Therapy, 41*(3), 465–485.

Franklin, A., Brown, S. & Brady, G. (2018). 'The use of tools and checklists to assess the risk of child sexual exploitation: Lessons from UK practice.' *Journal of Child Sexual Abuse, 27*(8), 978–997.

Franklin, A., Raws, P. & Smeaton, E. (2015). *Unprotected, Overprotected: Meeting the Needs of Young People with Learning Disabilities Who Experience, or are at Risk of, Sexual Exploitation.* London: Barnardo's.

Gilligan, C. (1982). *In a Different Voice.* Cambridge, MA: Harvard University Press.

Goff, P.A., Jackson, M., Di Leone, B., Culotta, C. & Ditomasso, N. (2014). 'The essence of innocence: Consequences of dehumanizing Black children.' *Journal of Personality and Social Psychology, 106*(4), 526–545.

Gunaratnam, Y. (2003). *Researching 'Race' and Ethnicity: Methods, Knowledge and Power.* London: Sage.

Hicks, S. (2008). 'Thinking through sexuality.' *Journal of Social Work, 8*(1), 65–82.

Hill, N. (2018). *Serious Case Review – 'Chris'.* London: Newham Local Safeguarding Children Board. www.newhamscp.org.uk/wp-content/uploads/2018/10/Serious-Case-Review-Chris-.pdf.

Hollinrake, S., Hunt, G., Dix, H. & Wagner, A. (2019). 'Do we practice (or teach) what we preach? Developing a more inclusive learning environment to better prepare social work students for practice through improving the exploration of their different ethnicities within teaching, learning and assessment opportunities.' *Social Work Education, 38*(5), 582–603.

hooks, b. (1989). *Talking Back: Thinking Feminist, Thinking Black.* Boston, MA: South End Press.

Long, R. & Danechi, S. (2019). *Language Teaching in Schools (England).* London: House of Commons Library. https://dera.ioe.ac.uk//34217.

Munro, E. (2011a). *The Munro Review of Child Protection. Interim Report: The Child's Journey.* London: Department for Education.

Munro, E. (2011b). *The Munro Review of Child Protection. Final Report: A Child-Centred System.* London: Department for Education.

Roper-Hall, A. (1998). 'Working Systemically with Older People and their Families who have "Come to Grief".' In P. Sutcliffe, G. Tufnell & U. Cornish (eds) *Working with the Dying and Bereaved* (pp.177–206). Basingstoke: Macmillan Press.

Stephens, D.L. (1999). 'Battered women's views of their children.' *Journal of Interpersonal Violence, 14*(7), 731–746.

Stone, A. (2017). 'Gender panics about transgender children in religious right discourse.' *Journal of LGBT Youth, 15*(1), 1–15.

Taylor, A. (2007). *Decision Making in Child and Family Social Work: The Impact of the Assessment Framework.* Unpublished doctoral thesis. University of Durham.

Webster's New World College Dictionary, Fourth Edition (1999). New York, NY: John Wiley & Sons.

Chapter 7

Has the Purpose Outgrown the Design?

Carlene Firmin and Rachel Knowles

Introduction

As outlined in previous chapters, safeguarding practitioners need to respond to a range of harms that young people experience in social contexts beyond family homes. Referred to in this chapter as 'extra-familial harm/s' (EFH), these experiences can feature severe and sometimes fatal risks in non-familial settings and relationships, including, but not exclusive to, exploitation (Barter, 2009; Brandon *et al.*, 2020; Catch 22, 2013; Firmin, 2017; Hudeck, 2018). For example, young people may be:

- sexually exploited by peers (e.g., in exchange for alcohol in local parks)

- physically assaulted in early romantic relationships

- stabbed by peers on their way to college

- groomed on high streets, the internet or at the school gates, then pressured to distribute drugs.

Over two decades, such young people have gradually been recognized as victims of abuse and as being in need of support (see Chapters 4 and 5). England's child protection system has been mobilized to offer that support (Brandon *et al.*, 2020; Firmin, Wroe & Lloyd, 2019), given its duty to protect children from harm, wherever the harm originates. But to what extent is England's child protection system, and the primary and secondary legislation on which it is built, designed for this purpose?

In this chapter, we compare England's child protection legislation, and associated policy and guidance, against system requirements for safeguarding adolescents from extra-familial harm. We focus on primary child protection legislation, and associated statutory guidance and regulations, while also making reference to youth justice legislation where relevant. Given our focus on EFH, we also attend to policy related to that harm, such as documents concerned with sexual exploitation and teenage relationship abuse. We recognize that there are elements of legislation and guidance in a wide range of other areas (e.g., the Making Safeguarding Personal agenda in adult social care, school exclusions, or young carers) that may contribute to a legal framework for safeguarding adolescents. However, it is not possible to consider them all sufficiently in this chapter, so we have tried to focus on the most relevant provisions.

First, with these parameters in mind, we outline the provisions in primary child protection legislation relevant to safeguarding adolescents in extra-familial contexts, making reference to specific sections of the Children Act 1989 (CA 1989), Children Act 2004 (CA 2004), and the Children and Social Work Act 2017 (CSWA 2017), as well as case law that best illustrates opportunities and challenges in the existing primary framework. We then reflect on the statutory guidance and policy landscape built on this primary base, asking whether elements of statutory guidance, and associated regulation or policy, utilize opportunities in primary legislation, or compensate for gaps. We close the chapter by reflecting on three practice questions that have emerged as local areas and partnerships design responses to safeguard adolescents from EFH. We highlight where these questions suggest levers or shortfalls in primary legislation and/or statutory guidance and regulation. Through this process, we draw conclusions about the extent to which, in responding to EFH, child protection systems are being used for a purpose that goes beyond their design.

Underpinning evidence base

Throughout this chapter, we draw on an emergent evidence base generated by the Contextual Safeguarding research programme at the University of Bedfordshire. Specific datasets include:

- The findings from two national roundtables (2018 and 2020) held with government departments (including legal representatives), child protection lawyers, local authority lawyers, regulators and inspectorates, family court judges and children's services leaders, to discuss the legislative foundations of adopting a Contextual Safeguarding approach (Firmin & Knowles, 2020; Firmin *et al.*, 2019), and a legal task and finish group that has formed thereafter.

- Emergent findings from a four-year embedded research project with ten local authority test sites which are piloting Contextual Safeguarding approaches in England and Wales, alongside consultative feedback from a further 41 who make up the Contextual Safeguarding Local Area Interest Network and Implementation Group. Data collected from these sites includes observations of strategy discussions, child protection conferences and other multi-agency operational and strategic groups, as well as the dip-sampling of cases at children's services' front door and following assessment to examine decision-making.

While much of this data is unpublished as of yet, the findings of both legal roundtables have been disseminated and are referenced in this chapter accordingly. Published material from test sites is also referenced and case study examples are utilized throughout.

A word from the designers

In a 2019 speech, Baroness Hale, one of the figures involved in the design of the Children Act 1989, detailed the purpose of the system that was created 30 years previously. Her summary included three points relevant to the question posed by this chapter.

The first was the ambition of creating a unified offer to children who required support; whether they were children with disabilities or those at risk of harm, 'the hope was that all would be seen simply as children in need of help' (Hale, 2019, p.6). In this respect, the Act had all young people (up to 18 years and, in some cases, 21 or 25) in mind, including those in need due to EFH. However, Hale made two other points, which arguably contest this assertion.

The Act sought to put some clear water between processes for 'respect of delinquent or naughty children. Those who were out of control, falling into bad associations or in moral danger' and those who 'were suffering or at risk of suffering neglect or abuse' (Hale, 2019, p.2).

For those behind the Act, the rationale was that, in cases of abuse, proceedings were brought against parents while, in matters of delinquency and children who 'were out of control [and] falling into bad associations' (Hale, 2019, p.2), proceedings were brought against the young person.

Hale also noted that the ambition had been for a welfare-orientated youth justice approach to this group of children, and not the one that saw increasing levels of youth incarceration in the 1990s (Prison Reform Trust, 2008). The Act, therefore, was built on a premise that when young people's behaviour, as opposed to their parents', was the cause of professional concern, these young people sat beyond the child protection system. These are some of the same young people who were practically ostracized from safeguarding processes after being sexually exploited or stabbed by peers, and who were supported primarily by voluntary sector agencies and youth justice interventions throughout the 1990s (Cockbain & Brayley, 2012; Pearce, 2013) – a reality which, in the case of serious youth violence and criminal exploitation, continues to this day (Hill, 2019; Lloyd & Firmin, 2019; Lloyd, 2019).

Finally, Hale reminded her audience of the 'threshold criteria' for state intervention via a court. For this criteria to be met, 'the child's welfare is not enough' (Hale, 2019, p.8). The harm experienced by the child must be 'attributable' to either the actions taken by the parents or because the child is beyond their control. Attribution implies a causal relationship, that is, this child is being sexually exploited by their parents, or they are being sexually exploited because they are beyond their parents' control, not that they are beyond their parents' control because they are being exploited, in which case one might address the exploitation to support the parents rather than address parenting behaviour to reduce exploitation.

It may be argued that a young person beyond their parents' control (due to EFH) is enough to demonstrate attribution. However, one might also question the value of this as such a reading situates the issue as being with parents and parenting while, in many cases of EFH, the response needs to look beyond parental control to peer relationships, the influence of adults beyond the family network, and victim-blaming cultures in schools or other social settings, to secure a young person's safety (Lloyd & Firmin, 2019; Firmin, 2020; PACE, 2020). This is a matter with which many local authorities are currently grappling (Firmin & Knowles, 2020). Hinging the threshold criteria on parenting places the capacity and care of parents as central to state intervention when, in cases of EFH, this may be a secondary factor.

Hale's summary therefore raises questions. On one hand, the 1989 Act had many adolescents in mind. It was intended to offer a unified response to *all* children and young people in need of help up until their 18th birthdays.[1] And yet, those designing the Act seemed to set aside young people whose behaviour, as opposed to that of their parents, could be viewed as attributable to the harm they experienced (a characterization of many young people affected by EFH). Furthermore, threshold criteria for state intervention (specifically s.31 intervention) hinged on harm being attributable to parenting or parental control. In cases of EFH, this is questionable. *Attribution* often sits beyond parenting/parental control (and beyond the decisions of young people), requiring a broader lens to develop meaningful responses: but what would be the legal basis and pathway to escalate in such situations? Throughout this chapter, we examine the extent to which primary legislation, and the steps to operationalize it through statutory guidance and regulation, entrenches or resolves these questions.

The foundations: Primary legislation

The Children Act 1989 (CA 1989) provides the contemporary legislative foundations for England's child protection system. The Children Act 2004 (CA 2004) and the Children and Social Work Act 2017 (CSWA 2017) built on, rather than replaced, this original legislation, adding (in 2004) and amending (in 2017) specific requirements related to inter-agency cooperation relevant to the ability of children's services to fulfil the duties introduced in the 1989 legislation. In this section, we explore this primary legislation with reference to:

- thresholds for accessing support and protection
- inter-agency working in leveraging a safeguarding response
- types of support considered in legislation.

Later in this chapter, we will consider how this foundation is interpreted in national statutory guidance, regulation and policy, and local practice.

---

[1]   And up to 21 or 25 for some young people with additional needs or who had been in care.

Thresholds for accessing support

Part III of the CA 1989 details the support that local authorities (LAs) are required to provide to children and families in England. S.17(1) of this part introduces a 'general duty' on LAs:

a. to safeguard and promote the welfare of children within their area who are in need; and

b. so far as is consistent with that duty, to promote the upbringing of such children by their families, by providing a range and level of services appropriate to those children's needs.

According to s.17(10), a child is defined as being in need if:

a. [they are] unlikely to achieve or maintain, or to have the opportunity of achieving or maintaining, a reasonable standard of health or development without the provision for [them] of services by a local authority under this Part;

b. [their] health or development is likely to be significantly impaired, or further impaired, without the provision for him of such services; or

c. [they are] disabled.

To this extent, adolescents affected by extra-familial harm are defined as children in need (for most up to their 18th birthday[2]), and LAs have a duty to safeguard and promote their welfare.

If LAs determine that a child is at risk of significant harm, part five of the CA 1989 becomes relevant. S.47 of part five outlines that an LA will conduct investigations related to the welfare of a child believed to be experiencing, or at risk of, 'significant harm' (EFH can create a risk of significant harm and so would fall within s.47 enquiries). However, the threshold for s.31 court-ordered interventions (i.e., care and supervision orders) that may follow an LA investigation narrows this reading.

This part of the Act requires that the significant harm is attributable to the care provided to that child or due to the child who is beyond their parents' control. However, as outlined in the introductory sections, in cases of EFH, attribution may rest elsewhere and, in such cases,

---

2   As noted previously, there are exceptions to this for children up to the age of 25 in regards to young people and some with special educational needs where adult social care will have a role to play.

interventions may need to assess attribution to extra-familial contexts/ relationships and intervene accordingly to safeguard a child. Furthermore, a child may be within their parents' control, and may be cared for by their parents, and still face significant harm when, for example, travelling to or at school (Lloyd & Firmin, 2019; PACE, 2020).

Other young people will experience some difficulties at home as a result of EFH, rather than familial issues being the cause of harm, and in such cases won't necessarily be 'beyond control' (Hudeck, 2018; PACE, 2020; Scott & McNeish, 2017; Shuker, 2017). Furthermore, the parents of young people affected by EFH may consent to statutory intervention, while the young people in question do not.

In all of the above situations, harm may also be beyond the influence of, for example, an individual local authority or company running a residential children's home, or a parent, and so may not be attended to via a care placement used either voluntarily or via a court order. In this regard, questions have been raised by local and national leaders as to whether s.31 care or supervision orders are the most effective route to safeguard the welfare of a young person who is at risk of significant harm due to EFH (Child Safeguarding Practice Review Panel, 2020; Firmin & Knowles, 2020; Lloyd & Firmin, 2019; Scott, Botcherby & Ludvigsen, 2017).

Conversely, youth justice services are accessible for young people affected by EFH aged ten and above. The Crime and Disorder Act 1998 s.37 states, 'It shall be the principal aim of the youth justice system to prevent offending by children and young persons', meaning that the system can intervene with young people who offend in the context of EFH (Cockbain & Brayley, 2012; Hudeck, 2018; Khan *et al.*, 2013) regardless of attribution to parenting or parental capacity. However, this route risks criminalizing young people. Furthermore, the goal is to prevent offending rather than safeguard young people's welfare, and while these not mutually exclusive, they are not the same thing.

A range of orders can be utilized in this area of practice under the Anti-social Behaviour, Crime and Policing Act 2014 including (but not limited to) civil injunctions for anti-social behaviour, criminal behaviour orders, and public spaces protection orders. These interventions (which are largely adversarial as opposed to strengths-based or welfare-orientated) are planned through a youth justice assessment and planning framework, AssetPlus, and can include requirements for a young person to:

- attend a support programme or education
- comply with a curfew
- avoid particular places
- receive treatment
- live in designated areas.

The primary legislation underpinning engagement in youth justice interventions means that youth offending teams can reach young people in ways that voluntary engagement via s.17 of the CA 1989 may not. At times, this has been appealing for those wanting to intervene with young people in need due to EFH, but yet to reach a threshold for statutory social work oversight. For example, a young person who is 'in need' (s.17) due to EFH, but not yet at risk of significant harm, or whose parents consent to support but the young person does not.

On other occasions, they may have reached a threshold of significant harm but local areas are still working through how to interpret s.47 and its associated plans in the context of EFH, so plans focus less on actions taken by parents and more on actions taken by a partnership to build safety in extra-familial contexts. Such tensions have meant that, in a 2020 report into criminal exploitation, the Child Safeguarding Practice Review Panel (2020) recommended the exploration of 'electronically tagging' young people who were being criminally exploited to prevent them leaving their homes at certain times. However, such an approach places legal requirements, with potential sanctions, on a child who has been abused as a route to safeguarding them. Furthermore, they disrupt the young person who has been abused and not the group or context in which that abuse takes place. This, combined with the consequences of criminalizing young people, especially young Black people due to the inherent bias in our criminal justice system (Lammy, 2017; Taylor, 2016), raises significant ethical questions about using youth justice legal pathways for safeguarding adolescents.

With the advent of the Modern Slavery Act in 2015, a legal lever was provided to recognize the victimization of young people identified as offending in the context of exploitation. In particular, s.45 provides a defence for victims of slavery or trafficking who commit an offence. Until 2018, when amendments were made to statutory guidance (discussed in more detail later in this chapter), local areas had minimal means to interpret this through a statutory safeguarding framework (and, as this chapter will demonstrate, the 2018 changes provide an insufficient roadmap in that regard). Furthermore, the legal tools provided by the Modern Slavery Act do not extend to all forms of EFH (such as serious youth violence, peer-to-peer sexual abuse, or teenage relationship abuse), and the use of them does not in itself remove the structural dynamics that problematize the situating of statutory responses to EFH within youth justice – rather than child protection – frameworks.

Therefore, most adolescents affected by EFH meet an s.17 threshold to be defined as a child in need. Many also reach a threshold for youth justice interventions. Some will also reach a threshold for statutory intervention following an s.47 enquiry, but the usefulness and sufficiency of the escalatory process that follows this is questionable.

For young people who continue to be at risk of significant harm due to EFH, but in ways that are not attributable to them being beyond parental control, local areas are querying whether increasing parental control even increases the protection of a young person and, if not, is the use of this pathway appropriate? Tensions have also surfaced about responses to young people (who offend or are at risk of offending due to EFH) reaching a threshold for a statutory (rather than voluntary) youth justice intervention, and not for a safeguarding one (though they could still be defined as children in need of a voluntary plan). It may be that a further legislative lever is required which offers statutory protection against EFH, does not criminalize them, and is not focused on housing them away from their parents (or changing the actions of their parents), therefore creating a range of solutions beyond s.31 or s.17.

Inter-agency working

Given its contextual nature, it is unlikely that the risks posed by EFH can be addressed by social workers alone. The legislative framework for inter-agency working is therefore important. Part 2 of the CA 2004 details the responsibilities of partners in supporting LAs in meeting their s.17 general duty. Indeed, it goes beyond this and extends certain duties to all children in the LA's area, not just children in need, and s.10 of the Act places a duty on LAs to make arrangements that 'promote co-operation' between them and their relevant partners to safeguard and promote the welfare of all children in their area. A number of partners are listed, including the police, health, education and voluntary sectors. S.11 of the Act states that all these partners must have arrangements in place so that they can discharge their functions while 'having regard to the need to safeguard and promote the welfare of children'.[3]

Many of these partners have greater reach into public places, peer groups and educational settings than local authorities, although it remains the responsibility of the local authority to establish arrangements for inter-agency work. Case law exemplifies these arrangements. In both J and L vs. Hillingdon (2017) and KS vs. Haringey (2018), judges concluded that LAs failed to meet their s.17 general duty, with reference to the specific duty under s.17(6) to provide accommodation. Although not related to EFH, both judgements emphasized that closing a case to children's services following a referral to a housing service was insufficient. Instead, social workers needed to oversee cases so that when the family's request for housing was rejected, and this decision compromised young people's safety, social care plans could be amended. Likewise, in the case of KS vs. Haringey (2018), housing colleagues were criticized for not appropriately weighting the evidence of a social work assessment in formulating a conclusion about a young person's housing needs.

The s.11 duty in the CA 2004 is to 'actively promote' the welfare of the child. The aforementioned judgements indicate that a decision by partner agencies not to provide services to families is reason enough to review assessments conducted under s.17 and formulate alternative plans. Not doing so is contrary to s.10 of the CA 2004.

The lack of attention provided by housing to social care assessments means that they also fall short with regards to s.11 of the CA 2004. To this extent, in addition to the duty to cooperate with enquiries under s.47 of the CA 1989, there is scope within s.17 of the CA 1989 and s.10 and s.11 of the CA 2004 to engage partner organizations in responding to the needs of adolescents affected by EFH. S.17 assessment and s.47 enquiries, as well as any child protection plans and care plans formulated as a result, could identify that a range of partners need to provide services to safeguard, and actively promote, the welfare of adolescents affected by EFH.

Following the introduction of the CSWA 2017, local authorities

---

3   In addition, educational settings have their own specific statutory duty set out in s.175 of the Education Act 2002, and part 3 of the Education (Independent School Standards) Regulations 2014.

transitioned their local safeguarding arrangements, moving from a structure of 'local safeguarding children's board' to 'safeguarding partners and child death review partners'. This transition period ended in December 2020. The CSWA 2017 inserts a series of provisions into the CA 2004, setting out this inter-agency framework (see s.16E–16L of the 2004 Act). S.16E(1) states that:

The safeguarding partners for a local authority area in England must make arrangements for –

a. the safeguarding partners, and

b. any relevant agencies that they consider appropriate, to work together in exercising their functions, so far as the functions are exercised for the purpose of safeguarding and promoting the welfare of children in the area.

Safeguarding partners are defined as being the local authority, the police, and the local Clinical Commissioning Group (16E; 3). Reference to 'relevant agencies', defined as a person who exercises functions in relation to children and who is specified in regulations, could be used to expand partnership work. For example, The Child Safeguarding Practice Review and Relevant Agency (England) Regulations 2018[4] includes the provision, supervision or oversight of sport or leisure, charities and some religious organizations within the schedule of agencies with whom safeguarding partners would need to work. This allows for youth clubs, libraries and other leisure centres to be active safeguarding partners – a useful step towards building a framework for safeguarding in extra-familial contexts. However, private and independent commercial entities such as hospitality or retail businesses also have a potential contribution to make in safeguarding young people affected by EFH, but don't currently feature in the legislative framework.

A potential opportunity for contextual inter-agency working can also be found in the Anti-social Behaviour, Crime and Policing Act 2014 via the use of 'the community trigger and the community remedy'. The community trigger allows for a victim to request an anti-social behaviour (ASB) case review by relevant bodies (councils, the police, local clinical commissioning groups (CCGs) and local social housing providers) where there are repeated reports of anti-social behaviour

---

4   www.legislation.gov.uk/ukdsi/2018/9780111167540.

that the victim feels have not been addressed. A review can be sought directly by the victim or by someone on their behalf, such as a family member, councillor, MP or other professional. The purpose of the review is to 'give victims and communities the right to request a review of their case where a local threshold is met and to bring agencies together to take a joined up, problem-solving approach to find a solution for the victim' (Home Office, 2021).

As part of the review process, information is shared between the relevant partners, recommendations are then made as to how to address the ASB, and then the victim is updated. Such an approach is currently framed as being used to address ASB, but it could be reframed as a legislative route to increasing safety or addressing thematic safeguarding concerns that impact the welfare of multiple (unrelated) children in a local area, as opposed to case planning (child in need or child protection) which is currently reserved for use with individuals or sibling groups.

Support and interventions referenced in primary legislation

The elements of primary child protection legislation that promote inter-agency working refer specifically to the provision of services for children and families, not to children's peer groups, locations or public spaces where harm has occurred. A focus on family intervention, and the use of care placements on occasion, is often insufficient for addressing EFH.

This type of harm requires contextual as well as individual interventions to build safety (Brandon *et al.*, 2020; Fagan & Catalano, 2012; Firmin, 2020; PACE, 2020). One could argue that support for a peer group is a service for children, if it meets their needs. However, the individualized design and provision of many services available to children in need suggest that this is not how the duty has been interpreted on the ground (as will be explored later). This limitation is exacerbated by the aforementioned partners missing from the s.16E list, who are active in public spaces such as the retail and hospitality sectors.

Care placements are used as an intervention for some adolescents at risk of significant harm in extra-familial contexts (Ellis, 2018; Firmin, Wroe & Skidmore, 2020; Rees *et al.*, 2017). To address the contextual dimensions of EFH, and to create a physical distance between young people and the groups/contexts in which they have been harmed, they may, under an s.20 voluntary placement or s.31 care order, be moved great distances from their families and communities (placement availability may also determine the distance). S.11 of The Care Planning, Placement and Case Review (England) Regulations (2010)[5] require that distance placements are approved by a nominated officer and meet the needs of an associated plan. As explained previously, in most cases of EFH, risk of significant harm emanates from contexts/relationships beyond the family home, and is not situated in the relationship between the young person and their parents/carers. As such, relocation away from the family home in cases of EFH is a form of intervention often delivered on a voluntary basis, under s.20(1) of the CA 1989, which places a duty on LAs to accommodate any child in need in their area, where required and their parents are unable to do so. As long as the arrangement is not ordered by the court, parents can remove their child (if under the age of 16) from these placements. Children over the age of 16 can agree to these placements without their parents' consent.[6]

Young people affected by EFH often go missing, and an increase in frequency and length of missing episodes has been linked to increasing concerns about their welfare. As a result, secure placements are also used as an intervention in some cases. S.25 of the CA 1989 permits LAs to apply to the family court to use this type of intervention if:

a. he has a history of absconding and is likely to abscond from any other description of accommodation; and

b. if he absconds, he is likely to suffer significant harm; or

c. that if he is kept in any other description of accommodation he is likely to injure himself or other persons.

This route, alongside other mechanisms for deprivation of liberty, can also apply to young people who are over 16 and do not consent to another form of placement (Ruck Keene & Parker, 2020). Numerous

---

5   www.legislation.gov.uk/uksi/2010/959/contents/made.

6   Under s.20(3) of the Children Act 1989, a local authority must provide accommodation for a child over 16, even where a parent is able to do so, if their welfare will be seriously prejudiced otherwise. There is a further discretionary duty under s.20(4) for local authorities to provide accommodation for any child, if they consider that to do so would safeguard or promote their welfare. In many ways, these options address the lack of fit between s.31 and extra-familial harm as experienced during adolescence. Also, on consent, see s.20(7), (8) and (11), which make it clear that children over 16 do not require parental consent for accommodation.

questions, however, surround the efficacy of both distance and secure placements for safeguarding adolescents affected by EFH.

First, s.17 requires that LAs promote the upbringing of children by their families. The use of care and secure placements in cases of protective parenting appears to be at odds with this requirement. Although s.20 placements don't require a child to be beyond parental control before they are taken up, if parents remove their child from a voluntary placement and in so doing increase the risk of significant harm their child faces in their home community, this could arguably be attributable to their decision as parents and means the young person reaches a threshold for an s.31 care order. But this is difficult and ethically uncomfortable. The harm would still be posed by those outside the family and yet this creates a situation where the family (i.e., the parents) would be penalized (and in many senses blamed) for that harm.

Research has questioned the success of care placements for young people at risk of EFH (Scott, Botcherby & Ludvigsen, 2017), and social care innovations have been funded with the intention of reducing their use (Lushey et al., 2017; Scott et al., 2017). Given this, it could be that a parent's decision to bring their child home is an attempt to safeguard rather than harm them. If young people are safe within their families but unsafe beyond their front doors, how does living a distance away from their families reduce the risk that they face in a way that is commensurate with the potential harm caused by separating them from their parents?

Further to this, while the ambition of using such interventions is often to prevent escalating missing episodes and stabilize a situation for a young person, the extent to which this is realized is variable. Studies into the use of out-of-area and secure placements have questioned whether such interventions are consistently accompanied with a plan that will ensure that the placement meets the needs of the young person in question (Ellis, 2018; Firmin et al., 2020). After all, both secure and out-of-area placements can remove young people from relatively safe family, peer and community relationships as well as extra-familial risks. Without any legal requirement that the extra-familial risks in question be addressed (e.g., via a coordinated plan to increase the safety of a street or school in which that young person was unsafe, so as to restore connections between families and communities in a timely fashion), distance and secure placements threaten to undermine the ambition of the CA 1989 to promote the upbringing of children by their families.

Beyond questions about their efficacy, there are additional matters to be addressed regarding the specific use of secure placements in response to EFH. The use of such placements under s.25 of the CA 1989 may require complex legal considerations around deprivation of liberty. In particular, where 16–17-year-olds are confined but do not consent to the confinement, there is a clear need for the deprivation of liberty to be authorized by a court. This area of case law is still developing rapidly[7] and is too complex for us to address fully here. However, it is an important factor to be aware of. Moreover, there is a further practical hurdle of the lack of availability of secure placements.[8]

A possible alternative solution is for an entire family to be rehoused, away from the contexts posing a risk to the young person. This could be achieved under s.17(6) of the CA 1989 and by seeking collaboration from another LA housing department (under s.27 of the CA 1989) to facilitate an emergency housing placement or swap, for example. While this allows for the upbringing of children by their families, it also requires a family to be uprooted, often suddenly. Such an option will not always be appropriate for families where a move would:

- disrupt the lives of younger children

- take families a significant distance from critical local support structures

- fail to address other potentially confounding impacts on parents and their decision-making, such as poverty or racism.

For a young person and their family, moving areas would also mean changing the practitioners who have been supporting them, like their social workers, creating further instability.

In some respects, the ASB legislation noted previously provides a route for interventions that are more contextually focused and engage a broader set of community partners. However, the list of interventions that could be included, such as a 'community remedy', currently include acceptable behaviour contracts, restorative justice, targeted interventions or structured diversionary activities for individuals deemed to

---

7   For a recent summary of the position, please see the guidance note published by 39 Essex Row: https://1f2ca7mxjow42e65q49871m1-wpengine.netdna-ssl.com/wp-content/uploads/2017/12/Judicial-Authorisations-of-Deprivation-of-Liberty-July-2020.pdf.

8   See, for example, the judgment arising from *Lancashire CC v G (No3) (Continuing Unavailability of Secure Accommodation) [2020] EWHC 3280 (Fam)* (02 December 2020).

be causing harm, with court injunctions for non-engagement. Most of these target individuals, not contexts. The target of interventions, and associations to criminalization for non-compliance, would need to be addressed for such work to be viewed as part of a system where the safety/safeguarding of adolescents is the primary objective.

The potential shortcomings of the legislative framework

S.17 and s.47 of the CA 1989, and s.10 and s.11 of the CA 2004, are as relevant to the safeguarding of adolescents as they are to younger children, and for the most part can be used as such (for all those up to 18, and for some through to 25). Case law strengthens how these legal levers may be interpreted to build plans for interventions with groups/ within contexts beyond families in order to safeguard and promote the welfare of young people. However, it is equally clear that other sections of the legislation were not designed for this purpose, particularly when it comes to young people characterized as both 'villains and victims', and were instead, as Baroness Hale suggested, written to safeguard children from abuse that occurred as a consequence of the actions taken by parents, or by limited parenting capacity. The focus of service delivery, the grounds for statutory intervention, and escalation of responses associated to 'significant harm' in child protection legislation, all presume and foreground the responsibility of parents. A more contextual focus is found, to an extent, in youth justice and community safety legislation, but this framework was designed to reduce offending and crime rather than safeguard children, and, for the most part, only targets individuals associated with EFH (rather than the contexts in which it occurs) as a means of achieving safety.

This shortcoming is not reserved for the UK. Child protection systems across Europe, North America, Australia and New Zealand have been built on the same premise: the state intervenes via its child protection system when parental capacity is compromised (Merkel-Holguin, Fluke & Krugman, 2019). However, as concerns have increased about the nature of extra-familial harm, so too have the calls for child protection systems to respond, and with a focus beyond parenting. Policy makers have responded by amending and creating policy documents that align to primary legislation but speak to the wider needs presented by EFH. So, to what extent do these changes enable the use of the child protection system beyond its original design?

Statutory guidance, policy interpretations and appendages

The primary legislation outlined thus far is interpreted across two key policy areas that collectively detail England's approach to safeguarding adolescents from EFH. One is a set of statutory safeguarding guidelines and regulations that translate child protection legislation into practice. The other is a raft of issue-specific documents published to guide responses to forms of EFH such as child sexual exploitation, serious youth violence and domestic abuse.

Safeguarding guidance and regulation

Working Together to Safeguard Children was introduced in 1988 to provide statutory inter-agency guidance for England's child protection. Until 2018, it made no reference to EFH, or the specific developmental needs of adolescents accessing safeguarding systems. Some previous iterations featured appendices about forms of EFH, such as child sexual exploitation, but these issues were not in the main body of the document. In 2018, the following text was added to Chapter 1:

> As well as threats to the welfare of children from within their families, children may be vulnerable to abuse or exploitation from outside their families. These extra-familial threats might arise at school and other educational establishments, from within peer groups, or more widely from within the wider community and/or online. These threats can take a variety of different forms and children can be vulnerable to multiple threats, including: exploitation by criminal gangs and organized crime groups such as county lines; trafficking, online abuse; sexual exploitation and the influences of extremism leading to radicalisation. (HM Government, 2018, p.22)[9]

This change was accompanied by five sentence changes that acknowledged the need to:

1. Identify connections between young people affected by the same extra-familial context of thematic concern during assessments (Chapter 1, para 25).

---

9   This has since been updated to include teenage relationship abuse.

2. Identify risks faced by, as well as in, a young person's family during assessment (Chapter 1, para 53).

3. Offer early help responses to contexts as well as individuals (Chapter 1, para 12).

4. Identify contexts in which young people supported by youth offending services might also be at risk of abuse (Chapter 2, para 49).

5. Ensure a range of partner agencies, included in s.11 of the Children Act 2004, have arrangements in place for ensuring a culture of equality and protection within the services they provide (to address peer-to-peer harm within services) (Chapter 2, para 3).

More recent changes to the guidance include a specific suggestion that extra-familial harm should be considered as part of the assessment process (see p.22, para 41).

These insertions signalled that it was possible for local authorities to address EFH within the existing framework provided by primary legislation, primarily drawing on s.17 of the CA 1989. They also explicitly situated young people who had committed offences in the context of EFH within safeguarding responses to these issues, moving away from the aforementioned intentions of the CA 1989 designer to separate out responses to young people whose behaviour was the 'cause' of the harm they faced.

However, the above changes have not sufficiently addressed the previous question about how to interpret primary legislation when responding to EFH. Most notably, while all assessments are required to analyse a child's 'needs and/or the nature and level of any risk and harm being suffered by the child' (Chapter 1, para 45), specific actions listed in the guidance from a statutory investigation onwards are focused on the assessment of families. Professionals are required to share information about children and families during child protection conferences, but there is no mention of information-sharing about the peer group, school or public place where a young person may have encountered EFH. While consideration of peer relationships during assessments is recommended, no methodological framework is provided for this. The only assessment framework provided is for children and families. There is no description of how to integrate or co-manage responses to young people who are open to youth justice services but have safeguarding needs – and needs which may outlive the length of their court-ordered contact with a youth offending team. Finally, the multi-agency opportunities afforded by s.10 and s.11 of the CA 2014, for partnerships to respond to contexts as well as individuals in need of support, is not explored in the document at all, with requirements that agencies provide services to, and share information about, children and families only (not extra-familial contexts). These areas of safeguarding guidance reaffirm the idea that EFH cases can be managed under s.17, but with little guidance about how to do so, or any advice on how to escalate via statutory plans that aren't focused on parenting. In this sense, while changes to statutory guidance in 2018 acknowledged some of the specific considerations required to safeguard adolescents, and utilized s.17 and, to some extent, s.47 to do this, the guidance does not offer a roadmap of how to act on those considerations.

In a similar vein, statutory guidance such as the *Children Act 1989 Guidance and Regulations Volume 2* (Department for Education, 2015) has acknowledged the unique set of circumstances at play when placing children in care due to extra-familial (as opposed to familial) harm, but it does not resolve the challenges posed by such circumstances. For example, when exploring the conditions for using out-of-area place-ments to safeguard young people, the guidance states:

> …some relatives also live hundreds of miles from the child's home. While the chance of developing a secure attachment with a relative may be of key significance to a younger child, the same may not be true of a teen-ager who may resent being cut off from peer networks or being obliged to change schools at a critical time and lose the local roots which may become a protective factor later on… Moreover, those young people who have been drawn into a gang culture or become involved with a delin-quent peer group may benefit not from being near home but from being offered the chance to develop new relationships and skills in a different environment. (Department for Education, 2015, p.53)

Such a position simply points to what is already known in practice, that is, there are some reasons to keep a young person where they are and others for moving them away. But both of these reasons often apply to the same young person. Weighing-up each to make a final decision, and the type of plan needed to facilitate a young person's return to their communities, is not detailed in guidance at all. More specific guidance would be useful, guidance which identifies key factors to address when developing plans in cases of EFH, and the conditions that would need to be met in extra-familial contexts to allow for reunification with families.

With increasing numbers of over-12-year-olds entering care for the first time due to EFH (Association of Directors of Children's Services, 2018), it is likely that more thought is required from policy makers about how to support the development of practice when care placements are used with young people who are living in relatively safe families. As these matters, or at least the extent of them, were not a principal concern when the regulations or their corresponding guidance were developed, it is unsurprising that they fall short of speaking to the purpose for which they are now used.

Guidance related to extra-familial harm

Since 2000, government departments have published a range of issue-specific guidance on forms of EFH. In 2001, 2009 and 2017, the Department for Education published safeguarding guidance on child sexual exploitation. In 2010, the same department issued advice for safeguarding children from gang association. In 2019, the Home Office issued policy consultations on creating a duty for community safety partnerships to respond to serious violence (including youth violence), a duty included in the Police, Crime, Sentencing and Courts Bill 2021 (undergoing parliamentary readings at the point of writing). The Home Office in 2012 also included over-16-year-olds in a revised policy definition of domestic abuse, but did not extend any related guidance to those under 16. In 2016, the Ministry of Justice published guidance for frontline practitioners and Youth Offending Teams on county lines exploitation, and in 2018, the Home Office published guidance on criminal exploitation. At the start of 2021, there was no national safeguarding guidance available on harmful sexual behaviour – despite calls for this since 2010.

In short, there is no integrated safeguarding policy to guide responses to EFH and its impact on the welfare of adolescents. Some forms of harm are attended to, such as sexual exploitation, and others are not, such as harmful sexual behaviour. Furthermore, Home Office (policing) policy addresses some forms of harm while Department for Education (safeguarding) policy attends to others. Very few of these documents provide any sense of how to respond to EFH within a child protection legislative framework, despite safeguarding guidance stating that these are all 'child protection issues'.

The challenges this presents to local delivery and the required resolutions

Numerous practice challenges emerge from the shortcomings in legislation, guidance and policy outlined thus far. Other chapters in this book explore many of them, such as:

- definitions of 'victims', 'perpetrators' and those in need of support (Chapter 4)

- transitional services for adolescents aged 18–25 (Chapter 10).

But this is not the focus here. Instead, this section examines three practice challenges specific to the extra-familial dynamics of adolescent safety (and the policy framework outlined above):

1. How to recognize and respond to cases of escalating risk faced by families who are relatively protective.

2. How to build partnerships with services with a reach into the places and spaces where extra-familial harm occurs.

3. How to integrate information about peer relationships into social care processes.

To overcome each of these challenges, local areas, including safeguarding partnerships, have written innovative policies, designed their own services and even instructed their own legal advice to offer a sufficient response to EFH. Such examples illustrate the direction of travel for adolescent safeguarding systems in England, and the primary legislation and statutory guidance that may be required in the process.

Escalating cases of extra-familial harm with largely protective families

In 2020, amid the inconsistent policy landscape detailed above, Ofsted released a blog outlining its expectations of local responses to risk beyond the family home:

> All the children that we're discussing here would be classed as 'children in need' under section 17 of the Children Act 1989, regardless of whether they have a child protection plan or not. (Stanley, 2020)

At the point of writing, a number of local authorities are testing this premise in various ways (Firmin & Knowles, 2020), and the fact it appeared in a blog rather than formal guidance is perhaps indicative of the questions that persist around this position. However, it speaks to a shift witnessed in local areas over the past five years, regarding how they hold and oversee cases of EFH within children's social care (Lloyd & Firmin, 2019).

Many local areas have moved from a position of closing EFH cases to social care and referring them to voluntary and policing organizations (Cockbain & Brayley, 2012; Firmin, 2020; Hill, 2019; Pearce, 2013), to one where EFH cases are overseen using s.17 arrangements. In some of these areas, professionals often reserve an escalation to s.47 enquiries and child protection plans for young people who are either at risk of significant harm within their families, or where the EFH they face is attributable to the care provided to them by their families (Firmin *et al.*, 2016).

However, in this process of shifting practices, a new question has emerged. How do professionals escalate actions for young people at risk of *significant harm* in extra-familial contexts compared to young people who are *in need of support* due to EFH, but whose physical safety is not at immediate risk, when both cohorts are safe with their families? The general duty to meet the needs of young people does not appear to confer the gravity of significant harm cases to the professional network involved, the young person or their family.

As a consequence, some areas have started using child protection plans in cases where a young person is at risk of significant EFH, even though parents are protective (Firmin *et al.*, 2016). Others have developed alternative plans for safeguarding adolescents such as My Safety Plan, trialled in place of child protection plans as part of the Greater Manchester Achieving Change Together (ACT) response to child sexual exploitation (Scott *et al.*, 2017).

These plans provide social work oversight in cases of EFH, while also being flexible and young person-led, in ways not always accommodated by statutory processes and timetables. Of the ten national sites piloting a contextual safeguarding approach in 2020, seven are exploring the idea of a 'third way' plan for young people who are at risk of significant harm (s.47) but who are in relatively protective families (s.17 or early help).

In creating alternative plans or using child protection plans with safe families, local areas are working around or in addition to the legislative framework, suggesting that either further detail is required in statutory guidance as to how to use the CA 1989 in these cases, or that further legislative levers are required. It could be argued that, despite fitting within the s.17 definition, young people who experience EFH sit outside most other elements of the CA 1989 (a natural consequence of the intentions behind its design). This means that, beyond the general duty, they don't apparently fit anywhere, preventing further routes to escalate concerns (with the exception of a s.20 voluntary placement away from their families, as discussed earlier) when they are not associated with parental care or control.

It could be that, with further statutory guidance and/or continuing innovation by local areas, escalation routes could be developed through the cooperation and the 'active promotion' of children's welfare under s.10 and s.11 of the CA 2004. Other specific duties in part 3 of the CA 1989 speak to examples of young people who are in need of support but not due to familial-abuse, for example young carers, young people with a disability, or young people in need of accommodation. It may be that young people in need due to EFH also require a specific duty, to hold the range of needs that may emerge from this experience, some of which could be significant. This could provide a clearer legislative underpinning for attempts to develop EFH plans.

Building information about peer relationships into assessment
As detailed earlier in this chapter, both *Working Together to Safeguard Children* (HM Government, 2018) and regulation and guidance related to out-of-area placements recognize the association between the nature of young people's friendships and their experiences of extra-familial safety. Both areas of policy promote the consideration of these dynamics when conducting assessments and formulating plans for young people. However, the statements on their own do not guide local areas on how best to assess and, where required, intervene in young people's peer relationships.

While the inclusion of friendships appears to be a common-sense feature of an adolescent safeguarding system, attempts to build frameworks and technology to support this activity unearth a lot of unanswered questions (Firmin, 2017; Johnson, 2013; Waltham Forest Safeguarding Children Board, 2020). For example, would every young person recorded on a peer map or wider assessment need to be supported by children's social care? How might parents and young people be informed that they are recorded on a peer map or wider assessment that has been drawn up to assess the needs of another young person, and what would be the confidentiality implications? How might peer assessments reflect the dynamic and fluid nature of young people's relationships?

This range of questions resulted in one LA instructing a QC for legal advice on their use of peer assessment and peer mapping within social care, and how this aligned, or not, to General Data Protection Regulation (GDPR) and human rights and child protection legislative frameworks (Contextual Safeguarding Network, 2019). The advice suggested that peer assessments could be conducted on the grounds of the 'protection of health' as opposed to the 'prevention of crime' (as they are undertaken when peers are mapped during police investigations). However, transparency about the process was also required, and decisions made about information-sharing on a case-by-case basis.

Given the technical, legal and ethical questions surrounding the use of peer assessment and associated mapping, one might think a 'threshold criteria' appropriate, to ascertain the circumstances in which a statutory body might undertake such work (especially without consent). There will, of course, be examples where social workers and other practitioners work with young people to map out, understand and assess their peer relationships. Such collaboration is likely to be already provided for and in many ways is as much an intervention as it is a form of assessment (Latimer & Adams-Elias, 2020). But for their broader use among professionals alone, peer assessments may require more boundaries than are currently defined in policy, and consideration in legislation where they are absent.

Broadening partnerships

To create safety in extra-familial contexts, children's services have looked for partnerships beyond those listed in s.11 of the CA 2004. While s.10 compels local authorities to establish the partnerships required to fulfil their s.17 duty, and the CSWA 2017 expands this list of partners, it isn't clear that all partners relevant to EFH are obliged to engage in the process.

Companies which run shopping centres and supermarket chains, transport providers, and individual managers of local pharmacies, shopping centres or parks have all featured in local responses to EFH (D'Arcy & Thomas, 2016; Firmin, 2020). Some of these partners, such as waste management or housing, may be part of council services and so fall within the duty under s.10 of the CA 2004. Organizations that have a contract with the local authority may be required under the contract to comply with safeguarding requirements. If some have signed up to the local child protection procedures then they will be expected to comply with these. Others, however, such as franchises of private supermarket chains, privately run transport companies and shopping centres, for example, are not covered as partners in existing legislation; their engagement in these activities is largely one of goodwill.

So, what can local authorities do if such goodwill is absent? If young people are at risk of significant harm outside and around a shopping centre but the owner of that shopping centre is not contributing to any child welfare assessments associated with its location, what options are available, if any? Some areas have sought to use licensing legislation to encourage engagement, for example requiring taxi drivers to undertake safeguarding training in order to renew their licences, or inviting local authorities to comment on alcohol licences. Such approaches have been led by local areas; they are not the result of a nationwide initiative or position. Ethical as well as legal questions may emerge regarding:

- the burden this places on organizations, particularly small ones which are not designed with a primary intention to safeguard adolescents

- the intrusion of state services into business operations

- the capacity implications for local authorities that engage with these processes.

These questions become even more pressing given that community-led, and less punitive, frameworks for engagement are far less developed. Legal and policy tools that might enable the engagement of private businesses in safeguarding processes likely require more thought. For example, one area developed information-sharing agreements for non-traditional partners who had agreed to attend a meeting about a location associated with serious violence (Hackney Contextual Safeguarding Project, 2019). These agreements sought to enable the attendance of local businesses at the meeting as the LA recognized that attending could open the businesses up to risks if they didn't have the technology, secure storage or other means to safely engage in, and share information at, the meeting.

The potential need to append health and safety, licensing or community safety legislation to facilitate wider partnership engagement illustrates the (perceived) limitations of using child protection legislation alone to broaden the partnerships involved in safeguarding adolescents. It also raises a question about whether this broadening agenda is symptomatic of safeguarding systems drifting into a community safety agenda. The latter is almost exclusively concerned with reducing community-based harm, crime and anti-social behaviour, whereas the former has historically focused on harm in familial settings.

By broadening the lens to assess and engage with harms, relationships and contexts that are extra-familial, children's social care and wider safeguarding partnerships have started to assess and engage with some issues that are simultaneously the responsibility of community safety partnerships. A legal framework for safeguarding adolescents would need to grapple with these tensions that, as outlined previously, are unresolved in policy as well as in practice. Arguably, the s.10 duty on local authorities to cooperate and develop partnerships could be used to further this area of work. If this happens it may make it easier to propose safeguarding relationships to new partners who are not obliged to engage, and go some way to resolving this impasse.

Conclusion: Reaffirming or reforming?

When legislated for in 1989, England's child protection system was designed to safeguard children (up to the age of 18, with exceptions up to 25) who were at risk of harm, and where that harm was attributable to either the care provided by their parents or the fact that the child was beyond a parent's control, or who were in need due to poverty or health-related reasons, such as having a disability, or being a young carer. EFH largely impacts adolescents and also affects young people beyond the age of 18, though this latter group has not been considered by the policy makers (Holmes & Smale, 2018). In some cases, young people affected by EFH were viewed as 'out of control, falling into bad associations or in moral danger' (Hale, 2019, p.2) and were therefore deemed to be out of scope.

Over three decades later, England's child protection system is being used for a much broader purpose. EFH has been framed as a child protection issue and young people affected by it have fallen under the remit of children's social care. This shift has been characterized by falling numbers of young people in youth custody, alongside an increase of young people in residential children's homes and welfare-based secure placements. Some young people who for aforementioned reasons fell outside the child protection system in 1989 are now positioned within it. However, this shift has occurred without amendment to primary legislation and with meagre adaptation of statutory guidance.

Many amendments to policy have surfaced, rather than resolved, questions about the legislative framework for safeguarding adolescents. They have also failed to:

- specify which elements of primary child protection legislation can be utilized for purposes beyond which they were designed

- unify wider legislative tools that may support or compromise this.

It is impossible to document all of these questions in one chapter. However, central ones that we have considered include the following:

- Whether the general duty under s.17 is a sufficient basis for responding to all young people at risk of harm in extra-familial settings/relationships.

- Stipulating the legal framework for peer assessment, including intersection with the Human Rights Act (1998) and GDPR.

- Clarifying whether s.10 and s.11 duties can be extended to non-traditional safeguarding partners and the relationship between licensing, community safety and child protection legislation in this regard.

At this stage, it is apparent that there may be much in s.17, s.47, s.10 and s.11 that could be tested and utilized further through statutory guidance to safeguard adolescents. Doing so would help us to ascertain whether or not we need to reaffirm or reform primary legislation to provide children's social care with a statutory framework designed for the purpose for which it is now used.

References

Association of Directors of Children's Services (2018). *Safeguarding Pressures 6*. Manchester: ADCS. https://adcs.org.uk/safeguarding/article/safeguarding-pressures-phase-6.

Barter, C. (2009). 'In the name of love: Partner abuse and violence in teenage relationships.' *The British Journal of Social Work*, 39(20), 211–233.

Brandon, M., Sidebotham, P., Belderson, P., Cleaver, H. *et al.* (2020). *Complexity and Challenge: A Triennial Analysis of SCRs 2014–2017: Final Report*. London: Department for Education.

Catch 22 (2013). *The Role of the Family in Facilitating Gang Membership, Criminality and Exit: A Report Prepared for Catch 22*. London: Catch 22.

Child Safeguarding Practice Review Panel (2020). *It was Hard to Escape: Safeguarding Children at Risk from Criminal Exploitation*. London: Department for Education.

Cockbain, E. & Brayley, H. (2012). 'Child sexual exploitation and youth offending: A research note.' *European Journal of Criminology*, 9(6), 689–700.

Contextual Safeguarding Network (2019). *Legal Framework*. www.csnetwork.org.uk/en/toolkit/legal-framework.

D'Arcy, K. & Thomas, R. (2016). *Nightwatch: CSE in Plain Sight. Final Evaluation Report*. Luton: University of Bedfordshire.

Department for Education (2015). *Children Act 1989 Guidance and Regulations Volume 2: Care Planning, Placement and Case Review*. London: UK Government. www.gov.uk/government/publications/children-act-1989-care-planning-placement-and-case-review.

Ellis, K. (2018). 'Contested vulnerability: A case study of girls in secure care.' *Children and Youth Services Review*, 88, 156–163.

Fagan, A.A. & Catalano, R. (2012). 'What works in youth violence prevention: A review of the literature.' *Research on Social Work Practice*, 23(2), 141–156.

Firmin, C. (2017). 'From genograms to peer-group mapping: Introducing peer relationships into social care assessments.' *Families, Relationships and Societies*, 8(2), 231–248. https://doi.org/10.1332/204674317X15088482907590.

Firmin, C. (2020). *Contextual Safeguarding and Child Protection: Rewriting the Rules* (first edition). Abingdon, Oxfordshire: Routledge.

Firmin, C., Curtis, G., Fritz, D., Olaitan, P. *et al.* (2016). 'Towards a contextual response to peer-on-peer abuse.' *Research and resources from MsUnderstood local site work 2013–2016*. Luton: University of Bedfordshire.

Firmin, C. & Knowles, R. (2020). *The Legal and Policy Framework for Contextual Safeguarding Approaches*. Luton: Contextual Safeguarding.

Firmin, C., Wroe, L. & Lloyd, J. (2019). *Safeguarding and Exploitation – Complex, Contextual and Holistic Approaches: Strategic Briefing*. Totnes: Research in Practice.

Firmin, C., Wroe, L. & Skidmore, P. (2020). *A Sigh of Relief: A Summary of the Phase One Results from the Securing Safety Study*. Luton: University of Bedfordshire.

Hackney Contextual Safeguarding Project (2019). *Information Sharing Protocol and Guidance for Community or Council Identified Stakeholders and Community Guardians*. www.csnetwork.org.uk/assets/images/Hackney-Information-Sharing-Protocol.pdf.

Hale, L. (2019). *30 Years of the Children Act 1989, Scarman Lecture*. Law Commission.

Hill, N. (2019). *Serious Case Review – Chris*. London: Newham Safeguarding Children Board.

HM Government (2018). *Working Together to Safeguard Children and their Families*. London: The Stationery Office.

Holmes, D. & Smale, E. (2018). *Strategic Briefing: Transitional Safeguarding – Adolescence to Adulthood*. Totnes: Research in Practice.

Home Office (2021). *Reform of Anti-Social Behaviour Powers: Statutory Guidance for Frontline Professionals*. London: HMSO. www.gov.uk/government/publications/anti-social-behaviour-crime-and-policing-bill-anti-social-behaviour.

Hudeck, J. (2018). *County Lines: Scoping Report*. London: St Giles Trust.

Johnson, F. (2013). *Redacted Overview Report on the Serious Case Review Relating to Tom and Vic*. Kingston LSCB.

Khan, L., Brice, H., Saunders, A. & Plumtree, A. (2013). *A Need to Belong: What Leads Girls to Join Gangs*. London: Centre for Mental Health.

Lammy, D. (2017). *The Lammy Review: An Independent Review into the Treatment of, and Outcomes for, Black, Asian and Minority Ethnic Individuals in the Criminal Justice System*. London: The Stationery Office.

Latimer, K. & Adams-Elias, C. (2020). *Opportunities for Peer Safeguarding Intervention: A Briefing Following Fieldwork with Safer London*. Contextual Safeguarding Programme. Luton: University of Bedfordshire.

Lloyd, J. & Firmin, C. (2019). 'No further action: contextualising social care decisions for children victimised in extra-familial contexts.' *Journal of Youth Justice, 20*(1–2), 79–92.

Lloyd, S. (2019). '"She doesn't have to get in the car...": Exploring social workers' understandings of sexually exploited girls as agents and choice-makers.' *Children's Geographies*. https://doi.org/10.1080/14733285.2019.1649360.

Lushey, C., Hyde-Dryden, G., Holmes, L. & Blackmore, J. (2017). *Evaluation of the No Wrong Door Innovation Programme*. London: Department for Education Children's Social Care Innovation Programme.

Merkel-Holguin, L., Fluke, J. & Krugman, R.D. (2019). *National Systems of Child Protection: Understanding the International Variability and Context for Developing Policy and Practice* (first edition). Cham, Switzerland: Springer.

PACE (Parents Against Child Exploitation) (2020). *Parents' Experiences of the Children's Social Care System When a Child is Sexually Exploited*. Leeds: PACE.

Pearce, J. (2013). '"What's going on" to safeguard children and young people from sexual exploitation: A review of local safeguarding children's boards' work to protect children from sexual exploitation.' *Child Abuse Review, 23*(3), 159–170.

Prison Reform Trust (2008). *Criminal Damage: Why We Should Lock Up Fewer Children*. London: Prison Reform Trust.

Rees, A., Luke, N., Sebba, J. & McNeish, D. (2017). *Adolescent Service Change and the Edge of Care: Children's Social Care Innovation Programme – Thematic Report 2*. Oxford: The Rees Centre.

Ruck Keene, A. & Parker, C. (2020). *Deprivation of Liberty and 16–17 Year Olds: Practice Guide*. Totnes: Research in Practice.

Scott, S., Botcherby, S. & Ludvigsen, A. (2017). *Wigan and Rochdale Child Sexual Exploitation Innovation Project*. London: Department for Education.

Scott, S. & McNeish, D. (2017). *Supporting Parents of Sexually Exploited Young People: An Evidence Review*. Centre of Expertise on Child Sexual Abuse.

Shuker, L. (2017). *Empowering Parents: Evaluation of Parents as Partners in Safeguarding Children and Young People in Lancashire Project 2014–2017*. Luton: University of Bedfordshire.

Stanley, Y. (2020). *Dealing with Risks to Children outside the Family Home*. Blog published by Ofsted. https://socialcareinspection.blog.gov.uk/2020/03/06/dealing-with-risks-to-children-outside-the-family-home.

Taylor, C. (2016). *Review of the Youth Justice System in England and Wales*. London: Ministry of Justice.

Waltham Forest Safeguarding Children Board (2020). *Serious Case Review. Child C: A 14-Year-Old Boy*. London: WFSCB.

Chapter 8

Learning to Love and Trust Again: A Relational Approach to Developmental Trauma

Kristi Hickle and Michelle Lefevre

Introduction

Sam, a White male aged 15, came to the attention of children's social care when his adoptive parents started reporting him to the police regularly as going missing from home. His parents described him as defiant and outside their control. A strategy discussion was held at an early stage because of concerns about possible sexual exploitation; Sam had been observed meeting regularly with adult males in the community and having money and expensive goods for which there was no obvious explanation.

The referral for Sam offers a common account of how young people experiencing exploitation and other extra-familial risks and harm come to the attention of the agencies involved with safeguarding. The focus of such referrals, and subsequent work, is often on how parents, carers or professionals involved in their lives see the young person in a 'problem-first' way – as either troubled or causing trouble, at risk or creating risks, vulnerable or harmful (Lefevre, Hickle & Luckock, 2019). These polarized perspectives reflect how adults do not always see what lies beneath young people's behaviour and social relationships, nor connect with young people's trauma and their unmet developmental needs.

This chapter will consider how viewing trauma through a developmental and relational lens can enable us to better make sense of young people's worlds and the impact of their experiences. This enhanced understanding can then enable professionals and carers to provide a facilitating environment within which young people can heal from their trauma and find productive ways of engaging with safer and more healthy relationships and environments. We will illustrate the theoretical discussions through excerpts from interviews with Sam and his social worker, Anne, which were conducted during earlier research by the first author. All names have been anonymized.

The impact of developmental trauma

Sam was adopted as a baby and lived with his adoptive parents until the age of 15, when it became apparent that a long, undetected history of neglect at home had resulted in escalating missing episodes as Sam sought to get his emotional needs met by adults who were sexually exploiting him in the community. When his parents refused to let him come home after a missing episode, and the extent of neglect in their home became evident, he was taken into care. Anne said: 'They were horrendous about him. There was no warmth there. They were so blaming of him for absolutely everything. They just neglected him on an absolutely massive scale and, yes, it was atrocious.'

Sam initially spent several months in a children's home, but struggled with managing his feelings: 'I had anger issues and I just kept on knocking people out, decking people, losing my temper, putting a fist through the walls, fist through windows, TVs broken...because when I lash out I don't stop.' When his biological father suddenly surfaced, Sam was eager to connect with him and was looking for a way out of the children's home. He went to live with his father for a year, but the placement eventually broke down as his father struggled with the challenging behaviours connected with Sam's learning difficulties and traumatic childhood.

It is evident that establishing physical, emotional and relational safety (Shuker, 2013) for Sam remained an ongoing challenge after he went into care. The challenges Sam faced in regulating his behaviour and engaging in social relationships are common among children who have experienced what van der Kolk (2014) called 'developmental trauma'. Drawing on Felitti and colleagues' (1998) landmark study on adverse childhood experiences (ACEs), van der Kolk (2014, 2017) and colleagues at the American National Traumatic Stress Network brought new attention to what many frontline mental health and social service professionals had perhaps long known: experiencing trauma in childhood through neglectful parenting and maltreatment within the context of community or familial relationships (Bush, 2018) can result in lifelong problems with physical and mental health and interpersonal relationships. While the methodology and application of the research on ACEs has been necessarily critiqued in recent years (e.g., Asmussen *et al.*, 2020), developmental trauma remains a useful concept for understanding the distinct impact of trauma in childhood.

Developmental trauma is characterized by impairment across several domains of human development, including attachment, cognition, self-regulation and biological functioning (Teague, 2013). As children exposed to multiple traumatic events grow and develop, their bodies' best efforts to keep them safe often translate to behaviours that are challenging and disruptive to themselves and others. These might include: extreme mood shifts (e.g., from anger and/or aggression to flat, emotionless detachment); agitation and difficulty focusing or being still; physical pain; sleep disturbances; sensitivity to touch or sound; self-harm; and difficulties with motor coordination, cognitive development and language processing (van der Kolk, 2014).

Children's capacity to respond to new stressors and challenging events is often reduced, and is lower than for peers who have not been exposed to childhood trauma. The absence of safe caregivers and/or an environment that facilitates their ability to self-soothe in times of distress means they don't develop a frame of reference for managing their impulses, regulating emotions, paying attention and experiencing safe and healthy relationships (D'Andrea *et al.*, 2012; Teague, 2013). Developmental trauma can shape how children conceptualize themselves as part of the world, and they come to understand who they are in the world through a framework characterized by low self-worth (Burack *et al.*, 2006), shame, guilt, reduced self-efficacy and an external locus of control (D'Andrea *et al.*, 2012). Herman (1992, p.96) explained:

> Repeated trauma in adult life erodes the structure of the personality already formed, but repeated trauma in childhood forms and deforms the personality. The child trapped in an abusive environment is faced with formidable tasks of adaptation. She must find a way to preserve

a sense of trust in people who are untrustworthy, safety in a situation that is unsafe, control in a situation that is terrifyingly unpredictable, power in a situation of helplessness.

Despite the significant challenges facing young people who have experienced developmental trauma, research on trauma recovery, post-traumatic growth, attachment and trauma-informed practice indicates the myriad possibilities for helping children and young people mitigate the impact of these experiences in their lives, and for providing opportunities for them to 'redraw their inner maps and incorporate a sense of trust and confidence in the future' (van der Kolk, 2014, p.109). In order to make best sense of how to meet the needs of individual children and young people, it is essential to understand first how their life experiences, including both early caregiving experiences and exposure to extra-familial harm within peer, school and community contexts, have either laid the foundations for resilience or have increased their vulnerability to risk and trauma.

Understanding the antecedents of resilience and developmental trauma

There is broad cross-disciplinary agreement that the ways in which children's cognitive, physical and emotional needs and experiences are responded to – or not – have a substantial influence on their developmental trajectory and future resilience (D'Andrea et al., 2012; Gregorowski & Seedat, 2013; Sroufe et al., 2009). The importance of early experiences in the development of the self was first elaborated in the 20th century by a branch of psychotherapy in the UK known as 'object relations'. Moving away from the earlier work of Freud, who had dismissed real experiences and relationships as less important than the gratification of inner drives and unconscious fantasies, psychoanalytic theorists such as Klein (1932), Winnicott (1965) and Bion (1962) postulated that children were primarily motivated by relationships with important others ('objects') rather than self-directed. The *actual* caregiving that children received was finally recognized as crucial to how children came to experience, understand and relate to themselves and the world around them.

Bowlby (1969) and Ainsworth and colleagues (1978) then built on this understanding through behaviourally oriented work, observing patterns and systems in how young children and their caregivers engaged and communicated with each other. They discovered that the provision of a 'secure base' by an emotionally engaged carer provides a facilitating environment from which children can begin to explore the world and engage with others (Allen, 2013). Their 'attachment theory' revealed the crucial role of safety and predictability in enabling children to start to organize their understanding of themselves and the world. Some critique of attachment theory is explored in Chapter 6.

Drawing on insights from object relations, attachment theory and neurobiology (how the brain and nervous system influence behaviour), Fonagy and colleagues theorized that infants require carers to comprehend and respond appropriately and consistently to their internal mental states (inner thoughts and feelings) in order to develop a solid sense of self (Fonagy, 2001; Fonagy, Gergely & Jurist, 2002; Fonagy, Gergely & Target, 2007). A 'mind-minded' or mentalizing caregiver is able to tolerate an infant's arousal, distress and frustration, make sense of their thoughts and feelings, and respond sensitively and empathically to their needs, mirroring, amplifying or soothing the child's affect as needed. Repeated experiences of such reliably attuned affect-regulation provide children with the message that their needs are valid, and their feelings can be borne and comprehended. An internal working model of the world and others as benign begins to be constructed and a pattern of what may be termed 'secure autonomous' relational behaviours might be observed (Landa & Duschinsky, 2013). These are associated with children who generally feel confident to approach others and are optimistic about receiving emotional warmth, protection and soothing. The seeds of self-identity, autonomy, confidence and relationality are hereby sown.

Having their needs and emotions understood and responded to consistently and congruently by the mentalizing caregiver – an experience of 'containment' (Bion, 1962) – helps children to learn experientially how to manage strong emotions and express thoughts and feelings constructively. This can enable children with neurotypical development trajectories to regulate their behaviour, tolerate their own frustration, control any aggressive, dangerous or damaging impulses and resolve conflicts with others in non-violent and non-coercive ways (Fonagy *et al.*, 2007). Through this they may begin to understand and assert their own needs and preferences, and recognize when others subvert these. Having been thought about in their own right, children are helped to begin to think for themselves and to comprehend other people. Their empathic engagement with the emotions, behaviours and intentions of others supports them in establishing and sustaining positive relationships (Collins *et al.*, 2006).

Reliable, responsive caregiving supports children in linking cause and effect, understanding right and wrong with regards to both their own and others' behaviour, and linking emotions to thoughts and behaviour (Coan, 2008). It then becomes more possible for them to assess safety and identify dangerous situations and negative behaviours in others. Their empathic engagement with the mental states of others also renders them less likely to want to cause harm themselves (Cook *et al.*, 2005). Children who have received encouragement and had their contributions valued tend to be more motivated to learn, more adaptable and more able to stick with challenges in the face of disappointment – capabilities that support them in managing school life successfully (Grossman & Grossman, 2019).

Of course, every child experiences a unique and dynamic set of circumstances; the lived life of the developmental journey is rarely neatly sequential or predictable (Wachs, 1999). Consistent and nurturing caregiving cannot prevent a child from experiencing challenging, unexpected or oppressive circumstances such as illness, bereavement, poverty and racism (Webb *et al.*, 2020). Disabled children all have their own unique potential and much more needs to be understood about which developmental outcomes might be realized in the context of particular conditions within optimal caregiving environments (Black & Lawn, 2018). While secure attachment relationships *seem* to make children less vulnerable to grooming and exploitation, they cannot guarantee a young person is safe from safeguarding risks beyond the family home, particularly during adolescence when peer relationships and external environments, including online, exert more attraction and influence (Firmin, 2020).

Nonetheless, there is reasonably robust evidence that the above mentioned elements are supportive of many children's future mental and physical health and wellbeing, creating a bedrock of resilience which means children are better able to weather the difficulties they encounter. Children without developmental trauma are more likely to have relationships with family and friends whom they trust and to whom they can go to for support, advice and protection (Shuker, 2013). Their stronger sense of self and capacity to recognize and value their own feelings will make them less vulnerable to grooming and coercion in adolescence (Lefevre *et al.*, 2017). Their more positive engagement in school and enhanced capacity for emotional self-regulation means they are less likely to get in trouble and be excluded – risk factors for engagement in criminality, anti-social behaviour and exploitative relationships and situations (Turner, Belcher & Pona, 2019).

When children's main caregivers are unable to provide this facilitating environment and emotional regulation, unthinkable levels of anxiety and distress can result. Winnicott (1965) described a state of 'primitive agonies' in the small infant who cannot integrate their sense of body, cognition and emotions because the (physical and psychological) holding and mirroring which knits these into coherent existence is absent. Children's sense of themselves as having validity and worth remains fragile and their affect is unregulated. Attachment theory suggests that children in such situations develop recognizable relational and behavioural patterns in an attempt to manage the overwhelming feelings generated, and to keep themselves as psychologically safe as possible.

Where the caregiver has been predictably misattuned or actively hostile, 'insecure-avoidant' strategies are thought to be more likely (Landa & Duschinsky, 2013). Children may learn to play down their needs and inhibit their affect in order to please their carers, or at least not antagonize them. Over time, they can become increasingly compliant and adaptive, failing to protest when their needs are ignored and their wishes over-ridden. Children may not develop an expectation that others will attend to their needs and so come to rely on themselves. The leap to imagining vulnerability to grooming by a future exploiter is not hard to make here.

'Insecure-ambivalent' strategies are more likely to develop for children whose parenting has been inconsistent (Landa & Duschinsky, 2013). At some points, the parent will have been warm and attuned, and at others preoccupied, emotionally volatile or overtly harmful. Because the child cannot predict their parent's response in any given situation, they cannot generate an ordered sense of the world. They may remain over-aroused, in an ongoing state of distress, and exaggerate their negative affect in an (often unconscious) attempt to bring the carer close and to generate holding and emotional regulation (Allen, 2013).

Neglect and abuse from those who should be most involved in nurturing and protecting a child disrupts these important developmental experiences still further. Some children who have experienced abuse have been noted to exhibit elements of both avoidant and ambivalent patterns alongside a disparate range of other behaviours. Hesse and Main (1999) categorized these strategies as 'disorganized attachment', theorizing that they resulted from the child's irreconcilable tasks of having to seek proximity with, and security from, caregivers who are actively frightening and/or do not have the wherewithal to protect them from danger.

Crittenden's (2000) dynamic-maturational model, in contrast, suggests that, in fact, this varied range of behaviours is highly organized in the face of extreme threat; it enables children to adapt and survive within the variety of home, peer, school and other social situations and relationships that children need to negotiate. The dynamic-maturational model aligns with Herman's (1992) understanding of early life trauma and the ways in which children find opportunities to organize their understanding of the world to keep themselves safe.

The diverse range of children's strategies noted by Crittenden includes compulsive caregiving or compliance (complex variations of insecure-avoidant) and punitive or submissive behaviour towards caregivers (complex variations of ambivalent) (Stacks, 2010). Whatever the categorization, these self-protective strategies prevent children from fully becoming who they are. Instead, they are left over-aroused and under-regulated, with a fragile sense of belonging, trust, self-esteem and self-efficacy (Landa & Duschinsky, 2013). Again, the links to developmental trauma and the resulting future vulnerability to extra-familial harm in adolescence can be readily made.

Some words of caution: foundations are not fate (Fraley & Roisman, 2019). Crittenden's model posits attachment as 'dynamic, that is, it is neither "hard-wired" nor fixed early in life, instead, it becomes increasingly complex with maturation and experience' (Stacks, 2010, p.211). A child's developmental trajectory is influenced by multiple, potentially competing, experiences and there is opportunity for change and growth through life, even when earlier experiences have been suboptimal, if the environmental conditions change (Sroufe et al., 2009).

We are learning more about these myriad influences all the time; disorganized attachment, for example, is now recognized to be correlated with 'grossly aversive' caregiver rejection, traumatic events, emotional dysregulation *and* the infant's own temperament (Duschinsky, 2018, p.27). Hence, we concur with White and colleagues (2020) that practitioners should avoid making concrete predictions about a child's future risk and vulnerability solely on the basis of earlier parenting experiences and/or childhood trauma.

We also caution against the tendency to attribute responsibility to parenting failures when a young person is caught up in risky, criminal or exploitative situations (Firmin, 2020). The varied social worlds of adolescents (both on- and off-line) offer multi-layered attractions and complexities for which many parents feel ill-equipped to prepare their children (Scott & McNeish, 2017). Even where caregiving has provided a child with a secure foundation, later experiences with peers and other extra-familial relationships and contexts may be sufficiently enticing, coercive or exploitative to override the self-awareness and resilience that this might have been expected to provide (Fraley & Roisman, 2019).

Nonetheless, an understanding of the extent to which a young person's psychosocial needs were met (or not) through their family life can provide important insights into both their vulnerability to risk in adolescence and to how professionals should intervene in developmentally reparative ways (Lefevre, 2008) if they are to engage and support young people who have experienced developmental trauma.

Reparative relationships

Sam's social worker Anne made long trips to visit him as often as she could while he was living with his father. When the placement broke down, she worked quickly to find supported independent accommodation. Sam occasionally got angry with Anne, refusing to work with her, but she persevered. The time she gave to their relationship was made possible by the lower caseloads given to her team, who all supported young people experiencing complex safeguarding risks. At one point, she brought in a colleague who would 'swap in and out a little bit', taking turns with her in an attempt to keep Sam engaged until he was ready to work solely with her again.

Anne's work with Sam continued to be characterized by persistence, an understanding of his behaviours as his own best efforts to stay safe, and genuine care for him as a child: 'I'm quite happy to say to Sam I absolutely love him to bits, and I do. I genuinely do, and I just think that is what allows you to effect any change in these kids' lives because, if you don't really give a shit and you're just being paid, and you see them once every six weeks, then why should they invest in anything that you're asking them to do? Why should they? This is their life and you're just this random person who's coming in and being paid to do so, and if you don't really care, then they see that. They can sniff you out a mile off.'

Sam's own description of his relationship with Anne several years later confirmed the strength of their relationship: 'No one can do this job, yeah, if you don't care, because every kid will look at you like…"Nah, fuck off, go away." I'm being real. I've told social workers to fuck off. I've told Anne to fuck off…but Anne was like, "No, I'm still worried about this kid." Still thinking about me after work. See, Anne will make sure where you're living, you're getting the right stuff, yeah, and everything's going correct, it's not going wrong. That's what Anne would do.' Anne reported how Sam had told her, several years down the line, 'Thank you for taking me out of that house… Thank you for taking me out of it, because other people didn't.'

Sam's latest placement is the most stable he has ever experienced, but he continues to struggle with anger outbursts. As Anne explained: 'It pops out of him, and why wouldn't it? When you hear what has happened to this boy, it's unbelievable that we don't see it more, I think.' She believed that the key element in facilitating his safety and positive progress thus far was relationships: 'They've saved that boy from spiralling more, because there's so much that he can spiral into, and, yes, those relationships have been absolutely key.' And Sam would probably agree. When asked what some of his strengths are, he replied: 'I'm strong and I'm determined. Everyone's said I'm, like, really brave and that I've come a long way. Like, my social worker's always saying I've come a long way. [And] it's about having the right people around you when you're surviving it.'

Sam's difficulty in accepting that Anne's warmth and positive regard was genuine is likely to have been connected directly with his earlier adverse experiences of caregiving. Sam could reasonably justify his lack of trust, as the people who should have loved and nurtured him (his adoptive parents) were not only withholding of care but actively abusive. A psychodynamic lens offers a further layer of understanding, though, when someone's responses are so fearful or hostile towards us as practitioners and substitute carers that it seems as if their emotions have no connection with who we are and what we are saying and doing. It is as if a malign relational template has been placed on us as a strong defence against the child or adult being hurt again: 'If I continue to think of you as bad, then I won't love you, and then I won't be destroyed when you leave me or harm me, as everyone always does.' Psychodynamic theory positions such as 'negative transference' are operating largely at an unconscious level as the intense feelings have come from very deep developmental trauma (Lefevre, 2008). The important implications of this are that healing also needs to happen at that deeper level, at a place of feeling rather than cognition (Fonagy *et al.*, 2002).

The account of Anne's working relationship with Sam demonstrates how she provided a facilitating environment over time that supported his recovery from developmental trauma. Anne listened to Sam with empathy, warmth and care over time, responding affectionately, reliably and persistently in the face of his hostility and resistance. He came to trust her and to understand that she cared about him in an authentic way. This experience of containment (Bion, 1962) is likely to have challenged Sam's internalized perception that he was not worthy of love, safety and nurture. It offered a space for him to think about himself and to understand Anne's motivations. As she accepted and worked with his affect, empathically attuning to his mood and managing the boundaries compassionately but firmly when he was angry, he came to recognize that his feelings could be borne, rather than needing to be denied, repressed or projected outwards. We might describe this as a reparative relationship – one that could start to address some of the ways in which the original parenting experience did not allow optimal development to be facilitated (Lefevre, 2008).

Understanding developmental trauma and attachment is essential in helping make sense of Sam's behaviour. As explored in Chapter 4, his story illustrates the constrained choices he faced in order to meet basic material and relational needs, and the sometimes counterproductive ways he sought to keep himself emotionally regulated and physically safe. This understanding enables professionals like Anne to recognize the primacy of relationships and the need to engage in relationship-based practice as essential to safeguarding him from future harm – taking time to get to know him, building trust, being open and congruent, and combining empathy, warmth and compassion with appropriate use of authority (Lefevre, 2018).

Trauma-informed practice

Professionals committed to relationship-based practice need a way of approaching traumatized young people that facilitates their ability to reconstruct a sense of safety and move forward with their lives. 'Trauma-informed practice' (TiP) recognizes the impact of prior trauma on behaviour and functioning, the role of relationships in creating safety, and the need for organizational culture change to ensure principles of safety, trust, choice, collaboration and empowerment (Harris & Fallot, 2001). It is a 'strengths-based framework grounded in an understanding of and responsiveness to the impact of trauma, that emphasises physical, psychological, and emotional safety for both providers and survivors, and that creates opportunities for survivors to rebuild a sense of control and empowerment' (Hopper, Bassuk & Olivet, 2010, p.82). The term was coined by Harris and Fallot (2001) who argued that health and human services in the United States had not been designed to account for the impact traumatic experiences have in people's lives. They described TiP as a paradigm shift, re-centring trauma survivors' strengths (i.e., their ability to stay alive and safe) and needs in order to mitigate the impact of trauma and facilitate their recovery (thus reducing the need to continue using these services). TiP guides a reorientation towards trauma healing and holistic wellbeing for staff and young people alike.

Research on TiP has developed throughout the last 15 years, with evidence of trauma-informed approaches implemented beyond the United States where it originated, into Canada, New Zealand, Australia and the United Kingdom (Sweeney et al., 2016). Evaluations of TiP interventions with children and young people indicate their effectiveness in reducing problem behaviours and trauma responses (Bartlett et al., 2016; Becker, Greenwald & Mitchell, 2011; Murphy et al., 2017). In order to adopt a trauma-informed approach to practice, professionals must begin by reconceptualizing negative or problematic behaviour as coping strategies that were once functional and even necessary during the traumatic experience (Levenson, 2017). Thus, the behaviours that might have previously seemed irrational or self-destructive (e.g., Sam's repeated punching of walls and destruction of property and his difficulty trusting adults) can be reframed for both professionals and young people as important survival skills that now inhibit their ability to manage stress, incorporate positive coping skills and make accurate assessments of safety in relationships and environments.

In addition to understanding the impact of trauma and the role of trauma responses in keeping young people safe, TiP also involves:

- ensuring that the environments where young people access services are physically and psychologically safe

- prioritizing trust, transparency and truthfulness, mutuality, and opportunities to interact with survivors of similar traumatic experiences via peer support

- recognizing the historical, cultural and gendered contexts that have contributed to young people's experiences of trauma

- whenever possible, facilitating access to trauma-specific care such as trauma therapy and specialist mental health services

- making every effort to avoid re-traumatizing young people, especially when safeguarding procedures are likely to do so

- offering opportunities whenever possible to enable young people to have choice and control over their lives.

(Christie, 2018; Knight, 2015; Levenson, 2017; Substance Abuse and Mental Health Services Administration, 2014)

The latter point, emphasized further in Chapter 9, was found to be particularly important in a recent study with young people receiving trauma-informed care (Hickle, 2020). When describing how professionals helped them feel safe, the 18 young people in Hickle's (2020) study spoke about being given choices (even when these were limited) and opportunities to participate in decision-making. They also described how professionals connected with them and built trusting relationships through persistence, authenticity, and in creating the physical and mental space for them to experience feeling calm, regulated and able to achieve things that mattered to them.

The emphasis on choice and control has particular relevance for young people victimized by exploitative relationships. Often, feeling unsafe begins while being controlled by perpetrators who make decisions for them in relation to what they did, where they went and who they could have contact with. Their feelings of unsafety (and maladaptive efforts to self-regulate) continue when professionals' efforts to keep them safe over-emphasize policing their behaviour (Hickle, 2018) via the use of out-of-home placements, curfews and mandates to avoid contexts where they may experience harm.

Young people are more likely to stay engaged when professionals engage collaboratively to create safety in partnership *with* them and prioritize making the contexts within which they live safer and freer from exploitation and abuse (Firmin, 2017). Indeed, McKenzie-Mohr and colleagues (2011) emphasize the need for services adopting TiP to incorporate an understanding of the ways in which structural conditions and the contexts in which young people live contribute to their intersecting experiences of oppression and trauma. As discussed in Chapter 5, a robust, holistic understanding of TiP necessarily involves engaging with the socio-political conditions that facilitate the abuse and trauma that young people experience. This includes designing trauma-informed interventions that encompass social and geographic contexts, identifying when structural conditions traumatize young people, and prioritizing resources to ensure safe housing and relational safety through engagement with staff who are culturally responsive (Treisman, 2018) and 'skilled in engaging with young people's intersecting experiences of oppression and trauma' (Hickle, 2020, p.547).

Conclusion

Throughout this chapter, we have proposed that understanding developmental trauma and attachment theory is useful for making sense of the feelings, motivations and behaviours of young people who have experienced caregiving privations or abuse in early childhood and who are encountering risky, anti-social, abusive and exploitative extra-familial contexts within adolescence. We offer relationship-based practice and trauma-informed practice as complementary frameworks that can provide professionals with the tools they need to facilitate relational repair and create conditions in which young people can heal, grow and thrive and be able to risk trusting and loving again.

It is important to note that this kind of transformative work can only be sustained within organizational contexts that provide practitioners with the practical support they need to be creative, flexible and persistent in engaging young people. Anne would have found it extremely difficult, if not impossible, to have provided this time and commitment without the support of her organization. The degree of emotional labour required in such emotionally charged environments can be intolerable for an individual to hold, potentially resulting in sickness, burnout and emotional detachment (Lefevre *et al.*, 2017). It is notable that Anne's team were given sufficient time to sustain their relationships with young people, and co-working was available to take the strain when Sam's hostility became hard to bear. Supervision is the other essential factor in ensuring that the container of the child is themselves contained, and workers can continue to 'mentalize' for the child (Ruch, 2007). Even in briefer working relationships, such interactions can help provide a foundation for the development of resilience (Iwaniec, Larkin & Higgins, 2006).

In considering the professional relationship between Anne and Sam presented in this chapter, we have been able to see how achievable trauma-informed practice can be. Anne was able to recognize some of Sam's challenging behaviours (e.g., 'anger outbursts') as evidence of his past trauma and reframe his adaptive survival instincts as strengths. She understood the importance of engaging persistently and authentically with Sam, and the centrality of providing a facilitative environment for healing. In adopting a trauma-informed approach, Anne was able to focus on helping Sam feel safe in his relationship with her, thus helping him acquire the capabilities he missed out on developing earlier in life (Hickle, 2020). Going forward, it is hoped that these will help Sam to manage stress, regulate his emotions and re-learn how to interact with the world from a place of safety, trust and possibility.

References

Ainsworth, M.D., Blehar, M., Waters, E. & Wall, S. (1978). *Patterns of Attachment: A Psychological Study of the Strange Situation.* Mahwah, NJ: Lawrence Erlbaum.

Allen, J. (2013). *Mentalizing in the Development and Treatment of Attachment Trauma.* London: Routledge.

Asmussen, K., Fischer, F., Drayton, E. & McBride, T. (2020*). Adverse Childhood Experiences: What We Know, What We Don't Know, and What Should Happen Next.* London: Early Intervention Foundation.

Bartlett, J.D., Barto, B., Griffin, J.L., Fraser, J.G., Hodgdon, H. & Bodian, R. (2016). 'Trauma-informed care in the Massachusetts child trauma project.' *Child Maltreatment, 21*(2), 101–112. https://doi.org/10.1177/1077559515615700.

Becker, J., Greenwald, R. & Mitchell, C. (2011). 'Trauma-informed treatment for disenfranchised urban children and youth: An open trial.' *Child and Adolescent Social Work Journal, 28*(4), 257–272. https://doi.org/10.1007/s10560-011-0230-4.

Bion, W.R. (1962). *Learning from Experience.* London: Heinemann.

Black, M. & Lawn, J. (2018). 'Early childhood developmental disabilities – data still needed.' *The Lancet, 6*(10). https://doi.org/10.1016/S2214-109X(18)30399-1.

Bowlby, J. (1969). *Attachment. Attachment and Loss: Vol. 1.* New York, NY: Basic Books.

Burack, J.A., Flanagan, T., Peled, T., Sutton, H.M., Zygmuntowicz, C. & Manly, J.T. (2006). 'Social perspective-taking skills in maltreated children and adolescents.' *Developmental Psychology, 42*(2), 207–217. https://doi.org/10.1037/0012-1649.42.2.207.

Bush, M. (ed.) (2018). *Addressing Adversity.* Young Minds.

Christie, C. (2018). *A Trauma-Informed Health and Care Approach for Responding to Child Sexual Abuse and Exploitation Current Knowledge Report.* London: Department of Health and Social Care. https://assets.publishing.service.gov.uk/government/uploads/system/uploads/attachment_data/file/712725/trauma-informed-health-and-care-approach-report.pdf.

Coan, J.A. (2008). 'Toward a Neuroscience of Attachment.' In J. Cassidy & P.R. Shaver (eds) *Handbook of Attachment: Theory, Research, and Clinical Applications* (second edition, pp.241–265). New York, NY: Guilford Press.

Collins, N.L., Ford, M.B., Guichard, A.C. & Allard, L.M. (2006). 'Working models of attachment and attribution processes in intimate relationships.' *Personality and Social Psychology Bulletin, 32*, 201–219. https://doi.org/10.1177/0146167205280907.

Cook, A., Spinazzola, J., Ford, J., Lanktree, C. *et al.* (2005). 'Complex trauma in children and adolescents.' *Psychiatric Annals, 35*(5), 390–398.

Crittenden, P. (2000). 'A Dynamic-Maturational Approach to Continuity and Change in Pattern of Attachment.' In P. Crittenden & A. Claussen (eds) *The Organisation of Attachment Relationships: Maturation Culture and Context* (pp.343–357). Cambridge: Cambridge University Press.

D'Andrea, W., Ford, J., Stolbach, B., Spinazzola, J. & van der Kolk, B.A. (2012). 'Understanding interpersonal trauma in children: Why we need a developmentally appropriate trauma diagnosis.' *American Journal of Orthopsychiatry, 82*(2), 187–200. https://doi.org/10.1111/j.1939-0025.2012.01154.x.

Duschinsky, R. (2018). 'Disorganization, fear and attachment: Working towards clarification.' *Infant Mental Health Journal, 39*(1), 17–29. https://doi.org/10.1002/imhj.21689.

Felitti, V.J., Anda, R.F., Nordenberg, D., Williamson, D.F. *et al.* (1998). 'Relationship of childhood abuse and household dysfunction to many of the leading causes of death in adults: The Adverse Childhood Experiences (ACE) Study.' *American Journal of Preventive Medicine, 14*(4), 245–258. https://doi.org/10.1016/S0749-3797(98)00017-8.

Firmin, C. (2017). *Abuse Between Young People: A Contextual Account.* London: Routledge.

Firmin, C. (2020). *Contextual Safeguarding and Child Protection: Rewriting the Rules.* London: Routledge.

Fonagy, P. (2001). *Attachment Theory and Psychoanalysis.* New York, NY: Other Press.

Fonagy, P., Gergely, G. & Jurist, E. (2002). *Affect Regulation, Mentalization and the Development of the Self.* New York, NY: Other Press.

Fonagy, P., Gergely, G. & Target, M. (2007). 'The parent–infant dyad and the construction of the subjective self.' *Journal of Child Psychology and Psychiatry, 48*(3–4), 288–328. https://doi.org/10.1111/j.1469-7610.2007.01727.x.

Fraley, R.C. & Roisman, G.I. (2019). 'The development of adult attachment styles: Four lessons.' *Current Opinion in Psychology, 25*, 26–30. https://doi.org/10.1016/j.copsyc.2018.02.008.

Gregorowski, C. & Seedat, S. (2013). 'Addressing childhood trauma in a developmental context.' *Journal of Child and Adolescent Mental Health, 25*(2), 105–118. https://dx.doi.org/10.2989/17280583.2013.795154.

Grossmann, K. & Grossmann, K.E. (2019). 'The Impact of Attachment to Mother and Father and Sensitive Support of Exploration at an Early Age on Children's Psychosocial Development through Young Adulthood.' In R.E. Tremblay, M. Boivin, R. DeV. Peters & M.H. van IJzendoorn (eds) *Encyclopedia on Early Childhood Development.* www.child-encyclopedia.com/attachment/according-experts/impact-attachment-mother-and-father-and-sensitive-support-exploration.

Harris, M. & Fallot, R.D. (2001). 'Envisioning a trauma-informed service system: A vital paradigm shift.' *New Directions for Mental Health Services, 89*, 3–22. https://doi.org/10.1002/yd.23320018903.

Herman, J. (1992). *Trauma and Recovery: The Aftermath of Violence from Domestic Abuse to Political Terror.* New York, NY: Basic Books.

Hesse, E. & Main, M. (1999). 'Second-generation effects of unresolved trauma in nonmaltreating parents: Dissociated, frightened, and threatening parental behavior.' *Psychoanalytic Inquiry, 19*(4), 481–540. https://doi.org/10.1080/07351699909534265.

Hickle, K. (2018). *Trauma Informed Evaluation Report.* YMCA Downslink Group/University of Sussex.

Hickle, K. (2020). 'Introducing a trauma-informed capability approach in youth services.' *Children & Society, 34*(6), 537–551. https://doi.org/10.1111/chso.12388.

Hopper, E., Bassuk, L.E. & Olivet, J. (2010). 'Shelter from the storm: Trauma-informed care in homelessness services settings. *The Open Health Services and Policy Journal, 3*(1), 80–100. www.mappingthemaze.org.uk/wp-content/uploads/2017/08/ARTL-Hopper-Et-Al-TIC-Homelessness-2010.pdf.

Iwaniec, D., Larkin, E. & Higgins, S. (2006). 'Research Review: Risk and resilience in cases of emotional abuse.' *Child & Family Social Work, 11*(1), 73–82. https://doi.org/10.1111/j.1365-2206.2006.00398.x.

Klein, M. (1932). *The Psycho-Analysis of Children: The Writings of Melanie Klein, Volume 2.* The International Psycho-analytical Library, No. 22.

Knight, C. (2015). 'Trauma-informed social work practice: Practice considerations and challenges.' *Clinical Social Work Journal, 43*(1), 25–37. https://doi.org/10.1080/07325223.2018.1440680.

Landa, S. & Duschinsky, R. (2013). 'Crittenden's dynamic–maturational model of attachment and adaptation.' *Review of General Psychology, 17*(3), 326–338. https://doi.org/10.1037/a0032102.

Lefevre, M. (2008). 'Assessment and Decision-Making in Child Protection: Relationship-Based Considerations.' In M.C. Calder (ed.) *The Carrot or the Stick? Towards Effective Practice with Involuntary Clients in Safeguarding Children Work* (pp.78–92). Lyme Regis: Russell House Publishing.

Lefevre, M. (2018). *Communicating and Engaging with Children and Young People: Making a Difference.* Bristol: Policy Press.

Lefevre, M., Hickle, K. & Luckock, B. (2019). '"Both/and" not "either/or": Reconciling rights to protection and participation in working with child sexual exploitation.' *The British Journal of Social Work, 49*(7), 1837–1855. https://doi.org/10.1093/bjsw/bcy106.

Lefevre, M., Hickle, K., Luckock, B. & Ruch, G. (2017). 'Building trust with children and young people at risk of child sexual exploitation: The professional challenge.' *The British Journal of Social Work, 47*(8), 2456–2473. https://doi.org/10.1093/bjsw/bcw181.

Levenson, J. (2017). 'Trauma-informed social work practice.' *Social Work, 62*(2), 105–113.

McKenzie-Mohr, S., Coates, J. & McLeod, H. (2011). 'Responding to the needs of youth who are homeless: Calling for politicised trauma-informed intervention.' *Child and Youth Services Review, 34*(1), 136–143. https://doi.org/10.1016/j.childyouth.2011.09.008.

Murphy, K., Moore, K.A., Redd, Z. & Malm, K. (2017). 'Trauma-informed child welfare systems and children's well-being: A longitudinal evaluation of KVCs bridging the way home initiative.' *Children and Youth Services Review, 75*, 23–34. https://doi.org/10.1016/j.childyouth.2017.02.008.

Ruch, G. (2007). 'Reflective practice in contemporary child-care social work: The role of containment.' *The British Journal of Social Work, 37*(4), 659–680. https://doi.org/10.1093/bjsw/bch277.

Scott, S. & McNeish, D. (2017). *Supporting Parents of Sexually Exploited Young People: An Evidence Review.* Centre of Expertise on Child Sexual Abuse. www.csacentre.org.uk/documents/evidence-review-by-sara-scott-and-di-mcneish-dmss-research.

Shuker, L. (2013). 'Constructs of Safety for Children in Care Affected by Sexual Exploitation.' In M. Melrose & J. Pearce (ed.) *Critical Perspectives on Child Sexual Exploitation and Related Trafficking* (pp.125–138). London: Palgrave Macmillan.

Sroufe, L.A., Egeland, B., Carlson, E.A. & Collins, W.A. (2009). *The Development of the Person: The Minnesota Study of Risk and Adaptation from Birth to Adulthood.* New York, NY: Guilford Press.

Stacks, A. (2010). 'Self-protective strategies are adaptive and increasingly complex: A beginner's look at the DMM and ABCD models of attachment.' *Clinical Child Psychology and Psychiatry, 15*(2), 209–214. https://doi.org/10.1177/1359104509355670.

Substance Abuse and Mental Health Services Administration (SAMHSA) (2014). *SAMHSA's Concept of Trauma and Guidance for a Trauma-Informed Approach*. https://ncsacw.samhsa. gov/userfiles/files/SAMHSA_Trauma.pdf.

Sweeney, A., Clement, S., Filson, B. & Kennedy, A. (2016). 'Trauma-informed mental healthcare in the UK: What is it and how can we further its development?' *Mental Health Review Journal*, 21(3), 174–192. https://doi.org/10.1108/MHRJ-01-2015-0006.

Teague, C.M. (2013). 'Developmental trauma disorder: A provisional diagnosis.' *Journal of Aggression, Maltreatment & Trauma*, 22(6), 611–625. https://doi.org/10.1080/10926771.20 13.804470.

Treisman, K. (2018). *Becoming a More Culturally, Adversity, and Trauma-Informed, Infused, and Responsive Organisation*. London: Winston Churchill Memorial Trust.

Turner, A., Belcher, L. & Pona, I. (2019). *Counting Lives: Responding to Children who are Criminally Exploited*. The Children's Society. www.childrenssociety.org.uk/what-we-do/ resources-and-publications/counting-lives-report.

van der Kolk, B. (2014). *The Body Keeps the Score: Mind, Brain and Body in the Transformation of Trauma*. London: Penguin.

van der Kolk, B.A. (2017). 'Developmental trauma disorder: Toward a rational diagnosis for children with complex trauma histories.' *Psychiatric Annals*, 35(5), 401–408. https://doi. org/10.3928/00485713-20050501-06.

Wachs, T. (1999). 'The nature and nurture of child development.' *Food and Nutrition Bulletin*, 20(1), 7–21. https://doi.org/10.1177/156482659902000103.

Webb, C., Bywaters, P., Scourfield, J., Davidson, G. & Bunting, L. (2020). 'Cuts both ways: Ethnicity, poverty, and the social gradient in child welfare interventions.' *Children and Youth Services Review*, 117(13), 105299. https://doi.org/10.1016/j.childyouth.2020.105299.

White, S., Gibson, M., Wastell, D. & Walsh, P. (2020). *Reassessing Attachment Theory in Child Welfare*. Bristol: Policy Press.

Winnicott, D. (1965). *The Maturational Process and the Facilitating Environment*. London: Hogarth Press.

Chapter 9

Nothing About Me Without Me

Nicky Hill and Camille Warrington

This chapter aims to provide an overview of how participation and empowerment-focused approaches can promote improved relational practice and outcomes for young people in safeguarding. It builds on learning from emerging practice in interrelated disciplines such as youth and community work, social work, youth justice and adult safeguarding.

Introduction

'I think what gets missed when we talk about safeguarding children a lot is this capacity that children have to keep themselves safe and they play a big role in that – I think that gets overlooked.' (Young Research Advisory Panel (YRAP)[1] member speaking in Hamilton *et al.*, 2019)

'Participation', 'empowerment' and 'co-production' represent familiar rhetoric in safeguarding and welfare support for adolescents. These terms are often used to communicate policy and service level intentions about young people's involvement in the planning, decision-making and implementation of actions which support an individual's safety and wellbeing (HM Government, 1989; United Nations, 1989). Yet meaningful demonstration of these concepts, and evidence of their integration within organizational cultures, remains patchy, superficial or tokenistic at best (Beresford, 2012; Brodie, 2016; Crowley & Larkins, 2018; Rosa *et al.*, 2019; Shuker, 2013; Warrington, 2016). In this

---

1   The Young Research Advisory Panel (YRAP) is a group of young people based at the University of Bedfordshire who support research, policy and practice relating to sexual violence and related forms of harm, drawing on youth perspectives and lived experience.

chapter, we reflect on this issue, presenting evidence of these gaps and considering:

- what we mean by 'participation' and 'empowerment-focused approaches' with adolescents

- the rationale for prioritizing these approaches when safeguarding adolescents

- key considerations and principles for implementing them in practice – including recognition of the need for systems level change.

Understanding participation and empowerment

Before thinking in more detail about the need for, and delivery of, participatory and empowerment approaches, it's important to consider what we mean by these contested terms. While it's clear there is no singular definition of either term, both reflect an interest in challenging traditional power relations and supporting the influence of those usually marginalized from decision-making processes.

In relation to children and young people, the language of participation remains strongly associated with Article 12 of the United Nations Convention on the Rights of the Child (UNCRC) (United Nations, 1989) but it is also a central principle of UK child protection, first seen within the Children Act (HM Government, 1989) and reflected in policy since (HM Government, 2018).

In these contexts, participation reflects the rights of individuals or groups to be involved in decision-making about issues affecting them, in keeping with their evolving capacity. Yet what this means in practice varies significantly. For example, at the individual level, this might mean a young person's presence and active involvement in a care review meeting (Diaz, Pert & Thomas, 2019) or, at a collective level, the influence of a young disabled rights group lobbying for educational policy change (Brady & Franklin, 2019).

As Lundy (2007) notes, interpretations also differ in the degree to which they limit participation rights to a focus on 'hearing children and young people's voices' strive for evidence of young people's influence, 'clout' (Houghton, 2018) and associated actions (Warrington & Larkin, 2019). Additionally, despite the presence of significant participatory rhetoric and examples of good practice, more systematic prioritization of participatory principles in work to support adolescents remains patchy, stymied as much by resource constraints and organizational cultures as individual will.

Arguably, the language of empowerment, though related, represents a more radical extension of this thinking. Adams (2008), writing in the context of adult social work, defines empowerment as 'the capacity of individuals, groups and/or communities to take control of their circumstances, exercise power and achieve their own goals and the process by which individually and collectively they are able to help themselves and others to maximise the quality of their lives' (2008, p.xvi). Whereas participatory approaches are often associated with the involvement of individuals in processes that are designed, instigated and controlled by those with institutional power, empowerment approaches may be taken to encompass work that enables individuals to achieve goals independently of institutional control, or community-led initiatives where professional roles are ancillary.

The language of empowerment also represents a foundational underpinning in the field of youth and community work (Jeffs & Smith, 2008) associated with the work of Freire (1970) and reflecting some shared ethos with adult social work practice (see Chapter 10). Unsurprisingly, empowerment initiatives within youth work often seek to address concerns straddling the lives of both young people and adults such as poverty, racism and other forms of structural injustice (Zheng, 2018). However, a consideration of empowerment is less evident within discourses associated with child protection and safeguarding. Where present, considerations of empowerment tend to be limited to work with parents and carers (McCallum & Prilleltensky, 1996). Perhaps, as noted elsewhere in this book, this reflects the legacy of a system historically focused on much younger children for whom such approaches seem a less obvious fit. Yet, in work with young people, the absence feels particularly notable, especially given the centrality of the principle of empowerment in both adult safeguarding policy (HM Government, 2014; Lawson, Lewis & Williams, 2014) and trauma-informed practice (see Chapter 8). Similarly, its importance has also been highlighted by adult service user movements, highlighting the need to counter oppressive and marginalizing tendencies in systems nominally designed to care (Adams, 2008; Beresford & Carr, 2012).

Unsurprisingly, approaches in practice to both empowerment and participation are fraught with tension. This is particularly true within the field of child safeguarding where protection and participation rights have long been noted as uneasy bedfellows (Archard, 2004; Coppock & Phillips, 2013; Lefevre, Hickle & Luckock, 2019; Warrington, 2013). Yet despite this seeming tension, growing calls highlight a need to further prioritize participatory and empowerment approaches in order to effectively safeguard young people, thereby better recognizing the interdependency of these concepts (Lefevre, Hickle & Luckock, 2019; Warrington & Larkin, 2019).

Square pegs in round holes: Adolescents in a child protection system

'[Social workers] don't talk to you as a human being – don't talk to you as an adult. They talk to you like a five year old or summat' (Phoebe, 17). (Warrington, 2013)

Another important part of the context for this chapter is recognition that adolescent safeguarding brings many unique challenges, not least the increasing focus on extra-familial and community-based harm reflected in revised *Working Together to Safeguard Children* documentation (HM Government, 2018 (and updated 2020)). As noted previously in this book, this shift brings many more adolescents under the radar of child protection systems, with different developmental needs from younger children and distinct experiences often rooted in fast-evolving contextual harms (Firmin, 2017). Learning from serious case reviews, rapid reviews and child safeguarding practice reviews has highlighted the disconnect between existing child protection structures and the needs, agency and evolving autonomy of adolescents (Firmin, 2018).

As noted in previous chapters and explored further in Chapter 10, one of the well-cited challenges facing both young people and those supporting them is the liminal and transitional status of adolescence – a kind of borderlands space in the life course when individuals are caught between the paternalistic structures and approaches designed for younger children, and the increasing responsibilities and expectations of adulthood. As the quote above from Phoebe indicates, for those using services this results in a sense of discord – a gulf between how they feel and how they are treated (Coleman, 2011; Raby, 2006).

A key aspect of this ambiguity is the degree to which adolescents are perceived and responded to as active citizens or as citizens in waiting – a consideration further complicated when their identities are also characterized as 'service users' or 'children in need of protection'. These dynamics in turn may be further exacerbated by other intersecting aspects of a young person's identity such as disability, ethnicity or class (considered in more depth by Davis and Marsh (2020) and in Chapter 6 of this volume).

For young people who have experienced forms of abuse, harm or exploitation, including experiences such as addiction or homelessness, these tensions are likely to have a heightened meaning – contrasting aspects of their lives which involved them in extremely 'adult' worlds with treatment according to a particularly narrow and restrictive concept of childhood. Evidence suggests that this in turn may contribute to young people's secrecy with professionals who they often feel simply don't understand them or the spaces in which they live, further distancing them from opportunities for support (Cossar *et al.*, 2013). In fact, as discussed in the previous chapter, when young people are moving from exploitative or highly coercive circumstances to supportive interventions, the need to maximize their sense of power and control is all the more pertinent, countering the abusive dynamics they are moving from and enabling them to engage with forms of support that feel distinctly different.

Yet we know that young people (both individually and collectively) remain distanced from many of the meaningful decision-making structures, designed to protect them, and subsequently are excluded from discussions about creating change in both their lives and their communities.

This means opportunities to further enable young people's safety are being missed. This happens in two, seemingly opposing, ways. First, minimizing young people's exposure to professionals who are, at best, a vital resource for young people and, second, preventing professionals' access to the expertise and insights that young people have into their own lives. Where this does happen, it can leave gaps in professional understanding and missed opportunities for developing relational working practices (White, Morris & Featherstone, 2014). Resulting interventions and risk mitigation approaches are subsequently often 'done to' young people, rather than 'with them', thereby minimizing the crucial 'buy-in' of young people to actuate change.

At an individual level, examples of how this operates can be seen in research demonstrating the patchy and inconsistent involvement of 'looked after' or sexually exploited young people in meetings about their care (Diaz, 2021; Warrington, 2013). Other particularly stark examples of young people's absence from decision-making spaces can be seen in serious case reviews, such as one following the murder of 'Chris' in Newham, London (Hill, 2018). This review notes the significant absence of both 'Chris' himself, or someone representing his views, from multiple meetings convened to explore, discuss and mitigate the risks he faced. This pattern is a familiar and long-standing one which overlooks both the rights of, and potential for, young people to work collaboratively with professionals to support their safety.

Yet we have also seen elsewhere in this book a parallel challenge – the dangers of 'adultification' (see Chapter 6) – overlooking adolescent vulnerability and their needs and entitlement for protection as children. At its core, the challenge is about striking the right balance to avoid either failing to recognize young people's skills and capacities and reinforcing their sense of being controlled, or overlooking their vulnerabilities and responsibilizing them.

Why does participation and empowerment matter when working to keep adolescents safe?

'I think what participation does is, it engages a young person in a process where their safety, their health, their wellbeing is thought about and cherished… It tells a young person that they are worth protecting.' (YRAP member speaking in Hamilton et al., 2019)

Having outlined our understanding of participatory and empowerment practices within adolescent safeguarding, and some of the associated challenges, we turn to think about the rationale for addressing these challenges. This feels particularly important given the implications for resources and organizational cultures. Arguably there are different (though interrelated) ways of approaching this, depending on whether we see participation and empowerment as a 'means' or an 'end' in themselves.

Participation and empowerment as an 'end'
On the one hand, we recognize that a young person's participation rights and their empowerment are clear 'ends' in and of themselves

– enshrined as rights in both national and international law (Children Act 1989; UNCRC 1989). This approach champions active and civic participation as an inalienable right which must be upheld by the institutions which govern and interact in young people's lives. However, and particularly for young people experiencing the most significant risks, when professionals are faced with competing 'asks' and limited resources, efforts to promote the active involvement of a young person in decision-making can be overlooked or there may be a struggle to prioritize it. This suggests there may also be merit in promoting an understanding of participation and empowerment as a 'means' to achieving broader organizational and policy goals relating to safeguarding.

Participation and empowerment as a 'means'

Understanding participation and protection rights as mutually dependent provides another clear rationale for a fuller integration of these approaches in adolescent safeguarding. Through this lens, participation and related empowerment approaches are a 'means' to achieving well-being and safety. Arguably, this works through a range of mechanisms.

Perhaps the most obvious of these is the aforementioned potential for participatory approaches to improve young people's motivation to engage actively in activities or initiatives designed to minimize risk and keep them safe (Hamilton *et al.*, 2019), thus bringing them into closer contact and more effective relational practice with the resource that is professional expertise and support. This echoes lessons from adult safeguarding (Preston-Shoot, 2020) where user involvement is positioned as key to active engagement with safeguarding.

As noted above, without the 'buy-in' of young people, professionals' efforts to fulfil safeguarding duties are likely to be significantly limited – even where professionals are able to enforce immediate physical safety on a young person. For example, placing a young person in secure accommodation or detaining them under the Mental Health Act (1983) provides no guarantee that their relational or psychological safety needs will be met (Shuker, 2013). Meeting this more holistic set of needs requires young people's active engagement, highlighting the need for more collaborative, relational and participatory approaches to enable longer term protection (ibid.).

Elsewhere, literature identifies the consequences for safeguarding when relational safety and support are not prioritized (Folgheraiter,

2004; Geddes, 2006; Ruch, 2005). This includes the myriad of ways in which young people can use their agency, in spite of institutional parameters or restrictions to 'resist'[2] the impact or intention of an intervention when they have not been granted influence or ownership over its nature. Such actions represent young people's exercise of agency independent of (and often in conflict with) the plans and intentions of the professionals charged to protect and care for them.

Research conducted with young people accessing support for child sexual exploitation identified a range of ways in which they minimized their engagement with an intervention if they felt a lack of trust and ownership over safeguarding processes nominally designed to support them (Warrington, 2013). Through avoiding or challenging services, failing to share information or providing partial information, young people described conscious efforts to minimize professional involvement and framed it as protective on their own terms. Understanding the protective motivations of actions that may appear to professionals as antagonistic or short-sighted aligns to trauma-informed practices, which recognize such behaviours as adaptive responses to trauma (Levenson, 2017).

These examples remind us that efforts to work in more participatory (and subsequently relational) ways do more than just uphold young people's rights. They also enable a professional's safeguarding role to be more meaningful and effective. Equally, they serve as an important reminder that the growing agency and autonomy of adolescents means increasingly *they* decide who to collaborate with and which professionals' authority they will allow in order to keep them safe.

Another way in which participation and empowerment can be viewed as a means of supporting young people to thrive, experience wellbeing and access social justice is through their role in countering a sense of powerlessness and supporting self-efficacy. Evidence tells us that experiences of powerlessness, such as those associated with exposure to trauma (Substance Abuse and Mental Health Services Administration, 2014), are regularly compounded through welfare interventions that fail to consider young people's need for maximizing choice and control (Hallett, 2017; Hickle, 2020).

In circumstances where welfare professionals speak for or silence young people, make decisions without young people and minimize their

---

2   In this context, resistance is understood as 'when youth resist interventions, dominant cultural norms, or pressures by caregivers' (Ungar, 2004, p.75).

influence (intentionally or inadvertently), the dynamics of so-called 'support' and 'care' may replicate or be reminiscent of abusive dynamics. Here, interventions may be experienced as triggering or re-traumatizing. This is seen within research on youth homelessness (Hickle, 2020), young people affected by sexual violence (Beckett & Warrington, 2015; Bovarnick & Cody, 2020), and care experienced young people (Ward, Skuse & Munro, 2005).

Efforts to counter these dynamics, through maximizing marginalized young people's involvement in decision-making and interventions designed to empower, are known to build self-efficacy[3] and address the impacts of trauma (Bulanda & Johnson, 2016; Hickle, 2020). Increased self-efficacy is itself regularly associated with an improved sense of wellbeing and the ability to cope (ibid.). As Ginwright (2010) notes, for individuals who have experienced different forms of trauma, healing and (subsequently) meaningful safety are only possible when they are supported to foster a sense of optimism and are empowered to claim their rights and access justice in its broadest sense.

Interestingly, the role of justice within safeguarding is rarely considered or discussed. Yet the threats to young people's wellbeing and safety which social care and wider welfare services are dealing with are almost always rooted in some form of injustice. Supporting young people to experience forms of active citizenship and demonstrating these processes within safeguarding can serve to model their ability to claim their rights and challenge individuals or structures that stand in the way of their realization.[4]

It also highlights recognition that many of the challenges and threats to young people's wellbeing (e.g., racism, poverty, inequality) require collective efforts to bring about change – not only self-efficacy but also collective efficacy (Bandura, 1982), a belief that working with others can influence change. In this way, young people's experiences of activism, campaigning and protest may themselves need to be considered as crucial aspects of creating a safe society for their peers and for future young people.

This presents a radically different view of what we mean by safeguarding, moving away from a solely individual focus. This, in turn,

---

3   Self-efficacy is understood as an individual's perception of their ability to effect change (Bandura, 1982).
4   For a more detailed example of this type of work see the Our Voices Youth Advocacy project outlined in Bovarnick and Cody (2020).

may align to approaches seen elsewhere in this book, which demonstrate the need to work with young people collectively within peer groups or communities to address particular contextual challenges to safety (Firmin, 2020). So too might we need stronger calls for more radical youth, community work and advocacy approaches, utilizing group work models and supporting young people's campaigning and activism skills (Davies, 2005).

Putting principles into practice

If, as we hope to have outlined above, participation and empowerment are fundamental for creating meaningful safety in young people's lives, how, then, do we realize and adopt these approaches in practice? As the evidence above suggests, there are relatively few blueprints for how to 'do participation and empowerment' meaningfully in the field of adolescent safeguarding. Yet elements of encouraging practice do exist and the evidence base points towards some key principles which might offer a framework for developing practice.

We have tried to suggest a number of these below, highlighting their significance and suggesting ways in which they may be fostered in safeguarding practice. We focus on seven areas:

- Relational practice

- Effective communication and active listening

- Supporting young people to make informed choices

- Strengths-based approaches

- Owning and sharing stories with care and purpose

- Supporting young people's involvement in formal decision-making

- Managing and holding risk and conflict.

This is not an exhaustive list; many of these principles overlap and intersect. Rather, this section hopes to stimulate thinking for practitioners, managers, policy makers and funders alike, and has relevance at local, regional and national levels, to support reflection on whether and how these principles can be made real for young people in need of protection.

Relational practice

'They [the police] were nice, don't get me wrong, but they were just … the way some of them looked at you…I felt like I were like a piece of meat, I was like "I don't like this", it were awful.' (16-year-old young woman, Beckett *et al.*, 2015)

We know that for effective participation and empowerment to take place, it requires a foundation of good relational practice. As noted above, so much of effective safeguarding practice relies on the nature of the working relationship between a young person and professional(s) as explored within the principles of relational social work (Folgheraiter, 2004).

This includes the ability for a professional to create felt safety and develop trust both within and beyond safeguarding structures. Similarly, we know that fostering agency for the young person from the outset can greatly assist the development of these relationships. This principle remains where contact and engagement may be brief, such as between young people and the police, for example (Beckett *et al.*, 2015). Though established by criminologist Edmond Locard in relation to forensics, the concept of 'every contact leaves a trace' also has relational relevance, and underpins new policing initiatives such as Divert and Engage within the Metropolitan Police Service, which seeks to ensure that interactions between young people and the police empower young people to identify and receive the support they need in order to avoid further contact with police.

Such approaches require a pool of professionals who are comfortable working with adolescents and taking an approach that significantly alters the traditional power dynamics of child protection and safeguarding. ACT[5] (Achieving Change Together) represents one example where these principles were embedded in statutory social care and supported through long-term investment in culture change and professional development.

ACT was first designed as a DfE-funded social care innovation project developed through co-design principles. It piloted a strengths-based approach to addressing childhood sexual exploitation in which relational practice was central, informed by consultation with young people, families and practitioners. Early indications from the evaluation

---

5   www.itsnotokay.co.uk/professionals/act.

(Scott, Botcherby & Ludvigsen, 2017) indicate promising results, but note the resource implications of delivering the service, and of its reliance on both small caseloads and culture change within organizations and systems, a point explored later in this chapter.

One challenge, however, for all professionals within statutory services is the fact that their role in young people's lives is rarely based on voluntary engagement, so young people's sense of agency may be diminished from the outset. Similar dynamics exist in other parts of the sector, including policing, education and health. In all these areas, the parallel issues of workload and staff turnover have the potential to undermine professional opportunities to develop trusting relationships with young people. Such limitations further the arguments for more partnerships between statutory services and the voluntary and community sectors, who can work within slightly different parameters and professional personas.

Examples of this include a number of youth work-informed models developed in response to this need for relationship-based and relational practice, working in partnership with and commissioned by local authorities. These include services such as Abianda, which work alongside gang-affected young women to address the barriers that stop them from seeking or accessing help, and to design and deliver services.[6] Elsewhere, mentoring provision represents another such model, including innovative approaches utilized by the Safer London Aspire programme and Yorkshire mentoring.[7] In these approaches, young people are involved in managing the mentoring relationship, selecting the person to support them based on key information about who they are and what they bring.

Effective communication and active listening

Effective communication can require some negotiation, as this young man describes:

> 'Yeah, she [the midwife] was cool actually, she was very cool. But at the beginning we wasn't on the same path because she tried to talk a certain way, but then we had to come to a middle innit and just compromise,

---

6   See www.abianda.com for more information.
7   See www.saferlondon.org.uk and www.yorkshirementoring.org.uk for more details.

so by the end of it she was very supportive.' (Young Dad from 'Young Dads Collective', quoted in Vemba, 2015)

Another key consideration for professionals keen to foster trusting relationships with young people is a need to promote open, meaningful and effective communication. While a seemingly obvious point, promoting respectful two-way dialogue that cuts across differences in status, role and institutional power is a skilled undertaking. Understanding and connecting with the language used by young people is a vital part of this. While there is a widespread recognition for high-quality translation and interpretation support where there are identified language barriers (NSPCC, 2014), there remain other linguistic barriers that are rarely identified and even less often addressed.

One recurring theme of adolescence throughout history is the creation of language and dialects 'owned' by the young and harder to access by older generations. Such dialects represent opportunities for young people to exercise power and assert boundaries in their relationships with older generations, often in contexts where their control may be limited. A modern example is the rise of multicultural London English (known as MLE), which is not, as the name suggests, limited to young people in London, but prevalent across the UK and drawing on language from various cultures. It is often used by young people from working class backgrounds, and like all accents and dialects, noted to be part of the basis by which young people are judged and responded to (Osmond, 2017).

Within adolescent safeguarding, the notion of young people being (and feeling) judged by professionals is ever present (Beckett *et al.*, 2015; Cossar *et al.*, 2013; Warrington, 2013). Though language and accent is only one dimension of this, it represents one of many markers of difference, power and hierarchy.

This highlights both the challenges and needs associated with communicating across (among others) generational, class and cultural differences. Effective communication, including active listening, requires ongoing focus and commitment by those supporting young people. It can involve sitting with the uncomfortable and also constantly clarifying and confirming meaning (Rogers & Farson, 1957). Ensuring that meaning is not lost across these divides is vital and the emphasis must be on the professional to overcome these barriers as an integral part of culturally competent and anti-oppressive practice.

Supporting young people to make informed choices

Another key aspect of effective communication is supporting young people to both understand the systems they are engaged with, at an interpersonal level as well as within broader cultural norms, and the forms of structural violence such as patriarchy and racism which constrain them. This means enabling young people to access information and perspectives which help them make informed choices both in relation to services and within their peer groups and communities.

Local safeguarding practice sits within systems that can feel impenetrable for many professionals, let alone young people and families. While localized approaches that meet local needs are to be encouraged, building on the deep knowledge that exists within communities at a micro-level, a real consideration must be given to the language that describes services and pathways, and how they are presented and explained to those using them.

Just to access a service, young people are invited through what might be called 'the front door', 'triage', 'multi-agency safeguarding hubs' or other screening services, gateways into complex systems that are hard to understand by virtue of unfamiliar language, and the use of acronyms and pathways that are not explained in accessible formats. Even the language of 'child protection' may be a barrier for young people who do not see themselves as either children or in need of protection (Hallett, 2017).

Service design must better consider how pathways are understood by young people, endeavour to make them accessible, and ensure that professionals are able to assist young people to navigate them where they remain hard to understand. The value of co-design and collaboration between those using services and those providing them is self-evident here, and innovative examples from social care (Scott, Botcherby & Ludvigsen, 2017), health (Association for Young People's Health, 2018; Brady & Graham, 2018) and criminal justice (Factor & Ackerley, 2019)[8] provide useful models to learn from.

Supporting young people's access to information about their wider social and cultural contexts is arguably more complex. It is likely to rely on approaches such as social pedagogy and critical consciousness

---

8   See also work as part of the MAC-UK INTEGRATE approach: a psychologically informed approach, delivering multi-level interventions that create change in social environments and co-produce services with those who have lived experience.

raising (Freire, 1970). Though relatively rare, examples are evident within youth activism, such as the work of Reclaim in Manchester which may offer a model that others can follow.

Strengths-based approaches

'I've learnt that I can do so much more than I thought I could. It's good for me because it gives me the courage and confidence to expand my knowledge and share and to keep on educating myself and build an empire!' (Abianda Young Trainer, 2016)

An aligned issue is the use of problematic language in safeguarding, with language such as 'troubled families' often linked to the policing of families rather than the support of children at risk (Lambert, 2019). Similarly, the language of 'anti-social behaviour', ubiquitous in policy and practice, is a deeply deficit-focused and blaming approach. These broad national policy terms undoubtedly influence local policy development and, in turn, practice. They create the lens through which professionals see young people and families, and, in turn, blind-spots around welfare and wellbeing needs.

An alternative approach to engagement starts by shifting the focus from professional labelling to a way of working that positions the young person as an expert in their life, recognizing their agency as a resource. Such an approach aligns with principles of strengths- or asset-based approaches to safeguarding (Oliver & Charles, 2016), increasingly apparent through models used with adults at risk and parents involved in child protection such as 'signs of safety' and 'motivational interviewing' (Forrester, Westlake & Glynn, 2012; Munro, 2011).

Interestingly, such models are also central in aforementioned practice models such as ACT (Scott *et al.*, 2017) and Abianda, both of which are founded on a belief in young people's competence, skills and strategies. These models are future rather than deficit focused, and position professionals as collaborators supporting young people to recognize their competence. Yet, equally, these approaches are not 'problem-phobic', acknowledging challenges or tensions, recognizing the cumulative experiences of young people, and acknowledging young people's skills and resilience to 'survive' such experiences.

Owning and sharing stories with care and purpose

When working to maximize young people's sense of control and influence in the context of safeguarding, approaches to information-sharing are critical, offering both opportunities for developing trust while also presenting significant challenge. Evidence suggests that professionals too often see information-sharing as something that is owned by them or entirely professional in its nature, overlooking the deeply personal and exposing nature of that information (Warrington, 2013). Being explicit from the outset about how information will be shared, with whom and for what purpose, is essential to building and maintaining trusted relationships.

Young people themselves highlight their right to know why information needs to be shared, and to understand why it has benefits for them and not just professional networks (Association for Young People's Health, 2014). There are additional challenges as children and young people are increasingly being viewed through a contextual lens and so information is held about peer groups as well as individuals.

Ultimately, information-sharing must be purposeful and serve to improve outcomes for that young person. Defining how this is achieved remains challenging, especially when 'effective information-sharing' remains a contested and poorly defined concept which differs considerably in the views of young people, families, communities and professionals.

Although there are professional frameworks that govern information-sharing, there remains a need to supplement these with ongoing reflective practice to consider what's appropriate for individual young people, for the professional network, and for the ongoing need to safeguard. The answers to these questions should help inform how, when and with whom information is shared.

Given the multitude of serious case reviews and other audits that have demanded greater sharing of information, there is a risk that professionals default to sharing everything with everyone. As well as contradicting best practice guidelines (HM Government, 2018), such approaches potentially create new risks for young people – a particular concern in the context of serious youth violence where risks associated with racial profiling and additional surveillance are well documented (Wroe & Lloyd, 2020). Equally, an undue focus within safeguarding activity on information-sharing rather than activities and interventions that actuate change for a young person and young people's ownership or involvement in that process is all too rarely considered.

In addition, professionals may overlook the fact that information-sharing starts with the young person offering information about themselves and their own lives, something best facilitated through the context of a trusted relationship between young people and professionals (Cossar, Belderson & Brandon, 2019).

Effective assessment of young people at risk should not just be a series of boxes to be filled in, but a record of how young people see themselves, their lives and the context in which they live. How people understand, internalize and express their 'story' has real value for those who wish to work with them to create change. This is no different for young people, and honouring their story is important when the goal is to change its direction or create a different ending to that which is unfolding.

Supporting young people's involvement in formal decision-making

Alongside the aforementioned relational and strengths-based principles that support participatory and empowerment principles within one-to-one support, there is also a need to consider how to support young people's involvement in more formal decision-making spaces. Multi-agency meetings represent one such space, a central means through which both information about a young person is shared and decisions about their support are made. And yet, as noted previously, all too often young people neither attend nor are properly represented within these spaces (Rosa *et al.*, 2019).

Interestingly, there is emerging evidence that the proliferation of different meetings designed to respond to widening the scope of adolescent safeguarding may have both further eroded young people's rights to privacy and created more decision-making spaces from which they are excluded (Lefevre *et al.*, 2019).

While it would be naive to assume that engaging young people in these decision-making spaces is straightforward, there are clear examples of approaches which facilitate this. These include work by Manchester Youth Justice Service which has recently developed a participatory service model that fundamentally changes the culture and practice working with young people at risk, centring them as experts in their own lives and able to identify what needs to change (Greater Manchester Youth Justice University Partnership[9]). This builds on historical approaches such as the Sheffield Safeguarding Children Board Sexual Exploitation Service (2010), which pioneered a uniquely collaborative approach to multi-agency 'sexual exploitation' meetings involving both young people and their families. The success of such models is about much more than simply inviting young people to attend. It rests on careful planning, considering how to support a young person to fully understand the process and professional roles, to feel safe, welcome and respected within the space, to find means to comfortably represent their views, and to ensure other stakeholders are prepared to support these processes and promote accessibility.

These meetings represent opportunities to shift traditional power dynamics and increase young people's sense of ownership and control. Traditionally, these are professionally chaired, often by highly experienced individuals independent from the case being discussed. While this has value in holding professionals accountable, it also creates the risk of the meeting drifting further away from the young person who is, or should be, the focus.

A number of pilot models have attempted to offer alternatives, such as those which allow young people to not just attend meetings but to co-chair them, as in Merton's looked after children review meetings,[10] and work in Derby which successfully involved young people in planning and managing 'sexual exploitation' meetings (Ofsted, 2013).

Such approaches are resource intensive, but noted to give young people the power to help shape the assessment and analysis of risk, to formulate plans, and to review progress and decide who will help them along the way.

Managing and holding risk and conflict

One challenge when inviting young people into decision-making processes is managing the conflict that occurs between them and professional perspectives. For some professionals, this may be a reason why it feels easier to leave young people on the 'side lines' – particularly when

9   www.mmu.ac.uk/mcys/gmyjup.
10 https://cyp.mertonpartnership.org.uk/march-april-2014/stay-safe/looked-after-child-reviews-the-childs-voice.

young people's perspectives feel ill-informed, short-sighted or at odds with what professionals consider to be 'safe choices'. However, young people deserve an opportunity to try and understand professional reasoning, and it is right that professionals should feel held to account by the young people they are paid to provide care and support for.

Meanwhile, for professionals, a chance to understand why a young person wants to return to an abusive relationship, maintain contact with exploitative gang members or make other seemingly 'un-protective choices' may be the key to a more meaningful assessment process and identification of needs. It may be a chance to understand the wider complex patterns of risk a young person is forced to negotiate – they may be trading one difficult circumstance for another that feels more manageable – described by Hallett (2017) as a young person's 'least worst option'. Professionals also need to recognize that there may be times when a young person's assessment of risk will be more nuanced and informed than their own, and based on a deeper understanding of their own circumstances.

Clearly, an anticipation of conflict must not override a young person's right to be involved in decision-making about their lives. Rather, it requires professionals who are able and supported to sit with and manage difference and conflict, enabled by approaches to improving reflective practice such as action learning and access to high-quality reflective supervision (Morrison, 2001). Professionals who are confident explaining to young people why they see things differently and challenge their perspectives respectfully without reducing a young person's pride or esteem are key to relationship-based safeguarding. This is also a reminder about the role and value of independent advocates for young people, supporting them to have their views heard and be taken seriously, particularly where they differ significantly to those of professionals.

Furthermore, professionals may have to accept a level of risk that is at odds with well-established and accepted ways of protecting children. While there is an irrefutable and necessarily relentless commitment to keeping young people safe, there is also value in recognizing that this is often a journey and not an output. As Pearce (2014, p.163), writing in the context of sexual exploitation, suggests, 'allow time to engage with the young person and to establish a supportive relationship despite episodes of "going missing"'.

This does not mean ignoring the missing episodes but encourages a parallel process of relational empowerment that aims to support the young person on their journey to improved safety. Long established in the field of substance misuse (Friedman *et al.*, 2007), harm reduction principles are beginning to be recognized as valuable in other areas of support and intervention, as the provision of resource, both practical and emotional, enables young people to develop safer and healthier behaviours (Stimson, 1998).

It aligns with increasing recognition that where exploitation and grooming are factors in harm, a 'rescue' response is unlikely to be effective and so requires an approach that creates safety where possible and reduces harm (Hickle & Hallett, 2016).

It is also important to consider that, ultimately, statutory roles including safeguarding duties mean professionals will continue to hold and wield power over young people's lives. It is vital that we acknowledge this and properly manage young people's expectations about the role of professionals in their lives.

Any attempt to invite young people to inform or share decision-making must be honest and realistic about the degree of influence they will be afforded and the terms under which their influence is sought. Equally, within initiatives labelled 'empowering', clarity about roles, funding and the ownership of objectives needs to be honest. Such honesty is the basis for trusting relationships and an important way of avoiding the type of tokenistic participation (Hart, 1992) in which young people's presence is co-opted to 'rubber stamp' a professional agenda.

Despite this proposed shift in role, such approaches still position professionals as a vital resource for young people, supporting them to problem-solve and access potential advice, resources and support to address seemingly intractable problems.

Conclusion

As noted above, participation and empowerment approaches urge us to move away from a solely paternalistic response to harm, and challenge ourselves to cede power and sit with risk in a different way. This is not easy work and must be built on a whole-system shift that not only empowers young people but also empowers and supports professionals. This requires a commitment to collaborative, strengths-based systems that are hopeful, both for professionals and young people. They must be systems which are rights-based and recognize and respond to both the context and impact of harm, including structural, systemic violence (Galtung, 1969).

Professionals need to feel that they are supported in their decision-making and have sufficient flex to assess, plan, intervene and review in creative and non-traditional ways. Meanwhile, young people need to feel that their needs are at the centre and that they are listened to, involved, respected and supported to access safe lives free from oppression in which they can thrive.

While we are still relatively early in our journey towards developing and embedding specific adolescent safeguarding frameworks, we have a unique opportunity to rethink our approach, drawing from principles of adult safeguarding and the centrality of principles of empowerment, partnership and accountability (HM Government, 2014).

Crucially, we must start by recognizing collaboration with young people and building self-efficacy as key to enabling safety, and subsequently position participatory and empowerment approaches as foundational requirements in any system change. This needs to run through policy, communications, case recording, management decision processes, supervision and support, and be properly resourced, in the broadest sense, to respond effectively to what young people tell us matters.

It also challenges us to think about how we expand our networks of safeguarding partners, drawing on the skills, experience and insights of those outside the 'usual suspects', such as the voluntary and community sector, and utilizing established ways of working within youth and group work practices.

Why can't we do assessments on a park bench to avoid venues that a young person does not feel safe within? Why can't we do home visits after a young person's curfew time, or prepare for a meeting while kicking a ball around? And why can't we engage young people themselves as creative partners in system change? There are a multitude of reasons why these things may feel understandably challenging, but a good start is the will to do it differently and the belief that it is possible.

References

Abianda (2016). Being an Abianda Young Trainer (webpage). www.abianda.com/voices?pgid=kgm2bvwb-2e299c8b-a44a-42d7-93bd-aef46a7880e6.

Adams, R. (2008). *Empowerment, Participation and Social Work* (fourth edition). London: Palgrave Macmillan.

Archard, D. (2004). *Children: Rights and Childhood* (second edition). London: Routledge.

Association for Young People's Health (2014). *Be Healthy*. AYPH/University of Bedfordshire. www.ayph-behealthy.org.uk.

Association for Young People's Health (2018). *Young People's Acute Care Flowchart*. www.youngpeopleshealth.org.uk/young-peoples-voices.

Bandura, A. (1982). 'Self-efficacy mechanism in human agency.' *American Psychologist, 37*(2), 122–147.

Beckett, H. & Warrington, C. (2015). *Making Justice Work: Experiences of Criminal Justice for Children and Young People Affected by Sexual Exploitation as Victims and Witnesses*. Luton: University of Bedfordshire. https://uobrep.openrepository.com/bitstream/handle/10547/347011/MakingJusticeWorkFullReport.pdf?sequence=1&isAllowed=y.

Beckett, H., Warrington, C., Ackerley, E. & Allnock, D. (2015). *Children's Voices Report: Children and Young People's Perspectives on the Police's Role in Safeguarding: A Report for Her Majesty's Inspectorate of Constabularies*. Luton: University of Bedfordshire.

Beresford, P. (2012). 'The Theory and Philosophy Behind User Involvement.' In P. Beresford & S. Carr (eds) *Social Care, Service Users and User Involvement* (pp.21–36). London: Jessica Kingsley Publishers.

Beresford, P. & Carr, S. (eds) (2012). *Social Care, Service Users and User Involvement*. London: Jessica Kingsley Publishers.

Bovarnick, S. & Cody, C. (2020). 'They Need to See the People they are Affecting by their Decision-Making.' Developing Participatory Advocacy with Young People on Sexual Violence in Albania, Moldova and Serbia. Monitoring and Evaluation Report: Our Voices Too Project. Luton: University of Bedfordshire.

Brady, G. & Franklin, A. (2019). 'Challenging dominant notions of participation and protection through a co-led disabled young researcher study.' *Journal of Children's Services, 14*(3), 174–185. https://doi.org/10.1108/JCS-03-2019-0016.

Brady, L.M. & Graham, B. (2018). *Social Research with Children and Young People: A Practical Guide*. Bristol: Policy Press.

Brodie, I. (2016). *Literature Review: The Participation of Young People in Child Sexual Exploitation Services*. Luton: University of Bedfordshire.

Bulanda, J. & Johnson, B.T. (2016). 'A trauma-informed model for empowerment programs targeting vulnerable youth.' *Child and Adolescent Social Work Journal, 33*, 303–312. https://link.springer.com/article/10.1007/s10560-015-0427-z.

Coleman, J. (2011). *The Nature of Adolescence* (fourth edition). London: Routledge.

Coppock, V. & Phillips, L. (2013). 'Actualisation of children's participation rights.' *Global Studies of Childhood, 3*(2). https://doi.org/10.2304%2Fgsch.2013.3.2.99.

Cossar, J., Belderson, P. & Brandon, M. (2019). 'Recognition, telling and getting help with abuse and neglect: Young people's perspectives.' *Children & Youth Services Review, 106*. https://doi.org/10.1016/j.childyouth.2019.104469.

Cossar, J., Brandon, M., Bailey, S., Belderson, P., Biggart, L. (2013). *'It Takes a Lot to Build Trust' – Recognition and Telling: Developing Earlier Routes to Help for Children and Young People*. London: Office of the Children's Commissioner.

Crowley, A. & Larkins, C. (2018). *Children's Participation in Public Decision-Making: A Review of Practice in Europe*. Brussels: Eurochild.

Davies, B. (2005). *Youth Work: A Manifesto for Our Times*. Youth and Policy, 88. https://indefenceofyouthwork.files.wordpress.com/2009/03/youth-work-a-manifesto-for-our-times-bernard-davies.pdf.

Davis, J. & Marsh, N. (2020). 'Boys to men: The cost of "adultification" in safeguarding responses to Black boys.' *Critical and Radical Social Work, 8*(2), 255–259.

Department for Education (2018). *Working Together to Safeguard Children. A Guide to Inter-Agency Working to Safeguard and Promote the Welfare of Children*. London: HM Government.

Diaz, C. (2021). *Decision Making in Child and Family Social Work: Perspectives on Children's Participation*. Bristol: Policy Press.

Diaz, C., Pert, H. & Thomas, N.P. (2019). 'Independent reviewing officers' and social workers' perceptions of children's participation in children in care reviews.' *Journal of Children's Services, 14*(3), 162–173. https://doi.org/10.1108/JCS-01-2019-0003.

Factor, F. & Ackerley, E. (2019). 'Young people and police making "marginal gains": Climbing fells, building relationships and changing police safeguarding practice.' *Journal of Children's Services, 14*(3), 217–227. https://doi.org/10.1108/JCS-01-2019-0001.

Firmin, C. (2017). *Abuse Between Young People: A Contextual Account.* London: Routledge.

Firmin, C. (2018). 'Contextualizing case reviews: A methodology for developing systemic safeguarding practices.' *Child & Family Social Work, 23,* 45–52. https://doi.org/10.1111/cfs.12382.

Firmin, C. (2020). *Contextual Safeguarding and Child Protection: Rewriting the Rules.* London: Routledge.

Folgheraiter, F. (2004). *Relational Social Work Toward Networking and Societal Practices.* London: Jessica Kingsley Publishers.

Forrester, D., Westlake, D. & Glynn, G. (2012). 'Parental resistance and social worker skills: Towards a theory of motivational social work.' *Child & Family Social Work, 17*(2), 118–129.

Freire, P. (1970). *Pedagogy of the Oppressed.* London: Continuum International Publishing Group.

Friedman, S.R., de Jong, W., Rossi, D., Touzé, G. *et al.* (2007). 'Harm reduction theory: Users' culture, micro-social indigenous harm reduction, and the self-organization and outside-organizing of users' groups.' *International Journal of Drug Policy, 18*(2), 107–117.

Galtung, J. (1969). 'Violence, peace, and peace research.' *Journal of Peace Research, 6*(3), 167–191. www.jstor.org/stable/422690.

Ginwright, S.G. (2010). *Black Youth Rising: Activism and Radical Healing in Urban America.* New York, NY: Teachers College Press.

Geddes, H. (2006). *Attachment in the Classroom: The Links Between Children's Early Experience, Emotional Wellbeing and Performance in School.* London: Caspari Foundation.

Hallett, S. (2017). *Making Sense of Child Sexual Exploitation. Exchange, Abuse and Young People.* Bristol: Policy Press.

Hamilton, C., Rodgers, A., Howard, K. with Warrington, C. (2019). 'From the ground up: Young research advisors' perspectives on relationships between participation and protection.' *Journal of Children's Services, 14*(3), 228–234. https://doi.org/10.1108/JCS-07-2019-0037.

Hart, R.A. (1992). *Children's Participation: From Tokenism to Citizenship.* Florence: UNICEF.

Hickle, K. (2020). 'Introducing a trauma-informed capability approach in youth services.' *Children and Society.* https://doi.org/10.1111/chso.12388.

Hickle, K. & Hallett, S. (2016). 'Mitigating harm: Considering harm reduction principles in work with sexually exploited young people.' *Children & Society, 30*(4), 302–313. https://doi.org/10.1111/chso.12145.

Hill, N. (2018). *Serious Case Review – Chris: Overview Report.* London: Newham Local Safeguarding Board.

HM Government (1989). Children Act 1989. HM Government.

HM Government (2014). The Care Act 2014. HM Government.

HM Government (2018). *Information Sharing: Advice for Practitioners Providing Safeguarding Services to Children, Young People, Parents and Carers.* London: HM Government.

Houghton, C. (2018). 'Voice, Agency, Power: A Framework for Young Survivors' Participation in National Domestic Abuse Policy-Making.' In S. Holt, C. Overlien & J. Devaney (eds) *Responding to Domestic Violence: Emerging Challenges for Policy, Practice and Research in Europe* (pp.77–96). London: Jessica Kingsley Publishers.

Jeffs, T. & Smith, M. (2008). 'Valuing youth work.' *Youth and Policy, 100,* 277–302.

Lambert, M. (2019). 'Between "families in trouble" and "children at risk": Historicising "troubled family" policy in England since 1945.' *Children & Society, 33,* 82–91. https://doi.org/10.1111/chso.12309.

Lawson, J., Lewis, S. & Williams, C. (2014). *Making Safeguarding Personal: Guide 2014.* London: Local Government Association.

Lefevre, M., Hickle, K. & Luckock, B. (2019). '"Both/and" not "either/or": Reconciling rights to protection and participation in working with child sexual exploitation.' *The British Journal of Social Work, 49*(7), 1837–1855. https://doi.org/10.1093/bjsw/bcy106.

Levenson, J. (2017). 'Trauma-informed social work practice.' *Social Work, 62*(2), 105–113.

Lundy, L. (2007). '"Voice" is not enough: Conceptualising Article 12 of the United Nations Convention on the Rights of the Child.' *British Educational Research Journal, 33*(6), 927–942. https://doi.org/10.1080/01411920701657033.

McCallum, S. & Prilleltensky, I. (1996). 'Empowerment in child protection work: Values, practice and caveats.' *Children & Society, 10*(1), 40–50.

Morrison, T. (2001). *Staff Supervision in Social Care Making a Real Difference for Staff and Service Users*. Brighton: Pavilion.

Munro, E. (2011). *The Munro Review of Child Protection: Final Report*. London: Department for Education.

NSPCC (2014). *People Whose First Language is not English: Learning from Case Reviews. Summary of Risk Factors and Learning for Improved Practice around People Whose First Language is not English*. London: NSPCC Learning.

Ofsted (2013). *Inspection of Local Authority Arrangements for the Protection of Children*. Derby City Council. London: Ofsted. https://files.ofsted.gov.uk/v1/file/50004210.

Oliver, C. & Charles, G. (2016). 'Enacting firm, fair and friendly practice: A model for strengths-based child protection relationships?' *The British Journal of Social Work, 46*(4), 1009–1026. https://doi.org/10.1093/bjsw/bcv015.

Osmond, A. (2017, 15 September). *The Rise of Multicultural London English, Innit?* SOAS, Linguistics. https://study.soas.ac.uk/multicultural-london-english.

Pearce, J. (2014). '"What's going on" to safeguard children and young people from child sexual exploitation? A review of local safeguarding children boards' work to protect children from sexual exploitation.' *Child Abuse Review, 23*(3), 159–170.

Preston-Shoot, M. (2020). *Practical Examples of Making Safeguarding Personal from Commissioners and Providers of Health and Social Care*. London: Local Government Association.

Raby, R. (2006). 'Children in sex: Adults in crime: Constructing and confining teens.' *Resources for Feminist Research, 31*(3/4), 9–28.

Rogers, C.R. & Farson, R.E. (1957). *Active Listening*. Chicago, IL: University of Chicago, Industrial Relations Center.

Rosa, G., King, L., Stephens, M. & Smith, L. (2019). *State of Children's Rights 2018*. London: Children's Rights Alliance for England.

Ruch, G. (2005). 'Relationship-based practice and reflective practice: Holistic approaches to contemporary child care social work.' *Child & Family Social Work, 10*(2), 111–123. https://doi.org/10.1111/j.1365-2206.2005.00359.x.

Scott, S., Botcherby, S. & Ludvigsen, A. (2017). *Wigan and Rochdale Child Sexual Exploitation Innovation Project: Evaluation Report*. London: Department for Education.

Sheffield Safeguarding Children Board Sexual Exploitation Services (2010). *Annual Report: 1 April 2009–31 March 2010*.

Shuker, L. (2013). *Evaluation of Barnardo's Safe Accommodation Project for Sexually Exploited and Trafficked Young People*. Luton: University of Bedfordshire.

Stimson, G.V. (1998). 'Harm reduction in action: Putting theory into practice.' *International Journal of Drug Policy, 9*, 401–409. https://doi.org/10.1016/S0955-3959(98)00056-5.

Substance Abuse and Mental Health Services Administration's Trauma and Justice Strategic Initiative (2014). *SAMHSA's Concept of Trauma and Guidance for a Trauma-Informed Approach*. Rockville, MD: SAMHSA.

Ungar, M. (2004). *Nurturing Hidden Resilience in Troubled Youth*. Toronto: University of Toronto Press.

United Nations (1989, 20 November). United Nations Convention on the Rights of the Child (UNCRC). UNICEF. www.unicef.org.uk/what-we-do/un-convention-child-rights.

Vemba, R. (2015). *LEFT OUT. How Young Dads Access Services in North East London*. Young Dads Collective. London: Family & Childcare Trust.

Ward, H., Skuse, T. & Munro, E.R. (2005). '"The best of times, the worst of times": Young people's views of care and accommodation.' *Adoption & Fostering, 29*(1), 8–17.

Warrington, C. (2013). *'Helping Me Find My Own Way': Sexually Exploited Young People's Involvement in Decision-Making about their Care*. Doctoral thesis. University of Bedfordshire.

Warrington, C. (2016). *Young Person-Centred Approaches in Child Sexual Exploitation – Promoting Participation and Building Self-Efficacy*. Totnes: Research in Practice.

Warrington, C. & Larkin, C. (2019). 'Children at the centre of safety: Juxtaposition of protection and participation.' *Journal of Children's Services, 14*(3), 133–142.

White, S., Morris, K. & Featherstone, B. (2014). *Re-imagining Child Protection: Towards Humane Social Work with Families*. Bristol: Policy Press.

Wroe, L. & Lloyd, J. (2020). 'Watching over or working with? Understanding social work innovation in response to extra-familial harm.' *Social Sciences, 9*(4). https://doi.org/10.3390/socsci9040037.

Zheng, R. (2018). 'What is my role in changing the system? A new model of responsibility for structural injustice.' *Ethical Theory & Moral Practice, 21*(4), 869–885.

Chapter 10

Transitional Safeguarding: Bridging the Gap Between Children's and Adults' Safeguarding Responses

Christine Cocker, Adi Cooper and Dez Holmes

Introduction

Turning 18 is the point in most westernized societies where a child legally becomes an adult, in terms of legal and social constructs of rights and responsibilities. It is a time for celebration and marks a 'rite of passage' to adulthood. However, the reality for many young people is that they will continue to need support, as becoming an adult is a process, not a single event. Often, this is the time when eligibility for public services in England changes, as the legal frameworks (Children Act 1989 and Care Act 2014) that denote the duties and powers of statutory provisions for children and adults across health and social care services are different. For those young people who require ongoing health and social care support from social services because of their own needs and situations, many parts of this wider system (e.g., young people with special educational needs and disabilities, care-leavers and young carers) have already achieved or are working towards a more fluid/transitional approach. However, safeguarding is notable in retaining a binary notion of child/adulthood, despite evidence that the risk and harms young people experience respect no such boundaries (Holmes, 2022).

Previous chapters have explored the drivers for re-imagining how we support and safeguard young people. Here, we highlight the importance of adopting an expansive definition of 'young people' to include those up to 25, and argue for a transformation in the approach to the protection and safeguarding of young people during this transition period. We provide an overview of the term 'Transitional Safeguarding', and summarize the literature about this area of practice. We look at the inconsistencies between safeguarding services for children and adults before exploring how the safeguarding systems regarding children and adults could become better aligned so that young people don't fall through the gap at 18. In considering options for a radical realignment of local and national safeguarding systems, we include case studies to illustrate innovative practice in this area.

What do we mean by 'Transitional Safeguarding'?

In England, children up to and including the age of 17 are subject to child protection processes defined by the Children Act 1989, while the safeguarding response for young people over the age of 18 is underpinned by the Care Act 2014. However, neither of these safeguarding systems is designed to meet the developmental needs of young people. In this chapter, we define 'young people' by the United Nations description of 'youth', as those aged 15–24 (United Nations, 2020). The term 'adolescent' is used for those aged under 18 and when quoting the work of others. The children's safeguarding system in England and Wales is based on an original intention to protect young children from abuse and harm within a family context (Corby, Shemmings & Wilkins, 2012; HM Government, 2018). Within this framework, in recent years, there has been significant innovation regarding the safeguarding needs of adolescents (Firmin, 2020). The adult safeguarding system primarily focuses on those adults with care and support needs who are unable to protect themselves from abuse and neglect (Department of Health and Social Care, 2020). These are predominantly described as older people, people with physical disabilities, learning disabilities, or substance misuse or mental health problems.

In an effort to identify the shortcomings of these approaches to safeguarding for young people, Holmes and Smale (2018) discuss the reasons why rethinking young people's specific safeguarding needs is necessary. They describe Transitional Safeguarding as 'an approach to safeguarding adolescents and young adults fluidly across developmental stages which builds on the best available evidence, learns from both children's and adults' safeguarding practice and which prepares young people for their adult lives' (2018, p.3). This recognizes that, from a life-course perspective, young people occupy very different physical, social and emotional places and spaces than younger children, not least as adolescents often face safeguarding pressures and risks external to their home environments (Firmin, 2016b).

The needs and risks that they experience during this period can also be different from those that can occur later in adult life, and society's response to their vulnerability or harms can also be rather different. Central to this developmental period is the ability to understand risk and learn how to manage it in a way that enables a fulfilling and rewarding life. Transitional Safeguarding also recognizes that, as well as differences, there are strengths within the existing children's and adults' safeguarding systems that can be utilized to support young people from adolescence through to early adulthood. By exploring divergence, particularly around concepts such as 'wellbeing' and 'welfare', and underpinning approaches such as 'risk-enabling' compared with 'risk-averse' approaches, there is an opportunity to design a system that explicitly responds to this specific life stage.

However, when considering changes to the current safeguarding systems, it is worth remembering that 'childhood' and 'adulthood' are both social constructs, reinforced through legislation, and social and organizational structures. A variety of different professionals (e.g., social workers, youth workers, youth justice specialists, health workers) mediate relationships between the state and young people, but the interface between all three (young people, the professionals who work with them, and the state) can be problematic. This is particularly the case when young people encounter children and/or adult safeguarding services, which are currently separate from each other. Safeguarding policy and concordant practice guidance has tended to adhere to polarized notions of childhood and adulthood (Holmes & Smale, 2018).

An example of where this can be complicated is the binary construct of 'victim/perpetrator' for under-18s and over-18s. Under 18, a young person experiencing criminal exploitation, for example, is increasingly, though not always, seen as a 'victim', which is supported by statutory guidance (HM Government, 2020). However, at 18, the young person is likely to be seen as a 'perpetrator' despite their circumstances, vulnerabilities and needs remaining the same. While there is an emerging understanding that those aged over 18 can be criminally exploited, Home Office guidance states that criminal exploitation can happen to 'any child under 18' and to 'any vulnerable adult' (Home Office, 2018). The term 'vulnerable adult', originally used 18 years earlier in the *No Secrets* guidance (Department of Health, 2000) and since replaced by the Care Act 2014, tends to denote those adults with health needs or disabilities and so does not necessarily include young adults with experience of abuse, coercion or trauma. This binary categorization fails to capture the complexities of risk and vulnerability for many young adults, and can arguably lead to criminalization of young people rather than a safeguarding response.

Alongside the moral and ethical drivers, there is an economic argument for Transitional Safeguarding. Failing to address harm and its impact in adolescence can result in (often) costlier later interventions (Kezelman *et al.*, 2015). Both the Children Act 1989 and the Care Act 2014, with their emphases on prevention, are useful levers in this regard.

The system changes required to improve safeguarding practice with young people are complex. A re-configuration of the risk vs. rights paradigms that permeate societal responses to the protection of young people is required to challenge the exercise of power within organizations, along with the need to centrally involve young people as key stakeholders in developing appropriate responses, both at an individual and systemic level. This is consistent with a personalized approach in adult safeguarding (Lawson, 2017). These will be explored further in this chapter.

Current safeguarding systems in child and adult services

The histories of children's and adults' safeguarding systems have taken different pathways. Safeguarding children, set out in the Children Act 1989, is focused on protecting children from harm. It is associated with an often counterproductive mix of responses to specific highly publicized child deaths, changing policy agendas under successive governments, which affect the support available to families, and the overall attitude toward children and childhood within wider society (Cooper & Whittaker, 2014). Adult safeguarding has its roots in the protection of older adults (Institute of Public Care, 2013) and in scandals concerning the abuse of adults in institutional settings (Norrie *et al.*, 2014). Adult safeguarding duties and powers were set out in statute for the first time in history in the Care Act 2014.

Adult safeguarding work is concerned with people with care and support needs who are unable to protect themselves from abuse or neglect because of those care and support needs (Department of Health & Social Care, 2020). Making Safeguarding Personal is a human rights-based approach to adult safeguarding, which was incorporated into the Care Act 2014 Guidance (Department of Health & Social Care, 2020). In this approach, the person is considered to have rights to live their life, which need to be balanced with their right to/need for safety. This underpins risk-enabling approaches and the co-production of outcomes (Cooper, Cocker & Briggs, 2018). By contrast, in children's safeguarding, the construct of rights is arguably narrower. The focus is on reducing or even eradicating risks. This, together with presumptions that children lack competence and so cannot be bearers of their own rights (Cowden, 2012), leads to the conceptualization of children and young people under 18 as passive and lacking the capacity to make decisions about risks, and so lends itself to an expert-led/professionals-know-best approach rather than one that is person-centred. In terms of overall approaches to management of risk in these different safeguarding paradigms, children's safeguarding practice is often described as 'risk-averse' (Munro, 2019), whereas in adult safeguarding, it is described as 'risk-enabling', as it is designed to prioritize the outcomes identified by the person themselves (Cooper et al., 2018).

Taken on its own, neither approach is a good 'fit' for work with young people. First, neither child protection nor adult safeguarding is designed for, or responsive to, the developmental needs of young people. It is not 'one side' that needs to adapt and recalibrate its goals, it is a task for both systems to take into account young people's developmental needs and the evolving nature of harm and risk for this group, particularly extra-familial harms. These types of harms:

- often extend beyond 18

- may continue irrespective of whether a young person enters care (under 18) or has formally defined care and support needs (over 18)

- can arguably fuel a cycle of 'victim/perpetrator' more than many types of other abuse (Firmin, 2016a)

- present new challenges to child protection and adult safeguarding practices, all of which highlight the need for transformation.

Second, the child and adult safeguarding systems interface with other policies and legislation that highlight the contradictory understanding of childhood and adulthood. For example, the Mental Capacity Act 2005 and the Liberty Protection Safeguards (LPS) assume decision-making capacity (for purposes of many, but not all purposes), from age 16, while the definitions of child sexual exploitation (CSE) and child criminal exploitation (CCE) assert that someone under 18 cannot consent to their exploitation (HM Government, 2020). The Domestic Abuse Bill (House of Lords and House of Commons, 2020) defines domestic abuse as affecting anyone over 16 years old in an abusive relationship. A 17-year-old could be simultaneously a victim of domestic violence, and/or CSE, and equally be considered to be exercising their 'right' to make an unwise decision (a right which they only have if, in fact, they have capacity to make that decision). Further, there is a danger that practitioners will wrongly view young people's behaviour and harmful experiences as 'lifestyle choices' (Holmes & Smale, 2018). This is underpinned by the idea that it is a young person's informed choice to engage in 'risky' and 'harmful' activities, rather than recognizing the highly constrained nature of these perceived 'choices'. This can be further compounded by services that treat adolescents as having the same agency as adults, and while this may be true for narrow legal purposes, it does not recognize the realities of adolescence (Beckett, Holmes & Walker, 2017).

There are also structural factors that are relevant to safeguarding, for example the role that gender and gendered thinking can play in shaping professionals' response to criminal and sexual exploitation (Children's Commissioner, 2019; Violence & Vulnerability Unit, 2018). Linked to this, there are issues of systemic inequality that affect the safeguarding of young people from extra-familial harm. The final report of the Youth Violence Commission noted the authors were 'concerned by unduly high rates of stop and search imposed disproportionately on young people from Black and minority ethnic backgrounds. This has served to undermine many young people's trust and confidence in the police' (Youth Violence Commission, 2020, p.11). As such, issues of equality, diversity and inclusion are key aspects to consider in understanding young people's safeguarding, and form a central tenet of a Transitional Safeguarding response.

Life-course development

There is an emerging literature that argues for the safeguarding of young people to be reconsidered, taking into account their developmental needs and the evolving nature of harm and risk for this group. Within the life-course development literature, US-based researchers argue the developmental case for adolescence lasting from the age of 15 to 25 years (Rosenfeld & Nicodemus, 2003) or even 10 to 25 years (Sawyer et al., 2018). Arnett's (2000) model of 'emerging adulthood' conceptualized this as a response to demographic shifts in the activities of young people in westernized countries over the past 50 years. Consequently, the median age of marriage and the median age of first childbirth has increased. Arnett argues that, 'having left the dependency of childhood and adolescence, and having not yet entered the enduring responsibilities that are normative in adulthood, emerging adults often explore a variety of possible life directions in love, work and world views (2000, p.469).

Along with adolescence and young adulthood, 'emerging adulthood' is also a cultural construct. Arnett (2000) argued that individual experiences are not universal because they are diverse; some young people are now less limited by historical gender role expectations, although there are important class and cultural factors at play. Critics of Arnett's work argue that 'emerging adulthood' is not universal as his model under-emphasizes the impact of socioeconomic conditions on young people's options, leading to 'increasingly precarious trajectories' (Côté & Bynner, 2008, p.251). The delay in adulthood is a coping mechanism in response to social and economic conditions, rather than a choice (Côté & Bynner, 2008).

However, these demographic transition factors have little influence on what young people themselves say is important for them in becoming an adult. The evidence is that there are two individual factors that are consistently rated highest: accepting responsibility for oneself and making independent decisions (Arnett, 2000). These mark the move toward self-sufficiency and autonomy in some areas of life, recognizing that there are external constraints on personal autonomy. There is evidence that they also apply to young people whose journey to adulthood is difficult (Tyrell & Yates, 2018). When we consider the impact of these on developing appropriate safeguarding responses for young people aged 16–25, practice that involves young people in decisions that are made about them at every stage is critical (Cossar, Brandon &

Jordan, 2011). This involves encouraging choice and control alongside achieving the outcomes of safety and wellbeing (Jobe & Gorin, 2013; Warrington, 2016).

Arnett also argued that 'emerging adults can pursue novel and intense experiences more freely than adolescents because they are less likely to be monitored by parents and can pursue them more freely than adults because they are less constrained by roles' (2000, p.475). Enabling young people to take risks safely is not a contradiction in terms. However, not all young people experience risk-taking in the same way. Tyrell and Yates (2018) found that for young people leaving care, a number of core features affecting their experience of 'emerging adulthood' were not acknowledged. These included the 'self-focus' of these young people and the effect on their optimism for their future. Additionally, how young people explored their worlds was different and how they articulated this point of transition – this 'feeling in-between' – was also different, 'fraught with difficulty, constraint and worry' (Tyrell & Yates, 2018, p.1023). This is critical for considering Transitional Safeguarding – the safeguarding needs of young people at these different stages of adolescence, emerging adulthood and young adulthood require a nuanced and flexible response from services because of the particular needs and developmental stages of these young people, and this is often missing (Holmes & Smale, 2018).

Arnett (2000) identified 'risk behaviour' as activities such as drug-taking, unprotected sex, driving over the speed limit and driving while intoxicated. Over 20 years later, these behaviours are still understood to be risks that adolescents engage in. However, new risks and dangers for some young people have emerged. Examples include: CCE, CSE and 'county lines' (Glover Williams & Finlay, 2019).

While the term 'risk-taking' continues to be used in relation to these harms, this is arguably problematic as it can imply a sense of responsibility or decision-making on the part of the young person, which can obscure the abusive nature of the harm (Holmes, 2022). There is a danger that these adolescent activities, viewed as 'risky' and 'harmful' by practitioners, might be wrongly seen as 'lifestyle choices' that young people freely choose to engage in, rather than recognizing the constraints and influences on young people ensnared in these circumstances or behaviours (Holmes & Smale, 2018). Where this occurs, it follows that services may then treat adolescents as having the same agency as adults (Beckett et al., 2017). The problem is that services are not necessarily basing these decisions on what is known about engaging with risk in the context of adolescent development or development of 'emerging adults', rather, it is governed by a binary notion of child/adulthood, despite the clear evidence that the risk and harms respect no such boundary. It is equally problematic, therefore, that adults with previous experience of abuse or exploitation may not be recognized under the Care Act 2014 as having 'care and support needs' and so may not receive a safeguarding response.

A multi-agency response that transcends this child/adult binary is critical to addressing the types of harm described above. For example, regarding criminal exploitation and county lines, under-18s might be involved in moving and delivering drugs around the country. Additionally, adults who are vulnerable because of drug and alcohol addictions, learning disabilities, mental health issues, prior experience of abuse or social isolation may be subjected to 'cuckooing' behaviour, where gang members use their home as their base for drug dealing (Glover Williams & Finlay, 2019).

Other specific groups of young people also face particular challenges as they progress towards adulthood (e.g., young people with special educational needs and disabilities (SEND), care leavers and young carers), and many parts of the wider system have already arguably created a more fluid and transitional approach towards service provision. Despite recent policy developments for care leavers geared towards improving services (e.g., the *Care Leaver Strategy* – HM Government, 2013 – and the subsequent care leaver covenant), there are still specific issues. Concerns remain that many young people who are care experienced are 'focussed on running away from their previous experiences rather than toward new opportunities', which is the opposite experience of most other young people who have not experienced care (Tyrell & Yates, 2018, p.1024). These young people have experienced considerable adversity in their lives and view themselves as adults long before turning 18, yet they do not think they have been prepared well for adulthood (Tyrell & Yates, 2018).

However, it is not only care-experienced young people who may have additional support needs as they approach adulthood. Being in care is a poor proxy for a person's post-18 support, as it is an administratively (rather than clinically) defined population. Additionally, the use of care orders for young people is affected by policy drivers, such as the emerging understanding of extra-familial harm, rather than need

(Firmin, 2020). So, a young person might experience considerable harm and trauma and yet not be removed into care. For example, young adults with care experience are over-represented within the adult prison population (see Staines, 2016, for a summary of evidence regarding this correlation). The Prison Reform Trust (2017) among others has called for better support for care leavers within prison. More recently, attention has been paid to the prevalence of broader adversities among adults in prison, such as bullying, emotional abuse and family violence, with research in Scotland and Wales identifying high rates of adverse childhood experiences, and other difficulties such as educational exclusion, among prisoners (Ford *et al.*, 2019; Scottish Government, 2018).

This disproportionate experience of hardship is mirrored within the homeless population. According to research by Reeve and Batty (2011), 25 per cent of those who were homeless had experienced care at some point in their lives. The concept of multiple exclusion homelessness refers to factors that contribute to safeguarding risks. These include experiences of care and childhood trauma (Preston-Shoot, 2020).

As with becoming ensnared in criminality, there is an emerging understanding that it is not only being in care, but wider adversity, which intersects with homelessness or unsafe living arrangements for young people. For example, research undertaken for Centrepoint by the Cambridge Centre for Housing and Planning Research, exploring the experiences of 16–24-year-olds experiencing homelessness, found that 90 per cent of those who had ever been in the care of a local authority or had a social worker as a child said that they had 'sofa surfed' in 2013/14 (Clarke *et al.*, 2015). These factors, along with social exclusion and poor mental health, provide imperatives for developing a more transitional approach to supporting young people. However, it is inappropriate for any such approach to be contingent on having experience of care.

Changing the existing safeguarding paradigms for adolescents and young people

The goal of any safeguarding system with young people should be to protect *and* prepare them for adult life. This is not simply a practice issue that emphasizes practitioners doing more or different or better. It requires a whole-system response and adaptation. It can be helpful, therefore, to interrogate safeguarding for young people as a whole system.

Young people have distinct safeguarding needs (Hanson & Holmes, 2014). This is because they are much more likely than younger children to experience extra-familial harm, and the roots and drivers for extra-familial harms are often contextual. As noted in previous chapters, Contextual Safeguarding is an approach that encourages professionals to rethink working with young people (up to the age of 18), create new partnerships within communities, which draw from partners' knowledge about how place and space are used by young people, and meaningfully consult with young people about their communities (Firmin, 2019).

In using a binary understanding of child/adulthood at 18, there is an emphasis on age as the metric that determines need, understands vulnerability and affects co-production in safeguarding interventions. Importantly, harm and its effects do not stop at 18. The long-term impact of trauma is now recognized as affecting people throughout their lifespan (Levenson, 2017; Rutter, 1980), and working in a trauma-informed way can be key to supporting young people effectively, as discussed in Chapter 8. However, care must be taken to avoid simplistic interpretations of cause and effect, particularly using tick-box protocols/tools, which can obscure complexity and individual experiences.

Trauma-informed practice incorporates core principles of safety, trust, collaboration, choice and empowerment (Levenson, 2017). Many of these cross over into the key principles underpinning adult safeguarding, particularly the Making Safeguarding Personal (MSP) approach. These trauma-informed approaches to safeguarding are essential for Transitional Safeguarding practice. The way in which practitioners respond to harm, abuse and neglect must therefore take into account young people's development and the extra-familial risks that young people can experience, be fluid across arbitrary boundaries such as age, and embrace a relational approach at both a strategic and practice level.

All of this makes clear the need for a system that is 'contextual or ecological, transitional or developmental, and relational' by design (Holmes, 2018, p.2021). Rather than conceptualizing Transitional Safeguarding as a 'model', discrete from other approaches, Holmes (2022) argues it is through aligning key principles that a framework for Transitional Safeguarding begins to emerge. As Figure 10.1 illustrates, if we are to create a system that is fit for purpose for young people and the harms they face, it is necessary to adopt an evidence-informed stance. Doing so leads us to respond to the growing evidence base regarding extra-familial harm, adopting a Contextual Safeguarding or ecological lens, and additionally informed by the evidence regarding this developmental life stage and the fluid nature of transition. Responding effectively to young people and their contexts requires a relational and person-centred approach wherein the impact of trauma and the importance of empowerment are central to building young people's capacity to live safely. Linked to this, it is important to take an equalities perspective, so that structural disadvantages are identified and addressed alongside responding to individual circumstances. Importantly, both the practice and policy of safeguarding young people – together with the system design process itself – must be highly participative, with young people's expertise and rights honoured throughout.

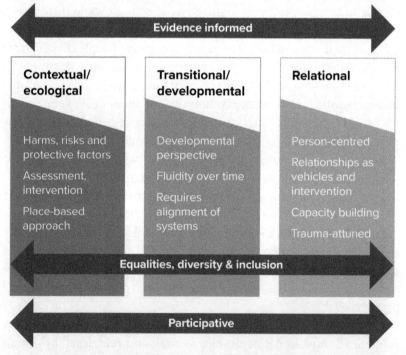

Figure 10.1: A framework for Transitional Safeguarding (Holmes, 2018)

One means of disrupting the current binary paradigm is to explore what might be adapted and adopted from safeguarding adults to inform a more developmentally attuned approach for young people under 18.

The six adult safeguarding principles are:

- proportionality

- protection

- prevention

- empowerment

- accountability

- partnership.

These underpin all adult safeguarding responses. The main differences in children's safeguarding, which impact on how a whole-systems approach might be applied to the safeguarding of young people, are:

- empowerment (a key factor in risk enablement, which involves giving people choice and control over decision-making)

- proportionality (which is, again, key to risk management)

- accountability (which exists at strategic levels across both children and adult partnerships).

(Care and Support Statutory Guidance 2020;
Children and Social Work Act 2017)

Arguably, developing a safeguarding response for young people that explicitly adopts the six key principles from adult safeguarding, using a 'making safeguarding personal for young people' approach, might provide the necessary link from one safeguarding system to another (Cocker *et al.*, 2021b). This means drawing on the safeguarding expertise of adult social care colleagues, alongside the adolescent development knowledge of children's sector colleagues (Cocker *et al.*, 2021a).

As Transitional Safeguarding is an approach encompassing practice and leadership, rather than a model, it is an emergent rather than a fully developed method. Just as, at practice level, Transitional Safeguarding aims to respond to the uniqueness of each young person and their situation, so too will local priorities and circumstances vary. It is important to recognize that the approach will and should be developed differently in different locations. Involving young people and those who work directly with them in co-producing a Transitional Safeguarding approach that reflects local context should help to identify and mitigate any unintended consequences.

Many local authorities across the country are addressing elements of Transitional Safeguarding and are doing so in different ways (Cocker *et al.*, 2021a). No one has yet achieved wholesale system change. Some have developed targeted services supporting specific groups of young people at risk of specific forms of abuse and exploitation. These may be developed as a result of local circumstances such as a police enquiry, a safeguarding adults review (SAR), or targeted funding for innovative practice. There are further examples where local strategic leaders, such as senior public sector officers, chairs of safeguarding boards and partnerships, see the development of the Transitional Safeguarding approach as key to improving services for young adults in their localities (Cocker, 2020).

The two anonymized case studies below illustrate different innovative local authority approaches to Transitional Safeguarding. Case study A examines one local authority's efforts to embrace whole-systems change, while case study B looks at practice changes within a local authority's provision that emerged from a SAR.

CASE STUDY A

Achieving the system and practice changes necessary for developing a Transitional Safeguarding approach requires leadership at all levels. In local authority A, which has a history of significant challenges in child protection, the Chief Executive brought together senior officers from the Council and partner agencies to engage with evidence collated by Research in Practice regarding Transitional Safeguarding. In response, both the Safeguarding Adults Board and the Children's Safeguarding Partnership agreed a joint priority in their respective annual plans to take the work forward. An officer group was set up, including the two principal social workers, led by the two assistant directors (one from children's services and one from adult services), who had both attended one of the Research in Practice Transitional Safeguarding workshops in 2019 (see Cocker *et al.*, 2021a).

They developed a programme of work, which included recommending a multi-agency 'vulnerable people strategy'. This included developing an operational protocol that addressed the safeguarding needs of young adults, which was then adopted by both Safeguarding Partnerships. This is one strand of the work intended to promote a Transitional Safeguarding approach. A challenge remains to meaningfully consult and embed young people's views on any proposed systems changes and ensure that their workforce has the necessary skills and knowledge to embed this change throughout their work across the child/adult service divide, or perhaps remove the divide altogether.

CASE STUDY B

A safeguarding adults review (SAR) was undertaken following the death of a 20-year-old young person, who had been in local authority care. She was well known to a range of different services including Adult Social Care, Children's Social Care, housing, police, NHS trusts, and drug and alcohol services. The SAR identified a number of key findings to support young adults in transition who also have safeguarding needs.

Areas to improve the safeguarding of care-experienced young people were identified, including:

- Services need to avoid having rigid threshold criteria, and the working relationships between services across the adolescent/adult divide need to be improved, for example between child and adolescent mental health services, and adult community mental health teams.

- Young people's support needs while experiencing care and leaving care require flexibility as threshold criteria had become obstacles rather than enablers.

- A risk-enabling approach should be used to understand the need and ongoing support requirements of particular young people, recognizing that not everyone is ready for independence at 18.

- Young people should be involved in decision-making about their lives.

This local authority received Innovation Programme funding from the Department for Education to develop services for young people that bridged these gaps. Young people co-produced the strategy, which emphasized education and employment opportunities for young people after leaving care. The local authority has set up a multi-agency planning forum for young people with complex needs, and developed an award-winning 'one-stop shop' multi-agency service centre for care-experienced young people. Relationships between centre staff and young people have been critical to its success. The challenge for this local authority is to build on the success of this engagement so that all young people in their area can have access to the safeguarding support they need.

Conclusion

This chapter has argued for a redesign of safeguarding systems for young people, and for that to start with a re-conceptualization of 'young people' which better reflects the fluid and individual process of transition into adulthood. Transitional safeguarding is not a model or an intervention, it is an approach to safeguarding that considers the developmental needs of young people and the extra-familial safeguarding risks that young people experience, and focuses on promoting person-centred practice at all levels of practice and policy.

Importantly, this type of flexible care and support for young people in the here-and-now provides practitioners with the opportunity to work with young people in their communities, to enable them to develop the supportive scaffolding and necessary skills they need for their future. However, there are challenges for organizational systems at every level when embedding this sort of approach. Strategic leadership is essential from leaders across the children's and adults' sectors, including multi-agency partners, to address this at a whole-systems level. The moral and ethical drivers are clear, and the economic argument supports this when we consider the costs – such as those associated with the criminal justice system, homelessness services and mental health support – of not supporting young people to make a safe and positive transition to adulthood.

Every local area will rightly approach Transitional Safeguarding differently, depending on the needs of their own communities, including equality and diversity factors, and their local priorities. Achieving lasting and effective change is not possible without involving all stakeholders. The involvement of young people and communities in the co-production of system transformation is central, as they directly experience the impact of this gap. Undertaking evidence-informed service change using a participative, relational lens throughout is complex and challenging, but anything less will not address the child/adult binary still present in safeguarding systems. Transformation is about removing this divide, and it is heartening to see that this work has already begun.

References

Arnett, J. (2000). 'Emerging adulthood: A theory of development from the late teens through the twenties.' *American Psychologist, 55*(5), 469–480.

Beckett, H., Holmes, D. & Walker, J. (2017). *Child Sexual Exploitation: Definition & Guide for Professionals.* London: Department for Education. https://bettercarenetwork.org/sites/default/files/Child%20Sexual%20Exploitation%20Extended%20Text.pdf.

Children's Commissioner (2019). *Keeping Kids Safe. Improving Safeguarding Responses to Gang Violence and Criminal Exploitation.* www.childrenscommissioner.gov.uk/wp-content/uploads/2019/02/CCO-Gangs.pdf.

Clarke, A., Burgess, G., Morris, S. & Udagawa, C. (2015). *Estimating the Scale of Youth Homelessness in the UK Final Report.* Cambridge Centre for Housing and Planning Research. www.cchpr.landecon.cam.ac.uk/Research/Start-Year/2014/Estimating-the-scale-of-youth-homelessness-in-the-UK/Report.

Cocker, C. (2020). 'Transitional safeguarding: Transforming how adolescents and young people are safeguarded.' *Practice: Social Work in Action, 32*(2), 85–87. https://doi: 10.1080/09503153.2020.1733826.

Cocker, C., Cooper, A. & Holmes, D. (2021a). 'Transitional Safeguarding: Transforming how adolescents and young adults are safeguarded.' *The British Journal of Social Work.* doi. org/10.1093/bjsw/bcaa238.

Cocker, C., Cooper, A., Holmes, D. & Bateman, F. (2021b). 'Transitional Safeguarding: Presenting the case for developing Making Safeguarding Personal for young people in England.' *Journal of Adult Protection, 23*(3), 144–157.

Cooper, A., Cocker, C. & Briggs, M. (2018). 'Making Safeguarding Personal and social work practice with older adults: Findings from local-authority survey data in England.' *The British Journal of Social Work, 48*, 1014–1032. https://doi.org/10.1093/bjsw/bcy044.

Cooper, A. & Whittaker, A. (2014). 'History as tragedy, never as farce: Tracing the long cultural narrative of child protection in England.' *Journal of Social Work Practice, 28*(3), 251–266.

Corby, B., Shemmings, D. & Wilkins, D. (2012). *Child Abuse: An Evidence Base for Confident Practice* (fourth edition). Maidenhead: Open University Press.

Cossar, J., Brandon, M. & Jordan, P. (2011). *'Don't Make Assumptions': Children's and Young People's Views of the Child Protection System and the Messages for Change.* London: Office of the Children's Commissioner.

Côté, J. & Bynner, J.M. (2008). 'Changes in the transition to adulthood in the UK and Canada: The role of structure and agency in emerging adulthood.' *Journal of Youth Studies, 11*(3), 251–268. 10.1080 / 13676260801946464.

Cowden, M. (2012). 'Capacity, claims and children's rights.' *Contemporary Political Theory, 11*(4), 362–380.

Department of Health (2000). *No Secrets: Guidance on Developing and Implementing Multi-Agency Policies and Procedures to Protect Vulnerable Adults from Abuse.* London: HMSO.

Department of Health & Social Care (2020). *Care and Support Statutory Guidance.* www.gov.uk/government/publications/care-act-statutory-guidance/care-and-support-statutory-guidance.

Firmin, C. (2016a). *Child Sexual Exploitation and the Victim-Perpetrator Overlap.* Luton: University of Bedfordshire. www.uobcsepolicinghub.org.uk/responding-to-cse/videos.

Firmin, C. (2016b). *Towards a Contextual Response to Peer-on-Peer Abuse: Research from MsUnderstood Local Site Work 2013–2016.* Luton: University of Bedfordshire.

Firmin, C. (2019). 'Relocation, relocation, relocation: Home and school-moves for children affected extra-familial risks during adolescence.' *Children's Geographies.* https://doi.org/10.1080/14733285.2019.1598545.

Firmin, C. (2020). *Contextual Safeguarding and Child Protection: Rewriting the Rules.* London: Routledge.

Ford, K., Barton, E.R., Newbury, A., Hughes, K. *et al.* (2019). *Understanding the Prevalence of Adverse Childhood Experiences (ACEs) in a Male Offender Population in Wales: The Prisoner ACE Survey.* Bangor University and Public Health Wales. https://phw.nhs.wales/files/aces/the-prisoner-ace-survey.

Glover Williams, A. & Finlay, F. (2019). 'County lines: How gang crime is affecting our young people.' *Archive of Diseases in Childhood, 104*(8), 730–732.

Hanson, E. & Holmes, D. (2014). *That Difficult Age: Developing a More Effective Response to Risks in Adolescence*. Totnes: Research in Practice; Association of Directors of Children's Services.

Holmes, D. (2018). *Working with Adolescent Risk and Resilience: A Relational Approach*. Presentation slides. Totnes: Research in Practice.

Holmes, D. (2022). 'Transitional Safeguarding: The case for change.' *Practice: Social Work in Action, 34*(1).

Holmes, D. & Smale, E. (2018). *Mind the Gap: Transitional Safeguarding – Adolescence to Adulthood*. Totnes: Research in Practice.

HM Government (2013). *Care Leaver Strategy: A Cross-Departmental Strategy for Young People Leaving Care*. London: HMSO. https://assets.publishing.service.gov.uk/government/uploads/system/uploads/attachment_data/file/266484/Care_Leaver_Strategy.pdf.

HM Government (2018, updated 2020). *Working Together to Safeguard Children: A Guide to Inter-Agency Working to Safeguard and Promote the Welfare of Children*. London: HMSO. https://assets.publishing.service.gov.uk/government/uploads/system/uploads/attachment_data/file/942454/Working_together_to_safeguard_children_inter_agency_guidance.pdf.

Home Office (2018). *Criminal Exploitation of Children and Vulnerable Adults: County Lines Guidance*. London: HMSO. https://assets.publishing.service.gov.uk/government/uploads/system/uploads/attachment_data/file/863323/HOCountyLinesGuidance_-_Sept2018.pdf.

House of Lords and House of Commons (2020). *Domestic Abuse Bill. HL Bill 124*. https://publications.parliament.uk/pa/bills/lbill/58-01/124/5801124.pdf.

Institute of Public Care (2013). *Evidence Review – Adult Safeguarding*. Leeds: Skills for Care.

Jobe, A. & Gorin, S. (2013). '"If kids don't feel safe they don't do anything": Young people's views on seeking and receiving help from Children's Social Care Services in England.' *Child & Family Social Work, 18*(4), 429–438.

Kezelman, C., Hossack, N., Stavropoulos, P. & Burley, P. (2015). *The Cost of Unresolved Childhood Trauma and Abuse in Adults in Australia*. Adults Surviving Child Abuse. www.qldfamilylawnet.org.au/sites/qldfamilylawnet/files/qflpn/The%20cost%20of%20unresolved%20trauma_budget%20report%20fnl.pdf.

Lawson, J. (2017). 'The "Making Safeguarding Personal" Approach to Practice.' In A. Cooper & E. White (eds) *Safeguarding Adults Under the Care Act: Understanding Good Practice* (pp.20–39). London: Jessica Kingsley Publishers.

Levenson, J. (2017). 'Trauma-informed social work practice.' *Social Work, 62*(2), 105–113. https://doi.org/10.1093/sw/swx001.

Munro, E. (2019). 'Decision-making under uncertainty in child protection: Creating a just and learning culture.' *Child and Family Social Work, 24*, 123–130.

Norrie, C., Stevens, M., Graham, K., Manthorpe, J., Moriarty, J. & Hussein, S. (2014). 'Investigating models of adult safeguarding in England – a mixed methods approach.' *Journal of Adult Protection, 16*(6), 377–388.

Preston-Shoot, M. (2020). *Adult Safeguarding and Homelessness: A Briefing on Positive Practice*. London: Local Government Association. www.local.gov.uk/sites/default/files/documents/25.158%20Briefing%20on%20Adult%20Safeguarding%20and%20Homelessness_03_1.pdf.

Prison Reform Trust (2017). *In Care, Out of Trouble*. London: Prison Reform Trust. www.prisonreformtrust.org.uk/Portals/0/Documents/Care%20review%20impact%20report%20Jan%202017%20UPDATE%20FINAL.pdf.

Reeve, K. & Batty, E. (2011). *The Hidden Truth about Homelessness: Experiences of Single Homelessness in England*. London: Crisis.

Rosenfeld, R.G. & Nicodemus, B.C. (2003). 'The transition from adolescence to adult life: Physiology of the "transition" phase and its evolutionary basis.' *Hormone Research in Adolescence, 60*(1), 74–77.

Rutter, M. (1980). 'The long-term effects of early experience.' *Developmental Medicine and Child Neurology, 22*(6), 800–815.

Sawyer, S., Azzopardi, P., Wickramaratne, D. & Patton, G. (2018). 'The age of adolescence.' *The Lancet Child and Adolescent Health, 2*(3), 223–228.

Scottish Government (2018). *Understanding Childhood Adversity, Resilience and Crime: Summary of Evidence on Links Between Childhood Adversity and Criminality in Adulthood.* www.gov. scot/publications/understanding-childhood-adversity-resilience-crime.

Staines, J. (2016). *Risk, Adverse Influence and Criminalisation: Understanding the Over-Representation of Looked After Children in the Youth Justice System.* London: Prison Reform Trust.

Tyrell, F.A. & Yates, T.M. (2018). 'Emancipated foster youth's experiences and perceptions of the transition to adulthood.' *Journal of Youth Studies, 21*(8), 1011–1028.

United Nations (2020). *Youth.* www.un.org/esa/socdev/documents/youth/fact-sheets/youth-definition.pdf.

Violence & Vulnerability Unit (2018). *County Lines – A National Summary and Emerging Best Practice.* www.local.gov.uk/sites/default/files/documents/County%20Lines%20National%20 Summary%20-%20Simon%20Ford%20WEB.pdf.

Warrington, C. (2016). *Young Person-Centred Approaches in Child Sexual Exploitation (CSE) – Promoting Participation and Building Self-Efficacy.* Totnes: Research in Practice.

Youth Violence Commission (2020). *Youth Violence Commission Final Report.* www.yvcommission. com.

Chapter 11

Concluding Thoughts

Dez Holmes

It is customary, in the final chapter, to provide a conclusion. Ordinarily this involves re-summarizing the chapters and crafting some pithy soundbites to ensure the reader draws the 'correct' conclusions.

That approach seems an ill-fit for a book that aims to help the reader think critically and draw their own conclusions from diverse perspectives. Instead, we offer some questions, designed to help the reader reflect on the key messages from this book. Depending on the context of their role, some readers will interpret these questions through the lens of direct practice or caring for young people, others from the perspective of operational management or strategic leadership.

- How do I ensure that alertness to risk does not obscure the importance of rights, when young people are being supported to be safe? Which rights tend to be prioritized, and are these the ones that matter most to the young person?

- What can I do personally in my role to ensure that a holistic understanding of a young person informs any assessment of risk *and* resilience? For example, considering their wider health behaviours, their peer networks, their early childhood experiences, their aspirations?

- Do I achieve the right balance in terms of recognizing the structural or systemic and the personal or individual factors regarding young people's safety and wellbeing? Which one do I tend to foreground, and why is that?

- How did it feel when reading the direct quotes from young people in Chapter 2? What does it make me think about how I seek and receive feedback from young people in my role? How do I make sure that lived experience informs my thinking, while recognizing that other forms of knowledge are equally important?

- How easy do I find it to hold a 'both/and' mindset? What helps me manage complexity and uncertainty? When facing uncertain or complex situations, do I have any unhelpful coping mechanisms that I need to be alert to?

- How do I understand my own multifaceted identity? How does my understanding of intersectional identities inform the way I approach my role? How would I know if I was inadvertently contributing to discrimination? How can I invite others to challenge me on this in a way that invites learning rather than defensiveness?

- Do I demonstrate a clear understanding of how resilience can be promoted, using internal and external resources in the face of adversity, and by affording a sense of self-efficacy? Do I give people enough choice and control, even when I am concerned or worried about the choices they might make?

- Do I have a tendency to want to fix things? Does this ever have a detrimental impact on others' sense of self-efficacy and agency? How would I know if I was inadvertently undermining another person's self-efficacy through my good intentions?

- Is a clear and knowledgeable understanding of adolescent development evident enough in the way I play my part in safeguarding young people? Do I need to know more about this life stage in order to play my part most effectively? If so, how can I develop this knowledge?

- What barriers do I encounter in terms of engaging the expertise of – and sharing power with – young people and their parents/carers? Are any of these barriers rooted in a previously adopted mindset or professional approach that I now need to revisit? Who could help me 'un-learn' anything that is no longer helpful?

- How did it feel to read some of the challenging or critical messages in some chapters? What does that make me think about how I deliver challenging or critical messages to others?

- How do I demonstrate my understanding of the importance of relationships in this field of work? Which relationships do I attend to most closely, and which ones do I find most challenging?

- How do I demonstrate and enable an understanding of trauma and the impact of trauma on young people, in the way I do my role? How do I demonstrate an understanding that, while trauma and early adversity matter, 'foundations are not fate'? What can I do to ensure that I and others are able to recognize and safely process the emotional impact of working with traumatized young people?

- How do I conceptualize adolescence and young adulthood? How much is my professional position informed by my own life experiences, and are there any downsides to this? What does the notion of transition mean to me, and how do I enact my understanding within my role?

- Do I sometimes inadvertently contribute to victim-blaming narratives, even in subtle ways? What would help me to be alert to this? How can I invite others to challenge me if it happens?

- What helps me to integrate protection and participation within my role, and how do I hold these in healthy tension? Which one do I tend to centre, and how would I know if the balance was not quite right?

- How do I demonstrate curiosity in my role, and encourage the same in others? How do I make it safe for others to make mistakes and demonstrate continuous learning?

- How do I demonstrate a boundary-spanning mindset in my role? How do I show that I learn from other disciplines, reach across traditional service boundaries and exercise influence across the wider system?

Author Biographies

Dez Holmes is the Director of Research in Practice, a not-for-profit organization that, since 1996, has been supporting those who work with children, families and adults to use evidence in their practice and leadership. She previously worked in local government, managing integrated early intervention services, and her practice experience is largely within youth offending services and early help. She is particularly interested in adolescence, transitions, risk and participatory practice. Dez introduced the concept of Transitional Safeguarding in 2018 and has been supporting local safeguarding professionals to design a more fluid and developmentally informed approach for young people facing harm. She is currently the Programme Director for the Tackling Child Exploitation Programme and also chairs the Contextual Safeguarding UK Advisory Group.

Dr John Coleman OBE is a psychologist with a long-standing interest in adolescence. He has had many different roles in his career, including running a therapeutic community for troubled teenagers, acting as Director of a research centre, advising government as a civil servant and taking various academic posts. Most recently he was a Senior Research Fellow in the Department of Education, University of Oxford (2006–2015). He is currently Visiting Professor at the University of Bedfordshire. His interests include parenting, the digital world, the teenage brain and young people's health. He has written a number of books on the teenage years, and has an international reputation for his work on adolescence. In 2001 he was awarded the OBE by the queen for his work on youth.

Dr Ann Hagell is a chartered psychologist with a specific interest in young people. She has a Masters in public health from the London

School of Hygiene and Tropical Medicine and a PhD from the Institute of Psychiatry. She has published widely on young people's health and has worked with a range of funders, think tanks and universities in the field of adolescent development. She was Editor in Chief of the Journal of Adolescence for 15 years and is an ad hoc reviewer for various journals and funders in the field. Ann is also a member of the World Health Organisation GAMA (Global Action for Measurement of Adolescent Health) Advisory Group.

Dr Helen Beckett is Director of the Safer Young Lives Research Centre and a Reader in Child Protection and Children's Rights at the University of Bedfordshire. She has 25 years' experience of researching issues affecting children and young people, across academia and the voluntary and statutory sectors. Although working across a range of adolescent harms, Helen holds particular expertise around young people's experiences of sexual harm. Her work has a particular focus on safely eliciting children and young people's perspectives on the harms they experience, and their views on service responses to identifying and responding to such harm. Her work also focuses on the ways in which social constructions of harm, and the young people who experience such harm, can serve to obscure or minimize the harms experienced in adolescence. Helen has published and presented widely on issues of adolescent harm and regularly consults on research, policy and practice in this field.

Dr Jenny Lloyd is Assistant Professor within the Department of Sociology at Durham University. Working within the contextual safeguarding team, her research focusses on extra-familial harm to young people during adolescence. As an embedded researcher, she works within child protection services to improve responses to harm including serious youth violence, child criminal exploitation and child sexual abuse. She previously worked in the Safer Young Lives Research Centre at the University of Bedfordshire, where her research explored harmful sexual behaviour in schools, peer-on-peer abuse and system change in child protection.

Lauren Wroe is a Social Work England registered social worker and an Assistant Professor (Research) at Durham University, working on the Contextual Safeguarding Programme in the Department of Sociology. Lauren currently works on a number of research projects exploring multi-agency responses to adolescents' experiences of harm in their communities. Lauren is interested in the relationship between structural inequalities and experiences of harm, and in particular in how structural inequalities shape young people's experiences of safety and harm reduction practices. Lauren is a co-founder of and a trustee at the charity Social Workers Without Borders, which provides pro bono independent social work assessments to support individuals and families impacted by border controls.

Jenny Pearce OBE is Professor of Young People and Public Policy at the University of Bedfordshire, where she works with the Safer Young Lives Research Centre. She runs an international university network, advancing engagement with children and young people in research on sexual violence. She is a Visiting Professor at Goldsmiths College, London, and an International Senior Research Fellow at the UNESCO Child and Family Research Centre, NUI Galway, Ireland. She is a trustee with the Association of Safeguarding Partners (TASP) and works as an independent scrutineer with Local Safeguarding Children Partnerships. Jenny's work focuses on questions of consent, representation and participation in local, national and international safeguarding research, policy and practice.

Jahnine Davis is an experienced child safeguarding practitioner and researcher. Jahnine's PhD research and practice expertise focuses on safeguarding Black children and young people from intra- and extra-familial harm. She is recognized nationally as a specialist in intersectionality and adultification. Jahnine is also the founder and director of Listen Up – an organization established to amplify lesser-heard voices in child protection research, practice and policy.

Nicholas Marsh is an experienced child protection social worker and researcher. Nicholas' PhD research and practice expertise focuses on safeguarding young people from exploitation and extra-familial harm. He specializes in translating research into practice and has led and supported the development and redesign of adolescent services across England. Nicholas is also the founder and director of Listen Up – an organization established to amplify lesser-heard voices in child protection research, practice and policy.

Dr Carlene Firmin MBE is Professor of Social Work at Durham University. Prior to this, Carlene was a Principal Research Fellow at the University of Bedfordshire, where she developed the Contextual

Safeguarding Programme. Since 2008 Carlene has researched young people's experiences of community and group-based violence and advocated for comprehensive approaches that keep them safe in public places, schools and peer groups. Carlene coined the term 'Contextual Safeguarding' in 2014, and in 2016 published the Contextual Safeguarding framework. Carlene is widely published in the area of child welfare, including through two sole-authored books. In 2011 Carlene became the youngest Black woman to receive an MBE for her seminal work on gang-affected young women in the UK.

Rachel Knowles is the Head of Legal Practice and Associate Professor (Teaching) at the UCL Centre for Access to Justice. She is responsible for running and supervising the UCL Integrated Legal Advice Clinic (UCL iLAC) and runs her own caseload of education and community care law work representing children and young people. She also teaches on the LLB and LLM Access to Justice courses at UCL. Prior to joining UCL, Rachel had been a practising solicitor since 2009, working in legal aid and the not-for-profit sector. She has specialized in representing children and vulnerable young children directly to access the support they need from statutory services. She is particularly interested in strategic cases which may make a more systemic change to children and young people's rights. Rachel was shortlisted as a Legal Aid Lawyer of the Year finalist in the category of Children's Rights in its inaugural year in 2015.

Kristi Hickle is a Senior Lecturer in Social Work at the University of Sussex, where she leads the Continuing Professional Development programmes for the Department of Social Work and Social Care. Kristi's research is focused on creative, participatory and trauma-informed approaches to working with young people experiencing extra-familial risk and harm. Current projects include the Economic and Social Research Council-funded Innovate Project, exploring innovation in social care to address extra-familial risks facing young people, and the Arts and Humanities Research Council-funded Imagining Resistance Project, using participatory photography to further develop understanding of resistance in the context of interpersonal and sexual violence among young people.

Michelle Lefevre is Professor of Social Work at the University of Sussex, where she is also Director of the Centre for Innovation and Research in Childhood and Youth. She leads the Innovate Project, a four-year pan-UK research study funded by the Economic and Social Research Council, exploring innovation in social care methods and systems to address extra-familial risks facing young people. Prior to her academic career, Michelle practised as a social worker and psychotherapist with children and families where there had been child protection concerns. Michelle was awarded a National Teaching Fellowship in 2015.

Nicky Hill is a freelance consultant with experience, expertise and passion in creating positive change for young people affected by violence and exploitation. She has been a practitioner for over 20 years and has held senior leadership roles within local government and the voluntary sector, including interim CEO posts for violence reduction charities such as StreetDoctors. Her work has a focus on enabling young people's voices to be heard in order to shape change within their own lives, within the communities they live and the systems in which they engage.

Dr Camille Warrington is a social researcher interested in participatory research practice in the field of children's rights and safeguarding based at both the University of Bedfordshire and University of Edinburgh. Her work explores children and young people's experiences of services and justice systems after experiencing violence and abuse and considers ways of collaborating with young people to produce new knowledge and understanding about these issues. Camille has a particular interest in the relationship between children's participation and protection rights; the role of group work and peer support in responding to individual or collective trauma; and building professionals' capacity and confidence to create participatory research and practice cultures. Prior to working in research, Camille worked as a youth and community worker and leaving care personal advisor.

Dr Christine Cocker is a Professor in Social Work and Head of School at the University of East Anglia, Norwich, and is a qualified social worker. Prior to academia, Christine practiced in child and family social work. She continues to have strong links with practice as an independent member of a local authority fostering permanence panel and as the Independent Chair for a local authority children's academy. Her research and publications are in the area of social work with looked after children, LGBTQ+ issues in social work and Transitional Safeguarding.

Dr Adi Cooper OBE is the Independent Chair of two safeguarding adults boards, Care and Health Improvement Advisor for London, the safeguarding lead for the Care and Health Improvement Programme (Local Government Association and Association of Directors of Adults Social Services) and Visiting Professor at the University of Bedfordshire. She has worked in adult social care for 30 years, including as a Director of Adult Social Services for nine years. She has contributed to national policy, service improvement and the Making Safeguarding Personal Programme. Her research and publications are in the areas of safeguarding adults, Making Safeguarding Personal and Transitional Safeguarding. Adi also works as an independent consultant in adult social care and adult safeguarding and is a Non-Executive Director on the board of Social Work England.

Subject Index

Author Index